TRAJECTORIES IN ARCHITECTURE

Trajectories in Architecture: Plan, Sensation, Temporality presents a compelling examination of underlying issues in late-twentieth-century architecture. Three formal preoccupations and conceptual orientations are used as guiding threads or trajectories. These three trajectories – the plan as conceptual device, a logic of sensation, and temporalities – serve to organise individual chapters in the central sections of the book and provide a new lens to the study of period work, revealing architectural conditions and consequent spatial effects little explored to date. *Trajectories in Architecture* adds to scholarship and expands our understanding of the role of conceptual and formal criteria in the analysis and creation of works of architecture. The book provides potentially transformative new interpretations of influential architects and key projects from the last half of the twentieth century to reveal new alignments and potentialities in architecture's recent past as a contribution to identifying future possibilities. In so doing, the book argues for the still-latent potential in modern architecture's traditions and design principles and their future expression. *Trajectories in Architecture* includes analysis of significant projects of Le Corbusier, Peter Eisenman, Zaha Hadid, John Hejduk, Louis I. Kahn, and I. M. Pei.

Michael Jasper is Professor of Architecture at the University of Canberra. Former Visiting Scholar at Columbia University's Graduate School of Architecture Planning and Preservation, and former Visiting Scholar at the American Academy in Rome, he is the author of *Architectural Possibilities in the Work of Eisenman*.

TRAJECTORIES IN ARCHITECTURE

Plan, Sensation, Temporality

Michael Jasper

LONDON AND NEW YORK

Cover image credit lines. Left: Diamond House A, 1963–1967, Sketch plan with red columns, John Hejduk, drawing in graphite with coloured pencil on translucent paper 50.9 × 76.3 cm, DR1998:0060:002:003 (John Hejduk fonds, Collection Centre Canadien d'Architecture/Canadian Centre for Architecture, Montréal). Middle: Morton H. Meyerson Symphony Center, Dallas, Computer model study of the lobby, I. M. Pei (courtesy Pei Cobb Freed & Partners). Right: MAXXI: Museum of XXI Century Arts, Rome, Study model in plexiglass, Zaha Hadid (courtesy Zaha Hadid Architects).

First published 2023
by Routledge
4 Park Square, Milton Park, Abingdon, Oxon OX14 4RN

and by Routledge
605 Third Avenue, New York, NY 10158

Routledge is an imprint of the Taylor & Francis Group, an informa business

© 2023 Michael Jasper

The right of Michael Jasper to be identified as author of this work has been asserted in accordance with sections 77 and 78 of the Copyright, Designs and Patents Act 1988.

All rights reserved. No part of this book may be reprinted or reproduced or utilised in any form or by any electronic, mechanical, or other means, now known or hereafter invented, including photocopying and recording, or in any information storage or retrieval system, without permission in writing from the publishers.

Trademark notice: Product or corporate names may be trademarks or registered trademarks, and are used only for identification and explanation without intent to infringe.

British Library Cataloguing-in-Publication Data
A catalogue record for this book is available from the British Library

Library of Congress Cataloging-in-Publication Data
Names: Jasper, Michael (Professor of architecture), author.
Title: Trajectories in architecture : plan, sensation, temporality / Michael Jasper.
Description: Abingdon, Oxon : Routledge, 2023. | Includes bibliographical references and index.
Identifiers: LCCN 2022052014 (print) | LCCN 2022052015 (ebook) | ISBN 9780367444259 (hardback) | ISBN 9780367444266 (paperback) | ISBN 9781003009641 (ebook)
Subjects: LCSH: Architecture, Modern—20th century.
Classification: LCC NA680 .J376 2023 (print) | LCC NA680 (ebook) | DDC 724/.6—dc23/eng/20221116
LC record available at https://lccn.loc.gov/2022052014
LC ebook record available at https://lccn.loc.gov/2022052015

ISBN: 978-0-367-44425-9 (hbk)
ISBN: 978-0-367-44426-6 (pbk)
ISBN: 978-1-003-00964-1 (ebk)

DOI: 10.4324/9781003009641

Typeset in Bembo
by Apex CoVantage, LLC

Printed in the United Kingdom
by Henry Ling Limited

CONTENTS

List of figures vii
List of tables ix
Acknowledgements x

    Continuities 1

TRAJECTORY I
Conceptual objects   **17**

1   Distancing: De Vore House by Louis I. Kahn   19

2   Displacements: House II and House IV by Peter Eisenman   33

3   Overcoming: Diamond Projects by John Hejduk   55

TRAJECTORY II
Sensation   **71**

4   Animate matter: Bryn Mawr College Dormitory by Louis Kahn   73

5   Elastic space: I. M. Pei's approach to form–space generation   93

TRAJECTORY III
Time   111

6   Diagonalities: Visual Arts Center by Le Corbusier   113

7   Group form: Meeting House and Philadelphia College
    of Art by Louis I. Kahn   130

8   Freedom: MAXXI by Zaha Hadid   148

    Discontinuity   163

Index   *167*

FIGURES

1.1	De Vore House, elevation study, Louis I. Kahn	23
1.2	De Vore House, plan diagram, Louis I. Kahn	24
1.3	Four-square variations in Louis I. Kahn's De Vore House	26
1.4	De Vore House, plan study, Louis I. Kahn	29
2.1	House II (Falk House), Hardwick Vermont, 1969–1970, conceptual sketches, Peter Eisenman, black ink on yellow paper 27.9 × 21.5 cm, DR1994:0130:015	37
2.2	House II (Falk House), Hardwick Vermont, 1969–1970, upper floor plan, Peter Eisenman, reprographic copy 63.5 × 65 cm, DR1994:0130:291	39
2.3	House II (Falk House), mock-up of a proposed cover for *Casabella* magazine, Peter Eisenman, ink and coloured ink on translucent paper 35 × 27.2 cm, DR1994:0130:301	41
2.4	Nine square variations in House II	42
2.5	House IV, Falls Village, Connecticut, circa 1970–1971, first-level plan, Peter Eisenman, drawing in ink with transfer type and traces of graphite on translucent paper, 79 × 92 cm, DR1994:0132:333:007	43
2.6	House IV, Falls Village, Connecticut, circa 1970–1971, section, Peter Eisenman, drawing in ink with transfer type and traces of graphite on translucent paper 79 × 92 cm, DR1994:0132:333:002	44
2.7	House IV, Falls Village, Connecticut 1970–1971, axonometrics, Peter Eisenman, mounted drawings in ink on paper 61 × 61 cm, DR1994:0132:193	45
3.1	Diamond House A, 1963–1967, sketch plan with red columns, John Hejduk, drawing in graphite with coloured pencil on translucent paper 50.9 × 76.3 cm, DR1998:0060:002:003	58
3.2	Diamond House B, 1963–1967, floor plan, John, ink over graphite on cardboard 50.9 × 76.3 cm, DR1998:0061:002:003	59

3.3	Diamond Museum C, 1963–1967, plan, John Hejduk, drawing in graphite on translucent paper 93 × 92 cm, DR1998:0062:003	60
3.4	Sketches for a fourth diamond house, 1963–1967, John Hejduk, drawing in graphite on translucent paper 60 × 84 cm, DR1998:0063:007	65
4.1	Bryn Mawr College Dormitory, floor plan, Louis I. Kahn	77
4.2	Bryn Mawr College Dormitory, photograph of entry hall, Louis I. Kahn	80
4.3	Bryn Mawr College Dormitory, photograph of exterior detail, Louis I. Kahn	83
4.4	Bryn Mawr College Dormitory, photograph of exterior, Louis I. Kahn	84
5.1	Everson Museum of Art, Syracuse, rendering of the interior sculpture court, I. M. Pei	100
5.2	Everson Museum of Art, Syracuse, sketch of external massing, I. M. Pei	101
5.3	National Gallery of Art East Building, Washington D. C., early concept sketch plan, I. M. Pei	102
5.4	National Gallery of Art East Building, Washington D. C., photograph of atrium from 1978. Architect: I. M. Pei, Sculptor: Alexander Calder	104
5.5	Morton H. Meyerson Symphony Center, Dallas, computer model study of the lobby, I. M. Pei	106
6.1	Visual Arts Center, Cambridge, site plan, Le Corbusier	118
6.2	Visual Arts Center, view from Prescott Street, Le Corbusier	124
7.1	Meeting House, Salk Institute, La Jolla, exploratory plan sketches of the perimeter duplication, Louis I. Kahn	135
7.2	Meeting House, Salk Institute, La Jolla, site plan schematic group form sketch, Louis I. Kahn	137
7.3	Philadelphia College of Art, Philadelphia, early site elevation sketch, Louis I. Kahn	139
7.4	Philadelphia College of Art, Philadelphia, site plan and elevation study, Louis I. Kahn	141
7.5	Philadelphia College of Art, project, Louis I. Kahn, section sketch of studios, Philadelphia, Pennsylvania, 1966. New York, Museum of Modern Art (MoMA), charcoal on paper 29 3/4 × 47 3/4' (75.6 × 121.3 cm) Gift of the architect 429.1967	142
7.6	Philadelphia College of Art, Philadelphia, site plan study, Louis I. Kahn	144
8.1	MAXXI: Museum of XXI Century Arts, Rome, master plan bird's-eye view, Zaha Hadid	151
8.2	MAXXI: Museum of XXI Century Arts, Rome, section on main lobby, Zaha Hadid	153
8.3	MAXXI: Museum of XXI Century Arts, Rome, study model in plexiglass, Zaha Hadid	154
8.4	MAXXI: Museum of XXI Century Arts, Rome, first-floor plan, Zaha Hadid	156

TABLES

2.1 Comparative table: design principles or devices and findings comparing House II and House IV   49
5.1 Conceptual and formal aspects of a perspective concept of space versus an elastic conception of space   96
6.1 Aspects of diagonal time versus linear time in certain works of architecture   126

ACKNOWLEDGEMENTS

My speculations around the questions tackled in *Trajectories* have been shaped and then sharpened over the decades by many others as is evidenced in individual chapter bibliographies. I must thus first underscore a debt to colleagues both academic and professional whose passion for architecture provoked and sustained a vigorous momentum.

I thank the executive staff at the University of Canberra who encouraged the research and provided material support to that endeavour at critical moments. This includes Faculty of Arts and Design Executive Dean and Professors Lyndon Anderson, Sally Burford, and Jason Bainbridge, Professor Dharmendra Sharma when Chair of Academic Board, and Heads of School Associate Professor Andrew Mackenzie, Professor Charles Lemckert, and Associate Professor Sam Hinton. The Faculty of Arts and Design Research Committee also provided financial support at important moments, and I thank successive committees for this.

The final stages of the present book benefited greatly from the collegial and financial support of the University of Canberra's Centre for Creative and Cultural Research, and I acknowledge in particular Centre Directors Professor Tracy Ireland, Associate Professor Bethaney Turner, and Katie Hayne.

The book's final drafting was initiated while on sabbatical in the first half of 2022. The leave from teaching and administration responsibilities was invaluable. I thank Vice Chancellor Professor Paddy Nixon, then Deputy Vice Chancellor Research and Innovation Professor Leigh Sullivan, and Deputy Vice Chancellor Academic Professor Geoff Crisp and their offices for their palpable commitment to the academic mission and for their endorsement of my sabbatical proposal.

Preliminary formulations of certain ideas and versions of some material in this book were trialled in various settings, both formal and informal. I benefitted from the engagement of all involved. My students in particular queried and helped reframe in seminars and studios the frequently odd early formulations and, as a

Acknowledgements **xi**

consequence, added needed focus to the research behind, and evolution of, this book.

I thank the conference organisers, reviewers, editors, and publishers for the opportunity to trial in-progress ideas and their permissions to recast some of that here. I acknowledge in particular the Society of Architectural Historians, Australia New Zealand for their permission to republish material from a paper presented in *Historiographies of Technology and Architecture*, The 35th Annual Conference of the Society of Architectural Historians, Australia and New Zealand, hosted by the School of Architecture, Faculty of Architecture and Design, Victoria University of Wellington, Wellington, New Zealand, 4–7 July 2018. I thank the editors of *Architectural Histories* for permission to republish work in progress material originally published as "Working It Out: On John Hejduk's Diamond Compositions," *Architectural Histories* 2 (1)/26 (2014). Elements in Chapter 4 are reprinted with permission of the publisher for material originally trialled as 'Bryn Mawr College Dormitory with Notes on Active Matter in Manuel De Landa's "Emergence, Causality and Realism",' *Architectural Theory Review* 17:1 (2012), publisher Taylor & Francis Ltd, www.tandfonline.com

I benefitted from periods of archival research in the 2010s at the Architectural Archives of the University of Pennsylvania, the Irwin S. Chanin School of Architecture Archives at the Cooper Union, and at the Canadian Centre for Architecture, Montréal and thank all the individuals who provided their friendly hospitality on those occasions. I must thank all those at the Canadian Centre for Architecture who provided advice and support on the ground in Montréal and when working remotely. I acknowledge and thank in particular Renata Guttman, Tim Klähn, Shira Atkinson, and Caroline Dagbert. A warm thanks to Céline Pereira and other colleagues at the CCA who provided invaluable assistance in the final image selection and digitisation which had to be completed remotely.

I also thank for their support in identifying and securing images Heather Schumacher, Archivist, University of Pennsylvania Architectural Archives, Emma Cobb, Senior Editor, Pei Cobb Freed & Partners Architects LLP, Malin in the press office of Zaha Hadid Architects, Cristina d'Alessandro at Scala Archives, and Arlette Martin of Copyright Agency. They were each patient in addressing my many questions and professional in helping secure the rights to use the respective images finally selected.

This book would not have been possible without the hospitality provided by many institutions over the decade-long gestation, and I acknowledge my thanks to the individuals and offices who made those institutional opportunities happen. My thanks in particular for enabling periods as visiting scholar to Professor Mary McLeod at Columbia University Graduate School of Architecture Planning and Preservation, to Professor John Ochsendorf, then Director of the American Academy in Rome, and to Professor Christopher Pettit, Director, City Futures Research Centre, University of New South Wales.

I am indebted to Taylor & Francis for the enthusiasm with which the initial proposal for this book was received, the engagement from the editor and reviewers who make detailed suggestions to the draft proposal that contributed to shaping the ultimate direction of the book, and the editorial and professional staff who have accompanied the development and production phases over the years. A large thanks to the team at Apex CoVantage LLC for their patience and care in the design and layout of the book. Back at Taylor & Francis, my special thanks to Senior Publisher Francesca Ford who was there at the beginning, Senior Editorial Assistant Trudy Varcianna, and Editorial Assistant Hannah Studd who saw it through the final project stages supported by a large team I did not meet directly but to whom I send my sincere thanks.

This book is dedicated to Jodette Kotz who buttressed with humour my efforts over years of cogitation.

CONTINUITIES

I Opening

In his 2014 Royal Academy of Arts lecture, Raphael Moneo surveys knowledge in architecture across the centuries.[1] Moneo finds architectural knowledge rendered in buildings, treatises, drawings, and encyclopaedias; in histories, construction technologies, and exhibitions. In what follows, I take a set of episodes alluded to but not elaborated on by Moneo as the point of departure. The episodes occur at different moments largely in the decades of the 1960s through the 1980s, a period when direct lines to the parallel legacies of Beaux-Arts planning, modernist form – space dynamics and neo-plasticist space concepts – are still vital. It is a moment when the practice of architectural composition and associated studio languages are sufficiently present such that potential disciplinary loss and threats to lingering vitalities can be sensed.

The moment is quietly signalled, for example, by Peter Eisenman in a little-cited text from the 1960s. In the text, Eisenman declares with emotion that the importance of the architectural plan as a conceptual device has been abandoned. The year is 1969, and Eisenman is reviewing a recent issue of *Perspecta*, the journal of the Yale School of Architecture. In the context of commenting on articles by Kenneth Frampton on the Maison de Verre, Alan Greenberg on Edwin Lutyens, and Antonio Hernandez on J. N. L. Durand, among others, the value of the architectural plan and its apparent demise in practice and education are highlighted.

'In the rush to embrace the tenets of "modernism," and to sweep away Beaux Arts academicism,' writes Eisenman, 'the importance of the plan as a conceptual device has been all but overlooked.'[2] Eisenman makes his position toward the plan even more emphatic when discussing approaches to architectural history 'as an analytical and theoretical medium,' with priority at least in part to be accorded to the interrogation of drawings and plans as manifestations of architectural ideas.[3]

In the same period, and as a further witness to perceived shifts in sensibility and temperament, John Hejduk announces another take on the continuing logic yet dissipating value of the plan as the locus of knowledge in architecture. Hejduk also signals without elaboration a palpable tension in architecture's relation to the past and specifically provides an argument for an alternative to a linear conception of time and evidence to equally counter perceived ideas of time as always already about progress and evolution.

Hejduk's text appears in 1965 in a tribute issue of *L'Architecture d'aujourd'hui* following the death of Le Corbusier. An expanded version is published in *a+u (Architecture and Urbanism)* in 1975.[4] The publication of 'Out of Time and into Space' serves as a hinge in Hejduk's own work, coinciding with the end of his nearly decade-long experiments on certain formal and theoretical issues in his so-called Texas House series. As partially documented in a catalogue accompanying a 1980 exhibition, Hejduk developed seven Texas House projects between 1954 and 1962, the 'Texas' appellation coinciding with Hejduk's entry to teaching, which occurred at the University of Texas at Austin in 1954.[5] At the end of the series, and confronted with the death of Le Corbusier, Hejduk sends out a missive through the 'Out of Time' essay. Hejduk's text, as I discuss in Chapter 3, announces a different or additional loss to that identified by Eisenman, one characterised by Hejduk as a slip in architectural time. It is a slip that also signals, I argue in what follows, a kind of abandonment in relation not only to time but also to sensation: an abandonment or relinquishment that is also an opening to different conditions.

A Beaux-Arts legacy of cross-axial, plaided composition is still present for Hejduk at that moment. However, cubist, post-cubist, or neo-plasticist formal ambitions and their consequent spatial effects equally inhabit and haunt architectural work and thinking at the time. All three sensibilities are present simultaneously: they are apart from and at the same time part of the contemporary for Hejduk. In this context, by Beaux-Arts planning, I refer to that compositional approach most closely identified with the nineteenth- and early-twentieth-century French tradition of architecture education propounded at the École des Beaux-Arts, Paris. Following Hejduk, we use the term 'neo-plasticist' as it is generally understood within art historical spheres when referring to a specific post-cubist practice and sensibility in painting and sculpture, one most closely aligned with the work and writing of Piet Mondrian.[6]

In the essay 'Out of Time and into Space', Hejduk discerns specific devices and conditions at stake in the plans of Le Corbusier's Visual Arts Center (Cambridge, Massachusetts, 1959–1963) and contrasts them with those at work in the earlier Villa Stein at Garches (1926). While this may be a part of the mourning process following the death of Le Corbusier, Hejduk finds something has been lost in the gap between the two Corbusian projects. Seemingly let go, according to Hejduk, are elements of a post-cubist or neo-plasticist knowledge exemplarily rendered in Garches.

What characteristics does Hejduk identify as differentiating cubist and neo-plasticist works? From a close reading of Hejduk's writings, four formal-spatial characteristics or composition effects can be discerned. The characteristics are peripheral tensions, boundless field extensions, voided centres, and spatial warps realised from right-angle relationships. These effects are contrasted by Hejduk with those at work in cubist paintings and thus provide a framework for him to differentiate a cubist space idea from a neo-plasticist idea of space.

According to Hejduk, then, architectural manifestations of the two viewpoints are realised – though never in a pure state – in Le Corbusier's Visual Arts Center and Villa Stein at Garches respectively. Confronted with the just-completed Visual Arts Center, Hejduk is perplexed, however, at sensing an apparent return to earlier cubist space concepts. He searches in vain for evidence of other conditions that, he claims, would signal more current neo-plasticist sensibilities. These conditions include, as alluded to earlier, peripheral tensions and voided centres, compression and expansion, the blurring of any stable figure/ground dichotomy in favour of simultaneous figure/figure conditions, and spatial warps generated from right-angled systems. For Hejduk, the Visual Arts Center exists in a state of temporal as well as perceptual ambiguity.

While this is going on, and in order to further expand the field of inquiry, we need to turn more directly to another topic of interest – that surrounding sensation – and another protagonist. Colin Rowe can be called in to introduce the theme of sensation and architecture. Rowe, in endeavouring to get a handle on what is at stake in a different project by Le Corbusier, in this case the Monastery of Sainte-Marie de la Tourette (1953–1961, hereafter La Tourette), is compelled to call up the problematic of sensation. La Tourette, for Rowe, provides an expression of Le Corbusier's difficult and rare ability to balance 'thought and sensation,' in contrast to the tendency in some critical and historical accounts to favour thought.[7] I return to and expand on the theme of sensation and Rowe in the next part of this chapter.

Vincent Scully, in the same years and to turn to another leading figure, opens a different though-related disquisition peripherally touching on sensation and more discernibly into the couple architecture and time. Not stated so boldly, and with a point of view on time that differs from Hejduk's puzzlement at the possibility of Le Corbusier refuting time's progression discussed previously, Scully brings to the surface a different point. In this instance, Scully is prompted by a confrontation with materials from architecture's past that manifestly or potentially work – given the right reading – to inflect architecture's present as well as its destiny.

The occasion is Scully's identification of the reflex diagonal as a new kind of architectural design sensibility, one he locates in Michelangelo's Florence fortification drawings. Scully charts this new sensibility which, he argues, led Michelangelo to resort not to rational but to reflexive drawing, to embrace not static but dynamic shape. What Scully discerns, in short, is an inaugural display of a diagonal method. The first question may be to attend to what effect Scully had in mind when sending his field report on the Florence fortification drawings.

Clearly moved by Michelangelo's drawings for improvements to the Florentine fortifications, Scully's description aims to capture an energy of ideas and forms that his text will in turn try to recreate and channel. In his Italian envoi, Scully displays an all-consuming fire, relaying a message that the real significance of the drawings, beyond their incredible beauty, is as heralds of a new kind of architectural design. The drawings, writes Scully, 'explode': they 'consume the paper.'[8]

The prose here is especially dense, Scully dancing, according to a close observer, as if himself 'a man on fire' mimicking the impact and power of the drawings.[9] A close reflection, however, also suggests which takeaways are really at issue for him. Such as they are, the lessons can be arranged in terms of composition (devices, tools) or consequence (character, effect), and as evidence of a different temperament in architecture independent of stylistic division.

Certainly, Scully appears to have been ready to receive the message. Or perhaps he was ideally placed to transmit it, even if not fully in control of the reach and extent of the impact such lessons might have on contemporary practice. For his singular temperament was characterised by its difference from a design mentality that, by contrast, favours 'static completeness, spatial definition and rhythmical symmetry.'[10]

On display in the Michelangelo drawings, by contrast, according to Scully, is a design temperament that is out of time: a cast of mind that favours instinct over intellect, reflex over reason, one turning to a dynamic diagonal over static right-angled relationships. The inheritance of that temperament follows a lineage for Scully that will still be in evidence in certain projects of Louis Kahn, and one that we return to in relevant chapters later.

———

We focused on three themes: architecture as a theoretical object with a focus on the plan as a conceptual device; a foray around projects that prefer sensation over thought; and architectures which disrupt time's meter: time out of joint, or out of time, not linear, and unable to be explained by such modern tropes as the architectural promenade. These thematic poles are taken to provide a loose order that we can, in turn, productively use when revisiting late-twentieth-century architectural events with the ambition of revealing heretofore little-considered qualities.

So, let us take Eisenman at his word and accept that knowledge swerved from the plan. Likewise, let us adopt as our own Hejduk's parallel claim that the conceptual, formal, and temporal powers to disrupt linear time found in certain neo-plasticist experiments such as those rendered in the plan of Garches have been forgotten or, at best, not fully exploited in practice. And let us embrace Rowe and Scully as witnessing trends and temperaments more in tune with the senses rather than the intellect, and thus occupying a situation that might force one to recognise a time out of joint. Assuming these and others would deploy the conceptual and formal powers in their own writing and work, by what means and with what forms did these and other architects engage with such themes in practice? Might a close reading of period projects reveal related conceptual and formal preoccupations, whether explicit or latent?

In starting to respond to these observations, I postulate that there are specific qualities characterising architectural thought and practice in the late twentieth century and rendered by the plan as a conceptual device and the locus of knowledge in architecture specifically. I conjecture, secondly, that different from a formative force, there is evidence not of theory in the making but of theory in deformation and dissipation, one that favours sensation over thought and thus is less susceptible to categorisation. This is to suggest that by the 1960s, the architect, critic, and historian start to lose sight of the plan, sensation comes out of focus in favour of thought, and they are distracted from time's real and positive ambiguities, their attention directed elsewhere. It is also to suggest that such terms merit our attention, if only to reveal qualities too little considered.

A number of propositions accompany what follows, broadly conceptual, formal, and methodological in their emphasis, though each might fairly be claimed to carry traits of one or more of the others. A central proposition holds that the questions raised by the architectural works examined are significant for their potential to add to our understanding of the general reach and impact of their architects. These include Le Corbusier, Peter Eisenman, Zaha Hadid, John Hejduk, Louis Kahn, and I. M. Pei.

Another proposition is that the questions raised in the study of such topics are equally significant for their potential to add to our understanding of specific architectural acts as they are for their capacity to contribute to promulgating swings in the two-way traffic of knowledge in architecture. This might include a swing away from the architectural histories that have dominated much of the twentieth century according to Raphael Moneo and back toward other manifestations.

Stated differently, this is to suggest that certain architectural acts or events are significant for their capacity to contribute to catalysing a swing in the bifurcating commerce of architectural knowledge. In certain instances, this will manifest as a swing away from a prioritisation of histories of architecture as the locus of knowledge and back toward other instances of knowledge, as hinted at earlier. This is to adopt as our own an argument made by Moneo in his 2014 Royal Academy of Arts lecture regarding the state of knowledge in architecture, and referenced at the beginning of this chapter. Moneo reinforces this position in his 2017 Soane Medal lecture. In the latter, Moneo argues that since at least the late nineteenth century, and up to today, 'knowledge in architecture has moved from the treatises of the past to the histories we now rely upon.'[11] In the same lecture, he challenges critics and scholars, as well as those in practice, to contribute to 'an explanation of today's architectural world without a reference to the past.'[12]

In order to approach these propositions and perhaps contribute to responding to Moneo's challenge, and before beginning properly, we need to introduce other protagonists and other references, and take the ideas and possible effects through a sieve of case studies. This is appropriate in order to make more palpable possible ways of expression and reveal diverse manifestations of one or more of the proposed trajectories. To that end, in the next section, key figures are called up, broad contexts set, and case studies identified for each trajectory.

II Trajectories

We have proposed three formal preoccupations, three conceptual orientations as guiding threads or trajectories to our inquiry into aspects of late-twentieth-century architecture. These three trajectories concern the plan and other manifestations

6 Continuities

as conceptual device, a privileging of sensation over thought, and relationships to time that distance conventions of progress and evolution such that they displace and even abandon the privilege accorded to movement as a generator of meaning to reference other manners of thinking about time and architecture. The three serve to organise sets of individual chapters in the central sections of the book. The three thematic lines also provide, we argue, an additional lens to the study of period work, revealing architectural conditions and consequent spatial effects too often running under the radar. In what follows, an overview of each is provided.

To attend to all these acts is not just propaedeutic to looking at architecture generally, whether current, past, or yet to come. It is also to recognise that deep in the ways of thinking about and practising architecture, there are residues and still active elements of other architectures.

Statedly differently, our approach assumes that some energetic elements of any thinking about or with architecture might be revealed in an analysis that adopts different categories to more conventional concerns, including those of place, of use, of material expression. As such, we suggest that it might be helpful to turn our focus to different acts or criteria and, in so doing, open other conditions of possibility, expose latent qualities in past works, as well as release immanent potentialities that might inform works of architecture to come.

II.i Conceptual objects, or the plan as theory device

To begin, let us start with another figure, French philosopher and art historian Hubert Damisch, and another term, that of theoretical object. In a conversation that took place in 1988, Damisch gets to the nub of it. Launched by a question about his activities and fields of research, Damisch comes to position himself as someone working to displace the objects of his reflection. The consequence of such displacements is such that the deviation causes the objects under his scrutiny to 'gain their function as theoretical objects.'[13]

Let us bracket another end of our approach and take up Damisch's notion and use of 'theoretical object.' The idea of architecture as a theoretical object provides a different elaboration to those ideas and concerns raised by Eisenman and Hejduk discussed earlier. Following Damisch, then, the relation of thinking to the plan and other architectural manifestations requires one to go beyond an interpretation of the plan as the generator of surface and volume. It is a call to go beyond what Damisch characterises as 'the constraint of the plan' in order to take on the plan as a thinking vehicle in its own right. Damisch alludes to the constraint of the plan as an aside in an essay treating the reconstruction of Mies van der Rohe's Barcelona Pavilion.[14]

By taking on the floor plan and other architectural phenomena, we further extend the logic of the plan as a device according to the limited but important emphasis of Eisenman and Hejduk discussed at the opening of this chapter. In so doing, we adopt a concept and an approach that Damisch constructs, that of reading certain architectural phenomena as manifestations of what he designates as theoretical objects. Damisch deploys the term 'theoretical object' in relation to works of art as early as 1958 in an essay on Mondrian. In the domain of architecture, the notion and analytic lens of the theoretical object appears in print as early as Damisch's 1964 article on Viollet-le-Duc.[15]

According to Damisch, the architectural work is in the realm of a theoretical object – whether building, drawing, or treatise – when that work 'gives pause for thought' or 'opens the way for reflection.'[16] In generating space for thinking, a theoretical object escapes the gaze of the critic and the historian as well as the techniques of the architect. In other words, following Damisch, certain works of architecture create thought or provide a model for thinking. Different from other kinds of architectural manifestations, the theoretical object is 'inhabited' or 'haunted' by thought to such a degree that it eludes, escapes, and exceeds the discursive reductions of the critic and historian.[17]

Perhaps recuperating in part its potential complexities, a close reading of the plan as a theoretical object suspends a reading of structure and volume, of use and expression, and at least provisionally prioritises an interpretation of ideas and formal relationships. For Damisch, then, to simplify, the plan operates so that certain primary concepts interpenetrate without optical, or formal, or heuristic destruction of each other. These primary concepts constitute the architectural questions or problems the plan can be claimed to be working on. In that instance, such primary concepts exist in a state of simultaneity. In their simultaneity, these concept-conditions generate tensions so that the plan eludes discursive reduction, always escaping a single reading. In this state of internal ambiguity, the plan as a singular architectural manifestation is 'able to function as a model for thought,' a defining criterion according to Damisch.[18] In that capacity, not only does the architectural object 'escape the expertise' of history and theory; it is potentially able – with the help of the analyst – to rework theory. According to Damisch, the architectural object is even potentially able to put theory 'to the test,' without however qualifying what that might look like or how that might operate.[19]

With such a Damischian apparatus provisionally constructed, and taking as material of study the period projects to be interrogated in Chapters 1, 2, and 3, I return to my first proposition. This can now be restated: the analysis of the floor plan and other architectural phenomena as theoretical objects renders or reveals a set of formal and conceptual configurations in the guise of architectural conditions. A close reading of the plan and other architectural manifestations can, in certain instances, also rejuvenate such architectural conditions. What such conditions or figures might be will be trialled in a set of investigations in the relevant section in what follows.

To illuminate aspects of the qualities and possible expressions of this line of inquiry, we take on three case studies to explore this theme. Each contains, as we show, a level of tension such that they elude discursive reduction and thus hypothetically meet Damisch's criteria as theoretical objects. Louis I. Kahn's project for the De Vore House, House II and House IV by Peter Eisenman, and the Diamond Projects of John Hejduk are examined in Chapters 1, 2, and 3 respectively.

8 Continuities

Individually and as a group, the projects delimit, we argue, diverse manifestations of architecture as a theoretical object.

II.ii Sensation

In an essay first published in 1950, and as already alluded to earlier, Colin Rowe calls out a pair of terms, presumedly incompatible. In a shorthand that is given different formulations, Rowe suggests that one symptom of twentieth-century architecture is an unresolved reconciliation between thought and sensation.

The comment comes at a point well into Rowe's essay 'Mannerism and Modern Architecture' and is claimed to delimit a blind spot in how architecture sees its programme. Located smack in the thick of Le Corbusier's thinking – at least the Le Corbusier of *Toward an Architecture* – the specific quality in architectural discourse that strikes Rowe at that moment is architecture's 'incapacity to define an attitude to sensation.'[20]

Years later, when again writing about Le Corbusier, Rowe returns to the problem of sensual expression. It occurs in an article devoted to Le Corbusier's Monastery of La Tourette. First published in 1961 under the title 'Dominican Monastery of La Tourette, Eveux-Sur Arbresle, Lyon,' the essay is expanded and tweaked here and there for inclusion in Rowe's 1976 collection of essays, *The Mathematics of the Ideal Villa and Other Essays*.

The dilemma of sensation surfaces again, evidencing the lingering currency for Rowe of the theme of sensation some three decades since 'Mannerism and Modern Architecture'. Over a number of paragraphs added to the 1976 publication of 'La Tourette,' the topic of sensation is foregrounded. It is Le Corbusier's capacity to balance out the demands of both sensation and thought that the now-older Rowe is compelled to acknowledge and comment on.

Over and above the many singular plastic achievements on display and animating the La Tourette monastery, Le Corbusier's feat is significant for Rowe as a demonstration of that rare temperament of one who has 'suppressed the demands of neither sensation nor thought.' Rowe continues: 'Between thought and sensation, he [Le Corbusier] has always maintained a balance; and therefore – and almost with him alone – while the intellect civilizes the sensible, the sensible actualizes civility.'[21]

Other formulations of the sensation versus thought dialectic can be listed. All will be called up more or less explicitly in the chapters dedicated to this trajectory. They include flesh versus word, physique over morale, perceptual compulsions against conceptual arguments, sensational aspects over rational ones, perceptual intricacies over or against wholly conceptual criteria, sensation versus rationale. These latter two pairs come directly from Rowe's 'La Tourette' article.[22]

What might be revealed by foregrounding that which is sensed over conditions that give themselves to be intellectualised? What different kinds of formulation and, in turn, expression might be called up depending on the orientation or priority? What is brought to the fore in considering architecture from outside this framework?

To broaden the context, we consider other commentators and critics who have remarked on the sensation – thought dilemma. Just staying with the Rowe factor, Robert Maxwell, for one, further suggests in support that the hook of sensation can function as a shorthand for much of Rowe's judgement and posture. For Maxwell, then, it was in part Rowe's ability to see and explain architecture as always already 'at the intersection of thought and feeling' that created part of Rowe's ongoing legacy.[23]

K. Michael Hays provides a helpful additional point of reference to an examination of the terms 'architecture' and 'sensation.' In Hays' *Architecture's Desire*, a critical survey of architectural impulses and attitudes more or less located in the mid-1960s to the mid-1980s, Hays calls up for notice a contradiction worked on by Bernard Tschumi. Under Tschumi's umbrella category of architectural questions, Hays notes in particular the identification of an opposition between thought and sensation. From a set of essays written by Tschumi in that period, Hays isolates this specific meditation. Hays sees the essays as a reflection on differences in stance between 'architecture as a product of the mind – a conceptual and dematerialised discipline with its own consistent logic – and architecture as the sensual experience and practice of space – a spatial *punctum* that resists and exceeds study and analysis.'[24] Benefitting from Hays' interpretation, Tschumi thus provides another take on architecture as a conceptual matter versus architecture as a sensed space pair.

What might be gleaned from a reading of architectural projects from the framework of sensation over thought? In other words, which conditions might be revealed in a reading of late-twentieth-century architectural acts through the lens of an opposition between conceptual objects on the one hand and sensual experience on the other? What might such confrontations make palpable around architecture's complex relation to time, as history, as a rapport with the contemporary and a time yet to come? To also point toward a third trajectory, which operations might be called for to push the sensible to a condition truly outside time's rhythm to start?

To begin to frame a response to such questions, we examine two episodes under the lens of sensation. The first is Louis Kahn's Bryn Mawr College Dormitory. A second episode, a second approach, is that contained, we argue, in certain projects and statements of I. M. Pei.

As part of the effort, we recruit two thinkers – Ignasi de Solà-Morales and Giulio Carlo Argan – to provide contexts and to open up expanded views of what is at stake. Or perhaps, to state it differently, they are recruited to reveal what is latent and still to be exploited out of the force of modernity's experiment if one provisionally foregrounds the sensual and suspends the conceptual. In considering Kahn's Bryn Mawr College Dormitory, for instance, we explore a concern with materiality. As Solà-Morales demonstrates, this concern resonates with the values and the preoccupations both of the minimalists of the 1960s and of Mies van der Rohe. For Solà-Morales, Mies' work is developed not out of images nor out of deference to classical notions of totality. Perhaps these in part are also in play: for Solà-Morales, Mies' architecture is also a response to materials in the strongest sense of the word as well as a range of material-building problems. Such building problems include factors such as 'lighting, of structure, of sealing the outer skin of a building, and the satisfactory functioning of the building in relation to the use for which it was designed.'[25] The technique of extracting architectural content from material, varied as it is with every architect and every domain, calls for a method according to Solà-Morales.

The non-structuralist and non-deconstructivist method foregrounded by Solà-Morales provides an alternative to other predominant, closed tendencies in architecture. It also supports the appropriateness of taking on the theme of sensation. To start to grapple with what a 'method' in the sense of Solà-Morales might look like, we take up two instances in Chapters 4 and 5.

When exploring elements of Pei's work, we adopt Giulio Carlo Argan's distinction between perspectval and non-perspectival or elastic space. The pair recalls differently the division of thought and sensation, reshaped as divergent space conceptions, being on the one side perspectival (on the side of concepts) and on the other elastic (on the side of the perceptual). This is developed fully in Chapter 5.

II.iii Temporalities

In a third trajectory, we consider architecture's relationship with time as an additional framework for understanding aspects of late-twentieth-century architectural culture. To provide a point of reference for the terms used, we generally follow the *Australian Oxford Dictionary* which defines temporality as 'the state of existing within or having some relationship with time.'[26] We use interchangeably 'temporality,' 'modes of existing within time,' and 'relationships with time' in what follows.

How are buildings and projects conceived such that time is confronted? Is there a specifically late-twentieth-century concept of temporality, a late modernist mode for the creation and expression of time? Just as there are different kinds of architectural space, are there different architectural modes related to time, and if so, how do they work, and what are their distinguishing characteristics? What kinds of relationships with time are uncovered in buildings? In another formulation, which formal moves and compositional devices can be said to characterise different temporalities?

To begin to respond to these questions, let us take a minor detour outside the strict boundaries of disciplinary writing and consider the concept of direct time as formulated by Gilles Deleuze in *Cinema 2: The Time-Image*. Deleuze proposes in response to twentieth-century aesthetic phenomena that in certain post-1945 films, a new relationship of movement and time is made visible. Time is no longer subordinate to movement, he writes, and a reversal occurs such that 'time ceases to be the measurement of normal movement, it increasingly appears for itself.'[27]

Elsewhere, Deleuze further elaborates on this. As he describes it in *Cinema 2*: 'What characterises these spaces is that their nature cannot be explained in a simply spatial way. They imply non-localisable relations. These are direct presentations of time.' Deleuze goes on to isolate the terms when he writes: 'We no longer have an indirect image of time which derives from movement, but a direct time-image from which movement derives.'[28]

Can a phenomenon similar to that which Deleuze has discerned in the realm of philosophy and cinema, one he characterises as a pure time, one independent of motion's measure, be claimed for architecture? What kinds of relationships of time might be operating in buildings that release or make concrete a 'direct time,'[29] one not bound to a vision in motion, or to an architectural promenade? Which formal moves and compositional devices create the effects at work?

We hypothesise that in certain works of architecture, there is evidence of the phenomenon of direct time that Deleuze discerned in the realm of philosophy and cinema. Such temporal ambiguities – whether in relation to chronology (as in the case of Hejduk's reading of Le Corbusier discussed earlier in this chapter), or to the experience of a building independent of movement (and thus without the support of the trope of the architectural promenade) – are explored across diverse manifestations.

Examples of architectural phenomena are discussed that distinguish themselves by the capacity to generate a temporality with qualities that exceed narrative, that are not linear, that are not evolutionary. Each of the instances when inspected, then, can claim to create a gap or distance, putting in doubt architecture's stable relation to time. Such acts, we argue, question architecture's presumed capacity to be present, and the desire or need to be contemporary. A critique of the promenade; a critique of the now; and thus, a critique of fixed relationships to past and future states.

In other words, and reframed as an organising proposition, we suggest that there is a largely unexamined temporality specific to certain works of late-twentieth-century architecture, one independent of movement. A close reading of certain projects from the perspective of time may reveal the devices and formal moves deployed to achieve the characteristic effects of such a temporality. In addition, it is conjectured that over the second half of the twentieth century, time – understood as movement, circulation, and promenade and manifest as both a composition device and an interpretive lens – is progressively supplanted by space as a preferred term of reference. This latter proposition is only obliquely developed in what follows.

Three ambitions – loosely thematic, methodological, conceptual – inform our response to these opening propositions around the trajectory of time and architecture. The first is that Deleuze's notion of direct time provides an initial way to think about and test different architectural concepts of time. The second proposition: a close examination of the plan in particular provides the most immediate approach to the devices and formal moves deployed to achieve these effects, and thus used to describe what is at risk or in play.

As an illustration, and as we discuss in relation to Le Corbusier and Zaha Hadid in Chapters 6 and 8 respectively, these architects, for example, have made specific pronouncements on the plan-driven nature of their work, and both exploit the plan's formal potential to create temporal ambiguities. Alongside Le Corbusier's famous 'The plan is the generator. . . . The plan carries with it the essence of the sensation,'[30] Hadid similarly emphasises the plan-focused nature of her work. An early statement by the architect provides a shorthand for this working method, with far-reaching aims. Her ambitions extend, she states, to asking the question: 'How, then, do you liberate the plan?'[31] Calligraphy is how Hadid characterised at certain moments her approach to liberating the plan. The consequences for her were 'almost rewriting the script for architecture. And that script could be manifested on a plan. So it becomes a new calligraphy of a plan. And the implication of that is that it could make a new kind of life.'[32]

A final ambition: in certain works of architecture read from the lens of time, we argue that there is evidence of a condition of vibration and energy already contained or produced by the building independent of movement. Time, to take Deleuze's implied formula, has 'gone creative,' and this condition perhaps resembles or renders physical his concept of direct time in the realm of architecture. Deleuze does not specifically frame the consequence in exactly these terms, but their appropriateness is suggested. He writes, in relation to the cinema image: 'What is specific to the [time-] image, as soon as it is creative, is to make perceptible, to make visible, relationships of time which cannot be seen in the represented object and do not allow themselves to be reduced to the present.'[33] To that end, gleaning concepts of time is aligned with tracing – to borrow a phrase from Eisenman – the 'architectural energies'[34] at work.

To begin to respond to these propositions, we examine in relevant sections of the book a series of projects that engage either covertly or overtly with movement and thus, by implication, embed or release a concept of time. The projects examined are the Visual Arts Center, also known as the Carpenter Center for the Visual Arts, by Le Corbusier, the Meeting House and the Philadelphia College of Art by Louis Kahn, and MAXXI: Museum of XXI Century Arts by Zaha Hadid.

III The book

This book traces a section through a particular cast of mind, one twisting through a strand of architecture across the second half of the twentieth century. Symptoms in evidence across the selected conceptual and formal phenomena considered in individual chapters contain or render aspects of one or more of the three thematic trajectories. The three trajectories may or may not adhere to a larger sensibility or style of mind. Admittedly dispersed, and at first blush unlikely bedfellows, we suggest however that the diverse phenomena and architectural acts do find resonance amongst themselves, even if only by means of the juxtapositions afforded in this collection.

The resultant configurations – whether within the chapters collected under the heading of a trajectory or by proximity between trajectories – are necessarily loose and could admittedly coalesce differently in alternate patterns or clusters. In what follows, one cluster running across three themes is suggested.

The continuum alluded to by the title of this chapter thus has at least two characteristics, or two sides. On one side, it is about a sensibility branching out of certain experiments in architecture undertaken in the second half of the twentieth century. From this position, such efforts might be interpreted as maintaining continuities across certain modern movement attitudes.

On another side, the continuum is also about a momentum that still exists, even if faint, to continue the work of formal and conceptual experimentation in favour of never closing off freedoms and thus, following Hadid, always allowing the potential for new life. More pointedly, recognising that when given architectural expression, they bear little resemblance to the recent past or contemporary expressions, such acts may still maintain an ability to open new capacities in the discipline.

The book is organised into three parts. This opening chapter, the first part, is intended to set the stage. It is at the same time a retrospective overview of things going on more or less under the radar. The middle and by far largest part of the book is given over to the three trajectories, with case studies used to illuminate various ideas. Within each trajectory or section, I provide chapters focusing on a specific instance or characteristic as described previously.

As its title suggests, the final chapter is certainly not intended to be cumulative nor conclusive. The brief remarks in that chapter gather together more recent acts that are dispersed around a limited number of agendas. This final part of the book endeavours to adopt a prospective stance. It does this by identifying three trends, ambitions, or concerns that are preoccupying the discipline at the moment and will likely continue to do so through the coming decades.

The chapters of the book may be read independently. There is, however, a proposed rationale for the placement of individual chapters. Accepting the proposition of three thematic lenses – conceptual objects, sensation, time out of joint – as the central part of the book, each trajectory or section then holds two or three chapters which, if read together, may reveal in confrontation diverse takes on the theme and thus, in turn, amplify or add nuance to their meaning.

These chapters thus provide a record of, and occasion for, a retrospective look at the discipline's recent past without claiming to provide histories of the architects or the projects. It is the hope, rather, that they both illuminate heretofore little-regarded features and provide additional nuances when thinking about such works. It is also hoped that such efforts contribute to framing an approach to addressing Moneo's challenge evoked earlier in this chapter. The challenge as he framed it in his 2017 Sloane Medal Lecture, that is, to find a way to provide 'an explanation of today's architectural world without a reference to the past.'[35]

Stated differently, the survey of works, elements, and details that manifest one or more thematic lines of inquiry may provide a way for things from the remote and more recent past to become active parts of our present. This might then establish a proximity with the past that results from out of an interruption of the flight of time.

Notes

1 Raphael Moneo, "Annual Architecture Lecture 2014," a lecture delivered in London at the Royal Academy of Arts on 7 July 2014. Accessed 10 October 2018. www.royalacademy.org.uk/article/rafael-moneo-annual-architecture.
2 Peter, Eisenman, "The Big Little Magazine: *Perspecta* 12 and the Future of the Architectural Past," *Architectural Forum* 131 (1969): 75.

3. See Eisenman's discussion of Greenberg on Lutyens, for example, and the suggestion of the value of examining the plans of turn-of-the-century British architect Bailie Scott in this regard. Eisenman, "The Big Little Magazine," 75.
4. John Hejduk. "Hors du temps dans l'espace," *L'Architecture d'aujourd'hui* 122 (1965): xxi–xxiii. A longer version is published as "Out of Time and into Space," *A+U (Architecture and Urbanism)* 53 (1975): 3–4, 24, Japanese text with illustrations starting on page 147.
5. For background and further context, see Kenneth Frampton, ed., *John Hejduk: 7 Houses* (New York: The Institute for Architecture and Urban Studies, 1980), a catalogue from a 1980 exhibition of Hejduk's Texas Houses with catalogue entries and other statements by Hejduk and a preface and critical essay by Peter Eisenman.
6. Mondrian's self-characterisation of his painterly work as neo-plasticist is most fully developed in his essay "The New Plastic in Painting," in *The New Art – The New Life: The Collected Writings of Piet Mondrian*, ed. and trans. Harry Holtzman and Martin S. James (London: Thames and Hudson, 1987), 27–74. For additional development of these ideas, see also in *The Collected Writings*, "The Realization of Neo-Plasticism in the Distant Future and in Architecture Today (Architecture Understood as Our Total Non-natural Environment)," 164–72.
7. Colin Rowe, "La Tourette," in *The Mathematics of the Ideal Villa and Other Essays* (Cambridge: The MIT Press, 1976), 196. First published in 1961 in *Architectural Review* under the title "Dominican Monastery of La Tourette, Eveux-Sur Arbresle, Lyon"; the cited section was added to the original 1961 essay for the 1976 publication. All references which follow unless noted are to the 1976 version.
8. Vincent Scully, "Michelangelo's Fortification Drawings: A Study in the Reflex Diagonal," *Perspecta* 1 (1952): 39.
9. Jaquelin Robertson thus characterises a 'young Vincent Scully' of those years in a letter of 1974. See Robertson cited in Robert Stern, "Yale 1950–1965," *Oppositions* 4 (1974): 45.
10. Scully, "Michelangelo's Fortification Drawings," 40.
11. Raphael Moneo, "Soane Medal Lecture" given in 2017 on the occasion of being awarded the inaugural Soane Medal; excerpts of Moneo's talk have been published on the Sir John Soane's Museum website. Accessed 23 May 2022, www.soane.org/soane-medal/2017-rafael-moneo.
12. Moneo, "Soane Medal Lecture."
13. Hubert Damisch with Yves-Alain Bois, Denis Hollier, and Rosalind Krauss, "A Conversation with Hubert Damisch," *October* 85 (Summer 1998): 11.
14. Hubert Damisch, "The Slightest Difference: Mies van der Rohe and the Reconstruction of the Barcelona Pavilion," in *Noah's Ark: Essays on Architecture*, ed. Anthony Vidler (Cambridge: The MIT Press, 2016), see especially 220–221.
15. For the former, see Hubert Damisch, "L'éveil du regard," *les Lettres nouvelles*, série bimensuelle, 61 et 62 (juin et juillet – août 1958). This article is included in Damisch's *Fenêtre jaune cadmium ou les dessous de la peinture* (Paris: Seuil, 1984), 54–72. The 1964 article on Viollet-le-Duc was first published as "L'architecture raisonnée," the preface to *L'architecture raisonnée: Extraits du Dictionnaire de l'architecture française* (Paris: Hermann, 1964), and in English translation as "The Space Between: A Structuralist Approach to the *Dictionnaire*: Viollet-le-Duc as a Forerunner of Structuralism," in *Noah's Ark: Essays on Architecture*, ed. Anthony Vidler (Cambridge: The MIT Press, 2016), 92–109.
16. Hubert Damisch, "Against the Slope: Le Corbusier's La Tourette," in *Noah's Ark: Essays on Architecture*, ed. Anthony Vidler (Cambridge: The MIT Press, 2016), 178. The essay was first published in *Log* 4 (Winter 2005), 29–48, trans. Julie Rose. All references in what follows are to the publication in *Noah's Ark*.
17. Damisch turns to metaphors of inhabitation and haunting in the discussion of Le Corbusier's La Tourette in his essay "Against the Slope: Le Corbusier's La Tourette," see for example 179.
18. Damisch, "The Space Between," 107.
19. Damisch, "Against the Slope," 179.

20 Colin Rowe, "Mannerism and Modern Architecture," in *The Mathematics of the Ideal Villa and Other Essays* (Cambridge, Mass.: The MIT Press, 1976), 42. Originally published in 1950 in *The Architectural Review*, the "Mannerism" essay is amended in multiple ways for its publication in the 1976 collection. Unless otherwise noted, all references are to the 1976 version.
21 Rowe, "La Tourette," in *Mathematics of the Ideal Villa and Other Essays*, 196.
22 Rowe, "La Tourette," 192–193.
23 Robert Maxwell, "Mannerism and Modernism: The Importance of Irony," in *Reckoning with Colin Rowe: Ten Architects Take Position*, ed. Emmanuel Petit (New York: Routledge, 2015), 30–31.
24 K. Michael Hays, *Architecture's Desire: Reading the Late Avant-Garde* (Cambridge: The MIT Press, 2010), 136.
25 Ignasi de Solà-Morales, *Differences: Topographies of Contemporary Architecture*, ed. Sarah Whiting, trans. Graham Thompson (Cambridge: The MIT Press, 1997), 32.
26 Bruce Moore, ed., *The Australian Oxford Dictionary, Second Edition* (Oxford: Oxford University Press, 2004), 1328.
27 Gilles Deleuze, *Cinema 2: The Time-Image*, trans. Hugh Tomlinson and Robert Galeta (Minneapolis: University of Minnesota Press, 1989), xii.
28 Deleuze, *Cinema 2: The Time-Image*, 129.
29 Deleuze, *Cinema 2: The Time-Image*, xii.
30 Le Corbusier, *Toward an Architecture*, trans. John Goodman (Los Angeles: Getty Research Institute, 2007), 116.
31 Zaha Hadid, "The Calligraphy of the Plan," in *Architectural Associations: The Idea of the City*, ed. Robin Middleton (London: Architectural Association and Cambridge, Mass.: The MIT Press, 1996), 65.
32 Zaha Hadid, excerpt from an interview in *Deconstructivist Architects*, a film by Michael Blackwood, Michael Blackwood Productions, 1989, 58 minutes, colour.
33 Deleuze, *Cinema 2: The Time-Image*, xii.
34 Peter Eisenman, *Inside Out: Selected Writings 1963–1988* (New Haven, Yale University Press, 2004), 132.
35 Raphael Moneo, "Soane Medal Lecture," excerpts from Moneo's Soane Medal Lecture delivered in 2017, published on the website of the Sir John Soane's Museum London website. Accessed 23 May 2022. www.soane.org/soane-medal/2017-rafael-moneo.

Bibliography

Damisch, Hubert. "Against the Slope: Le Corbusier's La Tourette." In *Noah's Ark: Essays on Architecture*, edited by Anthony Vidler, 176–211, endnotes 350–352. Cambridge: The MIT Press, 2016.

Damisch, Hubert. "The Slightest Difference: Mies van der Rohe and the Reconstruction of the Barcelona Pavilion." In *Noah's Ark. Essays on Architecture*, edited by Anthony Vidler, 212–228, endnotes 352–353. Cambridge: The MIT Press, 2016.

Damisch, Hubert. "The Space Between: A Structuralist Approach to the Dictionnaire: Viollet-le-Duc as a Forerunner of Structuralism." In *Noah's Ark: Essays on Architecture*, edited by Anthony Vidler, 92–109. Cambridge: The MIT Press, 2016.

Damisch, Hubert, with Yves-Alain, Bois, Denis, Hollier, and Rosalind Krauss. "A Conversation with Hubert Damisch." *October* 85 (Summer 1998): 3–17.

Deleuze, Gilles. *Cinema 2: The Time-Image*. (Translated by Hugh Tomlinson and Robert Galeta). Minneapolis: University of Minnesota Press, 1989.

Eisenman, Peter. *Inside Out: Selected Writings 1963–1988*. New Haven: Yale University Press, 2004.

Eisenman, Peter. "The Big Little Magazine: Perspecta 12 and the Future of the Architectural Past." *Architectural Forum* 131 (1969): 74–75, 104.

Hadid, Zaha. "The Calligraphy of the Plan." In *Architectural Associations: The Idea of the City*, edited by Robin Middleton, 64–83. London/Cambridge: Architectural Association and The MIT Press, 1996.

Hays, K. Michael. *Architecture's Desire: Reading the Late Avant-Garde*. Cambridge: The MIT Press, 2010.

Hejduk, John. "Hors du temps dans l'espace." *L'Architecture d'aujourd'hui* 122 (1965): xxi–xxiii.

Holtzman, Harry, and Martin S. James, eds., trans. *The New Art – The New Life: The Collected Writings of Piet Mondrian*. London: Thames and Hudson, 1987.

Le Corbusier. *Toward an Architecture* (Translated by John Goodman). Los Angeles: Getty Research Institute, 2007.

Maxwell, Robert. "Mannerism and Modernism: The Importance of Irony." In *Reckoning with Colin Rowe: Ten Architects Take Position*, edited by Emmanuel Petit, 27–39. New York: Routledge, 2015.

Moneo, Raphael. *Annual Architecture Lecture 2014*. Accessed 10 October 2018. www.royalacademy.org.uk/article/rafael-moneo-annual-architecture.

Moneo, Raphael. *Soane Medal Lecture* (Given in 2017 on the occasion of being awarded the inaugural Soane Medal. Excerpts of Moneo's are published on the Sir John Soane's Museum website). Accessed 23 May 2022. www.soane.org/soane-medal/2017-rafael-moneo.

Rowe, Colin. "La Tourette." In *The Mathematics of the Ideal Villa and Other Essays*, 185–203. Cambridge: The MIT Press, 1976.

Rowe, Colin. "Mannerism and Modern Architecture." In *The Mathematics of the Ideal Villa and Other Essays*, 29–57. Cambridge: The MIT Press, 1976.

Scully, Vincent. "Michelangelo's Fortification Drawings: A Study in the Reflex Diagonal." *Perspecta* 1 (1952): 38–45.

Solà-Morales, Ignasi de. *Differences: Topographies of Contemporary Architecture* (edited by Sarah Whiting, translated by Graham Thompson). Cambridge: The MIT Press, 1997.

Stern, Robert. "Yale 1950–1965." *Oppositions* 4 (1974): 35–62.

TRAJECTORY I
Conceptual objects

1
DISTANCING
De Vore House by Louis I. Kahn

I

First published in 1955, Louis Kahn's De Vore House remains still today, some seven decades later, subversive and outside categorisation. Continuously fascinating to architects, critics, and historians as a cursory survey of select texts from that period confirms, it has yielded multiple interpretations as to its meaning and relevance ever since its appearance and been deployed in support of a variety of agendas. Four different approaches provide a way to launch into an analysis of the project.

Alison and Peter Smithson, searching for traces of originating architectural gestures, find in De Vore House a model that to their minds is uniquely neither temple nor barn. For the Smithsons, rather, De Vore stands as a kind of abstract frame which can accommodate what they characterise as different kinds of spectacle.[1] The Smithsons locate the measure of Kahn's project in a line of architectural experimentations that function to 'capture the empty air.'[2] Consistent with our gambit of sketching out qualities of a certain cast of mind, the Smithsons too seek to describe attributes of the architectural working of Kahn's 'geometric and symbolic imagination.'[3] To that end, and accepting the title of their reflections as designating a more general quality of American urbanism, one can start to situate the De Vore House project as a conjecture on the between. If evidenced, De Vore would thus share a quality that Hubert Damisch locates on the side of the theoretical object, as discussed in the opening chapter.

David Brownlee and David De Long portray De Vore House as affecting the rejuvenation of lost organisation strategies. According to Brownlee and De Long, such strategies include those distinguished by a capacity to operate on larger spatial-structural units, such as 'connected pavilions [in a] picturesque grouping.'[4] From this characterisation, Brownlee and De Long add further momentum to situating

DOI: 10.4324/9781003009641-3

the house project on the side of experimentations on the between. The authors reiterate the character of an informal grouping in the pavilion mode such that the tension is related to the relative proximity of individual units and, to a lesser degree, a concern for a clear formal logic to the grouping. That the De Vore project remained diagrammatic perhaps gives it an ability to provoke such a reading.

Susan Solomon is moved to provide additional observations. In the context of a book-length interrogation of the provenance and impacts of Kahn's Trenton Jewish Community Center, Solomon sees De Vore as an illustration of how 'articulated space could represent the hierarchical distinctions between primary and secondary uses.'[5] Solomon highlights the project's ability to create a never-totalising 'differentiation of space.'[6] Importantly for our purposes, Solomon feels no affinity or sense of a generative mood or generational model in Kahn. For Solomon, there is nothing cellular or grid-like about it. It is more about a sensibility that favours part-to-part (or whole-to-whole) relationships, remaining for Solomon a curiosity in its capacity to render a condition of separateness that does not lend itself to other models.

More recently, Peter Eisenman places De Vore House as one in a cluster of ten projects from the twentieth century whose shared traits include the capacity to still provoke. Situated between sections in Eisenman's *Ten Canonical Buildings 1950–2000* on Mies van der Rohe's Farnsworth House and James Stirling and James Gowan's Leicester Engineering Building, De Vore reveals for Eisenman an architectural manifestation of diachronicity, one critical of specifically linear notions about time.[7]

Eisenman's reading provides a provocative reframing of Kahn's mid-century project as achieving a condition Eisenman describes as 'an architectural text in diachronic space.'[8] This is brought about, claims Eisenman, by a superpositioning of different kinds of architectural space. The implications of this, the collateral possibilities for a renewed understanding of other mid-twentieth-century projects, give additional momentum to further research on the questions that are raised by, and that adhere to, De Vore. Independent of the narrower focus of the present chapter, Eisenman provides a fascinating hint at larger implications in his discussion of the critique of conventional part-to-whole relationships in the project's denial of a single unified whole.[9]

It is also perhaps a late implementation by Eisenman of a stated desire to give further momentum to certain vectors put in motion by modern architecture. This would include, for example, the 'capacity of its ideas to be regenerative,' picking up a statement from Eisenman in his editor's introduction to the Smithsons' text.[10] We return to Eisenman in greater detail in what follows.

Through an examination of De Vore House, we take up the provocation to identify and theorise composition strategies that differ from and even resist processes of division and separation. To that end, we hope to start to reveal in what follows those aspects of De Vore House that can be read as architectural manifestations of a conceptual object, as suggested in the opening chapter, 'Continuities.' The criterion or trope of distancing or spacing is here understood to refer to inaugural moments, simple actions, and, in certain instances, to singular shapes that are indivisible and distanced from the other. An architecture marked by a distancing sentiment in this sense perhaps manifests a temperament that is different from one grounded in part-to-whole logics. This would signal a sensibility that adopts strategies of form generation that also differ from the simple aggregation of a 1 + 1 + 1 + nature in favour of other strategies.

Three propositions motivate in part the analysis of De Vore. We conjecture, firstly, that Kahn's unbuilt project is characteristic of a swerve from modern movement morphological and space generation paradigms. This is to suggest, in other words, that at the time of its appearance, the project functioned as an unanticipated launch of a different sensibility or temperament, one that remained unrealised and untheorised some twenty years later at Kahn's death in 1974, and one still awaiting resuscitation.

We propose, secondly, that in De Vore House, an underlying temperament and composition strategy of spacing or distancing is at work, one that can be described as haunted by an invisible four-square plan. It is one revealed by gestures that differ from those resulting in dispositions better expressed through the more ubiquitous nine-square schema. Such gestures equally perhaps cannot easily be claimed to illustrate an additive strategy. We argue, rather, that Kahn's project resonates with, and shares traits of, a temperament that differs from a logic of dissociation and division in favour of a certain kind of simultaneity.

As a third proposition, we suggest that this other strategy of disposition signals what should be considered an expression in thinking about the plan that is on the side of the conceptual device. Unlike Beaux Arts cross-axial distributions, cubist collage-fragmentations, and the modernist free-plan point-column infinite grid or repetitive frame, this other approach is sufficiently different to remain largely ignored and unexploited to this day.

Within the limits of this foray, analysis and demonstration will perhaps be cursory, but we nevertheless hope to outline the elements of the investigation and contribute to approaching in De Vore the theme of figures of expression as a conceptual object. The overarching lens to this chapter, as well as that of Chapters 2 and 3, which together constitute this section of the book, is that De Vore House can be located on the side of what Damisch characterises as a theoretical object.[11] The chapter also aims to add to the existing literature on Kahn, expanding on and varying important findings of others, including those of David Brownlee and David De Long, Peter Eisenman, Romaldo Giurgola, Vincent Scully, and Alison and Peter Smithson. Their terms of reference and findings have been considered over the course of the study.

II Analysis

In 1955, Kahn published two drawings of De Vore House. Across a double-page spread are published an elevation sketch and a diagrammatic building and site plan. See Figures 1.1 and 1.2. The drawings are paired on the spread with drawings for

Kahn's Adler House from the same years and a short text by the architect. Publication of the drawings occurs in Volume 3 of *Perspecta*, the journal of the Yale School of Architecture. The issue also contains commentary about, and documentation of, Kahn's project for Adath Jeshurun Synagogue, Philadelphia, and the just completed Yale Art Gallery and Design Center, New Haven.[12]

Out of an examination of the drawings and text that accompanied Kahn's original publication of De Vore House, a number of architectural qualities and conditions are evident. While other qualities and conditions exist, a few stand out. First, what I call the disappearance of the line, understood not as an energy force but rather a contour, or a thin edge. A second quality is rendered by means of a strategy of disposition that favours the informal. A third condition in play is a singular approach to conceiving the plan with a commitment to what we characterise as an extreme freedom, one that finds expression in an experimentation with what we claim is the invisible figure of a four-square plan. These together can be said to serve as various figures of expression that together constitute a critique of unity and wholeness. In what follows, I develop each condition.

II.i The line and its disappearance

De Vore House comes after Kahn's time in Rome (1950–1951) as resident architect at the American Academy in Rome. Thus, the project comes after time spent with the Mediterranean archaeologist Frank Brown, also at the American Academy in Rome in the same years. De Vore comes after his travels to Egypt and Greece, and after completion of the Yale University Art Gallery in 1953.

As a signal placeholder in support of one of the design principles at work in De Vore House, we can take Scully's description of the differences between Kahn's manner of drawing before and after Rome and thus, in principle, present in De Vore. In an introduction to a published collection of Kahn's drawings and paintings, Scully writes: 'Moved, one might say driven by Le Corbusier's vision, Kahn moved to thin linear and planar perspectives in the 1940s, in which his architecture was clearly being drawn back and forth between poles of geometric discipline and physical attenuation.'[13]

This emaciated line – to take Scully at his word – would equally distract and drive Kahn for some years, awaiting a catalyst for change: a catalyst to more confidently develop an architecture of mass and shadow as opposed to an architecture of thin contours and transparency.

Scully continues: 'Le Corbusier's thin, pitiless, analytical line still helped direct Kahn's hand until an outward vision of the world and an inward vision of geometric order came together [for Kahn].'[14] That Kahn moved beyond what Scully dismissed as the line's physical attenuation in Kahn's earlier work can be seen and felt in the deep, physical shadows of the elevation study for De Vore House. See Figure 1.1.

In addition, Scully highlights the importance of Frank Brown's descriptions of the peculiar qualities of Roman architecture to Kahn's swerve away from that

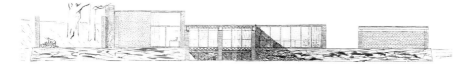

FIGURE 1.1   De Vore House, elevation study, Louis I. Kahn

Source: Louis I. Kahn Collection, University of Pennsylvania and Pennsylvania Historical and Museum Commission

modernist emaciated line. As Romaldo Giurgola and Jaimini Mehta note, this accompanies a departure from his house designs up to that moment.[15] A number of traits are evident in Kahn's work of the 1940s, and they are overturned or, at minimum, abandoned in the 1950s.

Key characteristics in overall temperament and ambition visible in De Vore House include a turn toward shadow and mass as distinct from a desire for transparency and lightness, a mindset in favour of isolation over fragmentation, and an attraction to pure geometries over free forms. These together can be described as signalling a shift away from the line, which can be used as a shorthand for a sensibility that, in certain histories of the period, had dominated modern movement thinking and expression in the previous forty years. In other words, the disappearance of the line in favour of mass and volume rendered in, and yielding, light and shadow was already underway during Kahn's time in Rome at the American Academy and in his travels through Egypt and Greece. And I would argue the project for De Vore House of 1955 is reflective of that shift.[16]

In a lecture some years later, Scully again turns to Kahn. And Scully is again compelled to call out a shift he claims to find in Kahn's sensibility, a shift that Scully argues occurs around the period of De Vore House. The occasion is a lecture given at the California Institute of Technology in 1993. Announced in the context of a lecture intended to trigger interactions and interferences of art with science, Scully states: 'Kahn wanted to deal with beginnings – with the primeval reality of architecture as physical mass.'[17] Perhaps closer to the direction of this chapter, Scully talks about Kahn's ability to capture and direct 'forces running through matter.'[18]

II.ii A spacing temperament

In Kahn's aphoristic text accompanying De Vore House's initial publication in *Perspecta*, there is a clue to a specific attitude toward form and space manipulation. The compositional strategy at work in De Vore, writes Kahn, is intended to avoid 'a predetermined total form.'[19] In its stead, Kahn advocates for singular architectural units that retain some kind of independence. At least theoretically.

Here again is Kahn: 'Might they [the rooms] not be separated a distance from each other theoretically before they are brought together.'[20] See the diagrammatic floor plan in Figure 1.2. It is a question we return to in what follows.

24 Conceptual objects

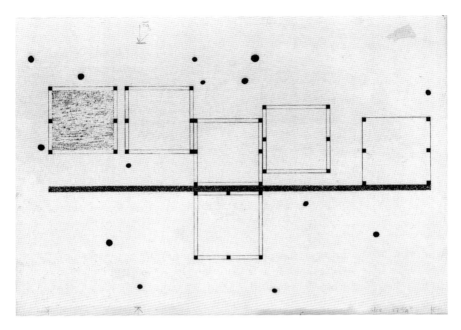

FIGURE 1.2 De Vore House, plan diagram, Louis I. Kahn

Source: Louis I. Kahn Collection, University of Pennsylvania and Pennsylvania Historical and Museum Commission

In lieu of a total form, Kahn argues for and draws a formal-spatial logic that favours the separation of units from each other. This state of remaining a certain distance apart, even if only temporarily, introduces specific conditions into the plan. It results in a holding pattern that remains open for an undetermined period of time before one assumes the units settle into some adjacency, however tentative and provisional the plan may appear. This strategy of separation or spacing is evident in Kahn's plan-diagram as published and to a degree in the published elevation.

What might this resistance to the total form reveal? Does it align, as Christian Bonnefoi has suggested, with something in the air at the time? Does Kahn's approach accord, that is, with a cast of mind, a temperament that manifests itself in those early minimalist artworks that would start to appear in art galleries just a few years later?[21] Let us explore the implications of this alignment with specific minimalist artists, as Bonnefoi conjectures. His analysis suggests parallels in the activities and, more directly, the formal and plastic problematics trialled in the work of Kahn when compared to artists such as Robert Morris, Jules Olitski, and Robert Ryman. Three qualities are highlighted by Bonnefoi: a practice of accumulation (as distinct from hierarchical composition), an anxiety around a priori totalities, and a bias toward simple, repetitive multiplication.[22]

If we accept this strategy of provisional spacing, then the De Vore House room-units, each some twenty-six feet (eight metres) to a side, can accordingly be read as if they are unmoored and in a state of permanent drift. The plan that we see, therefore, is only one possible stage in their drifting or floating evolution, such that one cannot really anticipate or claim a logic or a promise of progress, nor any final state. It is as if the stage of form development we witness is suspended at one particular freeze frame and the six square pavilion units might, at any moment, again start to drift away from each other or alternatively feel compelled to move toward each other. Such movement in this reading is buoyed by a desire for separation or alternatively an attraction to one another, moving or sliding to align alongside another of the rooms in some kind of configuration or basic accumulation. Bonnefoi again provides insight into Kahn's sensibility. The last term, that of accumulation, is one that Bonnefoi turns to as characterising Kahn's work as well as certain works of Robert Morris.[23]

Shifts can also be assumed more prosaically to be in response to topography and to existing trees, the latter appearing to orbit around piers both in plan and in elevation, their gravitational pull suggested in the relative calliper thickness of Kahn's drawing.

Following Kahn's desire for literal and conceptual distancing as one technique for resisting the total form, this plan diagram speaks with exceptional clarity of different kinds of relations. Such architectural relationships can be claimed to demarcate aspects of spacing that contain a nascent logic of alignment always in suspense, one resisting the passage of time because time is always already past. To this extent, De Vore House can be claimed to exist in a state of atemporality, that is, outside of or beyond a relation to time. This can be taken as another possible trait of the culture of architecture in the second half of the twentieth century: an alternative time that is never definitively closed. More will be said of this in Chapters 6, 7, and 8.

Coming back to De Vore, reading left to right and top to bottom, five plan-to-pier, or room-to-room, conditions are evident. See again Figure 1.2. These conditions can be characterised as gap, abut, slip, detach, and attracted by – or held together along – a third element, in this case a retaining wall. For the purposes of this chapter, these can be gathered under the general notion of distancing and together might delimit a strategy to avoid the total form.

How this range of formal-spatial relationships might have been maintained, or varied, or added to were Kahn to have continued with the project, can only be speculated on. The Louis I. Kahn Collection at the University of Pennsylvania contains at least two extant partial plan studies and one internal section with rooms occupied by use and furniture, suggesting possible configurations at the room-unit level if not at the level of the group form discussed in the next part of the chapter.

II.iii A four-square plan idea

To kick off this section of the chapter, let us start with a citation from Kahn about De Vore House, a characteristically allusive and evocative statement on the relation of built form to space. Kahn writes: 'In searching for the nature of spaces of house,

26 Conceptual objects

might they not be separated a distance from each other theoretically before they are brought together. A predetermined total form might inhibit what the various spaces want to be. . . . The order of construction should suggest an even greater variety or design . . . and more versatility.'[24]

As published by Kahn, the plan diagram renders the location and relative size of existing trees on the site and a potential contrapuntal relation with the piers of the future house. De Vore House suggests an exploration of architectural-tectonic structure as a series of spatial units, or spatio-structural units as the main ordering element. In the text that accompanies De Vore's original publication, Kahn characterises his general intent as one of spacing or distancing, as discussed earlier. It results in a plan form he calls a cluster.[25] As will be seen later in relation to Peter Eisenman's House II, discussed in Chapter 2, the idea of the cluster or aggregate is shared between the two projects. This quality in De Vore is briefly suggested by Brownlee and De Long.[26]

The first thing one notices in the published diagram is that there is no centre. Or if there is a centre, it has taken on the form of a line. Perhaps the edge of the retaining wall is the centre. The various spaces could then be described according to specific wall/edge relationships. The outdoor court and garage units are fully detached, the others slipping.

The absent centre, to take another starting point, perhaps justifies considering the plan as a modification of a four-square plan. Figure 1.3 diagrams possible variations or mutations in De Vore on the ideal four-square plan.

The four-square plan has a point, or a cross, at its centre. Kahn takes the ideal of the twenty-six-foot (eight-metre) spatio-structural unit and, perhaps partly in response to site conditions, including existing trees and a steep change in topography, places the house on top of a ridge or proposed retaining wall. The centre can be said to have shifted from a point to a line or wall. And the other spatial units are given distance, freed from the grip of the single point or cross, and drift or disperse, slipping one from the other, attracted or repelled. A gap or a gapping relation is realised between units, with that infamous wall or horizon line or edge inserted between.

The plan for De Vore as initially published is composed of six units in a group or cluster plan. Which kind of order is it? It has been characterised as being composed of informally grouped pavilions. There is, however, a doubling of the columns/posts in the six structural units. This introduces a direction in the otherwise

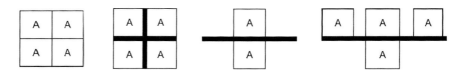

FIGURE 1.3 Four-square variations in Louis I. Kahn's De Vore House

Source: diagram by the author

supposedly neutral space, though it is hard to imagine any space really being, or feeling, neutral when one begins to examine the subtle inflections that always accompany Kahn's work. In the first published plan, for example, the sixth unit to the lower side of the wall rotates 180 degrees to introduce a cross-axial movement into the whole.

The figure of the built form to open space is ambiguous, not shaped into a pyramidal mass even with the extra height of the living room. The spatial or area units appear somewhat adrift, maybe even randomly placed, responding to no apparent single compositional order. To take the opinion of Alison and Peter Smithson, there are traces of Blenheim here, but differently expressed. This follows a lead announced but not expanded upon by Kahn, as discussed by the Smithsons.[27] And Kahn's observation about avoiding the constraints of that 'pre-determined total form' support this interpretation and, in turn, thus find expression. So, how might we describe the order?

Perhaps De Vore House should be read as simply additive. It works to deflect any reading of centralisation or hierarchy or part-to-whole relation. There is accordingly only a part-to-part logic at work, one different from the logic or structure of Peter Eisenman's House II and House IV, discussed in Chapter 2.

Confronted with the plan, one might ask if De Vore functions within the parameters of typical composition formats. Is it critical of them? Does it introduce new instruments or effects? Does it inflect old instruments and devices to create another kind of overall organisation, one whose logic is still to be named?

The drawings as published neatly render Kahn's concept of structure and architectural space as predicated on a constitutive element of a square room demarcated by square piers without, however, coalescing into a figure of repetitive parts. In another regard, they also revel in an experimental approach to form-space-making according to a logic of spacing in which the ideas are best read in plan over section or elevation studies, as argued. Accepting that interpretation, which kind of plan is it? An examination of De Vore House reveals a plan idea that bears little residue of, or resemblance to, the binuclear and pinwheel plans that characterised Kahn's work prior to the 1950–51 period in Rome. The Weiss House (1947–1950) is an example of the former; the Genel House (1948–1951) can be taken as an example of a pinwheel-type plan.[28]

The plan idea of De Vore is also some way away from a Beaux-Arts cross-axially organised plan. It is also specifically distanced from a Palladian nine-square disposition. That said, Eisenman has elegantly and with some conviction suggested that traces of a nine-square plan remain invisible, tucked away in De Vore House's unconscious, a lineage that follows in the wake of the project for the contemporaneous Adler House.[29]

For Eisenman, a critical reading of De Vore suggests much more. For Eisenman, De Vore provides a counter-stance against, or other than, a part-to-whole being. Here is Eisenman: 'The device of a single and identifiable point of origin also begins to critique the notion of the classical part-to-whole relationship.'[30] Plus, De Vore House varies from the, in theory, infinitely extendable and extensive flat-slab point-column free plan. As Brownlee and De Long point out, that is, De Vore departs from an order that would allow one spatial cell to extend to another in a cellular ordering of space.[31]

As additional testimony, consider again the Smithsons' turn to De Vore in an envoy published in 1974 and written, according to the editor, just prior to Kahn's death. Opening a different line of consideration, it is worth noting the Smithsons' resistance to classifying De Vore – Kahn's 'house of brick columns' – other than in opposition to what it was not: neither barn nor temple. Where my reading differs from the Smithsons' is thus specifically on this point. Their two points of reference (barn, temple) are both spatial-megaron volumes that potentially combine in a logic of free-standing structures. De Vore operates according to a different order, tied to but ultimately independent of that specific retaining wall. The Smithsons effectively, though without developing the implications, describe the house as a force machine, both radiating outwards in a centrifugal motion and at the same time capturing and pulling inwards in a centripetal movement that actively works on space such that the void framed by the piers is positively charged. As they think about the project, it is part of a group of projects whose architectural forms work to 'capture the empty air . . . such forms are double-acting, concentrating inwards, radiating buoyancy outwards.'[32]

Ultimately, the Smithsons are less interested in the role of the retaining wall, which for Eisenman, and I think correctly, is fundamental to the pavilion's identity. For Eisenman, it is the relationship to the retaining wall itself, one contrary to an idea of space as volume, the wall emblematising the only inside available to the project. While not exactly aligned with the terms of the present study, such an interpretation opens up another aspect, that of the missing centre. We will come back to this trait of the voided centre in relation to John Hejduk's Diamond House A, Diamond House B, and Diamond Museum C, as discussed in Chapter 3.

The plan-diagram so often published remains perhaps the truest capture of Kahn's inquiry; neither tent nor temple, not barn and not quite the bathhouse of the Jewish Community Centre in Trenton designed shortly after. Two sketches at least do remain and provide clues as to the further translations that might have been called up in the making of a developed house plan. A number of qualities and constraints are revealed: the division that results from populating the pavilions with use and furniture is the most striking. See Figure 1.4 for an example of this. The fourth pavilion (counting left to right, top to bottom) is split into two spaces. The pure wall is compromised: thickened such that it is neither wall nor simple thickness. There is rather little doubt that Kahn would have continued to refine. His Korman House (1971–1973) suggests one possible variation, though nothing of that 'De Vore drift' remains in Korman. Nothing, that is, of De Vore's contribution to orthogonal and diagonal ordering that resides in the published diagram of De Vore House.

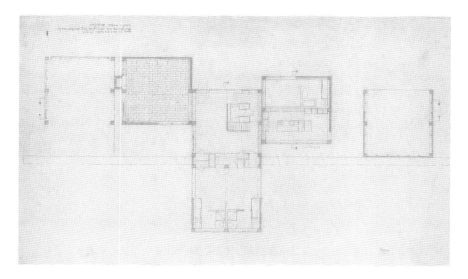

FIGURE 1.4   De Vore House, plan study, Louis I. Kahn

Source: Louis I. Kahn Collection, University of Pennsylvania and Pennsylvania Historical and Museum Commission

III

In a way, De Vore House is an exemplary theoretical object, accepting Damisch's description of a model work that puts theory to the test. Description never ceases circling the thing: or perhaps it is more accurate to say that theory never gives up the chase in pursuit of meaning without, however, fully gaining on it. Caroline Maniaque provides a further comment on De Vore that supports this interpretation. In an essay that cites the work of conceptual and formal experimentations, for Maniaque, Kahn's De Vore House constitutes a blurring of structure as poche. It's not about geometry nor about a cell.[33]

Maria Bottero adds a different dimension. Written much closer in time to the period of De Vore's conception, Bottero sees qualities of the non-dialectical and the contingent in Kahn's architecture and thought, writing of the works' 'ambiguous dimension.'[34] She also highlights the enigmatic characteristics, with Kahn's work proving the 'difficult coexistence of past and present, synchronous and diachronic.'[35] These qualities lead Bottero to qualify Kahn's architecture as 'fragile and powerful simulacra of the discontinuous and the non-homogeneous.'[36] Bottero's insistence on the untimeliness of Kahn's work is further considered in Chapter 7 in our exploration of the Meeting House, the Salk Institute, and the Philadelphia College of Art.

As described earlier, there are three or four – if we accept the missing centre as a fourth – architectural qualities at stake in Kahn's De Vore House. Together, they can be said to serve as figures of expression that more or less align with the defining criteria of a conceptual object. Accepting these findings from the analysis, provisional responses to the opening propositions can be made.

To the claim that De Vore House stands as further testimony of well-argued claims of Kahn's swerve from modern architecture paradigms toward an architecture of primeval, not classical, beginnings, the evidence contained in the published drawings is supportive. There is also evidence that form generation via a practice of spacing or distancing – one that can be read as a critique of division and separation – is at work and was a specific ambition for Kahn in this project. This is evidenced, as discussed earlier, in Kahn's text that accompanies the project's initial publication.

Finally, the plan and, by implication, the structure and space idea to all evidence still resist single categorisations, whether stylistic or aesthetic. This is in provisional support of an interpretation of De Vore as signalling or provoking a swing away from other plan categories toward a space concept whose potential is still being exploited.

As a form of provisional conclusion, three further lines of research are at least called out. The first would include an examination of De Vore House via the lens of the informal. As hinted at, the use of art-historical developments of the notion of the informal by Yve-Alain Bois and Rosalind Krauss, for example, may prove productive. Such a thematic study should also consider Hubert Damisch's idea of architecture as between 'form and formlessness.'[37]

A longer study should also properly interrogate as a second line of research the possible origins and implications of Kahn's aversion to the total form, announced so forcefully in the 'Two Houses' text of 1955. Recall his warning that a total form 'might inhibit what the various spaces want to be.'[38] Such a study might include for consideration whether this is a reaction in part to ideas and writings of the period, such as Walter Gropius's *Scope of Total Architecture*, published in the same year as De Vore House appeared in *Perspecta*. In further investigations, one might also consider Bonnefoi's provocative alignment of Kahn's approach with that of the nascent minimalist sculptors. This is a potentially rich and revealing take only briefly touched on. Such lines of inquiry are worth consideration and may deepen the study of De Vore House as contributing to thinking about the architectural plan as a conceptual device.

Notes

1 Alison Smithson and Peter Smithson, "The Space Between," *Oppositions* 4 (1974): 78.
2 Smithson and Smithson, "The Space Between," 77.
3 Smithson and Smithson, "The Space Between," 77.
4 David Brownlee and David De Long, *Louis I. Kahn: In the Realm of Architecture* (New York: Rizzoli International, 1991), 101. Bibliographic note: Two versions of *Louis I. Kahn: In the Realm of Architecture* have been published. The 1991 publication cited here is the first, full version that accompanied a major retrospective exhibition on Kahn's work initially mounted at the Museum of Contemporary Art, Los Angeles. A second, condensed version with the same title was published in 1997 by Thames and Hudson, London, and Universal Publishing, New York. Both versions have been used in the

preparation of this chapter. To avoid confusion, in relevant notes the publication year will be included along with the designation 'condensed' when referring to the 1997 version and 'full' to the 1991 version.
5 Susan Solomon, *Louis I. Kahn's Trenton Jewish Community Center* (New York: Princeton Architectural Press, 2000), 97.
6 Solomon, *Louis I. Kahn's Trenton Jewish Community Center*, 97.
7 Peter Eisenman, "From Plaid Grid to Diachronic Space: Louis I. Kahn, Adler House and DeVore House," in *Ten Canonical Buildings 1950–2000* (New York: Rizzoli International, 2008), 107.
8 Eisenman, "From Plaid Grid to Diachronic Space," 104.
9 Eisenman, "From Plaid Grid to Diachronic Space," 105.
10 Peter Eisenman, "Editor's Prefacing Comments to Alison and Peter Smithson, The Space Between," *Oppositions* 4 (1974): 75.
11 See the discussion by Damisch in Hubert Damisch with Yve-Alain Bois, Denis Hollier, and Rosalind Krauss, "A Conversation with Hubert Damisch," *October* 85 (Summer 1998), 8. Damisch provides further use of the idea of theoretical object in relation to architecture in, for example, the essay "Against the Slope: Le Corbusier's La Tourette," in *Noah's Ark: Essays on Architecture*, trans. Julie Rose (Cambridge: The MIT Press, 2016), see esp. 178–179.
12 For De Vore House and Adler House, see Louis I. Kahn, "Two Houses," *Perspecta* 3 (1955): 60–61. For Kahn's art gallery, see Boris Pushkarev with photographs by Sandford Meech, "Yale Art Gallery and Design Center," *Perspecta* 3 (1955): 47–58.
13 Vincent Scully, "Introduction," in *The Paintings and Sketches of Louis I. Kahn*, ed. Jan Hochstim (New York: Rizzoli, 1991), 17.
14 Scully, "Introduction," 17.
15 Romaldo Giurgola and Jaimini Mehta, *Louis I. Kahn* (Boulder, Colorado: Westview Press, 1975).
16 For a discussion of shifts in Kahn's attitude over the 1950s, see Brownlee and De Long, *Louis I. Kahn: In the Realm of Architecture*, condensed version 1977, 50–70; Scully, "Introduction," 15–17.
17 Vincent Scully, "Louis I. Kahn and the Ruins of Rome," *Engineering & Science* (1993): 3.
18 Scully, "Louis I. Kahn and the Ruins of Rome," 9.
19 Kahn, "Two Houses," 60.
20 Kahn, "Two Houses." *Perspecta* 3 (1955): 60.
21 Christian Bonnefoi, "Louis Kahn and Minimalism," trans. Dan Cooper, *Oppositions* 24 (1981).
22 Bonnefoi, "Louis Kahn and Minimalism," 7–11, and 25–30 respectively.
23 Bonnefoi illustrates this idea by reference to two works of Robert Morris: "Untitled, sculpture in thread, mirrors, asphalt, aluminum, lead, felt, copper, and steel" (1968), and "Untitled, sculpture in timbers, concrete, and steel" (1970) in "Louis Kahn and Minimalism," 6–7.
24 Kahn, "Two Houses," 60.
25 Kahn, "Two Houses," 61.
26 Brownlee and De Long, *Louis I. Kahn: In the Realm of Architecture,* full version 1991, 58, and condensed version 1997, 151.
27 Smithson and Smithson, "The Space Between," 78.
28 Brownlee and De Long, *Louis I. Kahn: In the Realm of Architecture,* full version 1991, 39–40, for reproductions of floor plans for the Weiss, Ehle, Roche, Tompkins, and Genel Houses.
29 Eisenman, "From Plaid Grid to Diachronic Space," 105.
30 Eisenman, "From Plaid Grid to Diachronic Space," 105.
31 Brownlee and De Long, *Louis I. Kahn: In the Realm of Architecture* (condensed version, 1997), 66.
32 Smithson and Smithson, "The Space Between," 77.

33 Caroline Maniaque, "Louis Kahn: La maison Comme Laboratoire d'expérimentation," *AMC: Le Moniteur Architecture – Revue Mensuelle* 108 (2000): 96.
34 Maria Bottero, "Louis Kahn e l'incontro fra morfologia organica e razionale/Organic and Rational Morphology in Louis Kahn," *Zodiac* 17 (1967): 51–243, page numbers referring to the Italian and then English texts.
35 Bottero, "Organic and Rational Morphology in Louis Kahn," 51–243.
36 Bottero, "Organic and Rational Morphology in Louis Kahn," 52–244.
37 Hubert Damisch, *Noah's Ark: Essays on Architecture*, ed. Anthony Vidler (Cambridge: The MIT Press, 2016), 255.
38 Kahn, "Two Houses," 60.

Bibliography

Bois, Yve-Alain, and Rosalind, Krauss. *Formless: A User's Guide*. New York: Zone, 1998.
Bonnefoi, Christian. "Louis Kahn and Minimalism." (Translated by Dan Cooper). *Oppositions* 24 (1981): 2–25.
Bottero, Maria. "Louis Kahn e l'incontro fra morfologia organica e razionale/Organic and Rational Morphology in Louis Kahn." *Zodiac* 17 (1967): 47–53, 240–245.
Brownlee, David, and David, De Long. *Louis I. Kahn: In the Realm of Architecture*. London: Thames and Hudson, 1997 (the condensed version).
Brownlee, David, and David, De Long. *Louis I. Kahn: In the Realm of Architecture*. New York: Rizzoli, 1991 (the full version).
Cadwell, Michael. *Strange Details*. Cambridge: The MIT Press, 2007.
Damisch, Hubert. *Noah's Ark: Essays on Architecture*, edited by Anthony Vidler. Cambridge: The MIT Press, 2016.
Damisch, Hubert, with Yve-Alain, Bois, Denis, Hollier, and Rosalind, Krauss. "A Conversation with Hubert Damisch." *October* 85 (Summer 1998): 3–17.
Eisenman, Peter. "From Plaid Grid to Diachronic Space: Louis I. Kahn, Adler House and DeVore House." In *Ten Canonical Buildings 1950–2000*, 102–127. New York: Rizzoli International, 2008.
Giurgola, Romaldo, and Jaimini, Mehta. *Louis I. Kahn*. Boulder: Westview Press, 1975.
Gropius, Walter. *Scope of Total Architecture*. New York: Harper, 1955.
Hochstim, Jan, ed. *The Paintings and Sketches of Louis I. Kahn*. New York: Rizzoli, 1991.
Kahn, Louis I. "Two Houses." *Perspecta* 3 (1955): 60–61.
Maniaque, Caroline. "Louis Kahn: La Maison Comme Laboratoire d'expérimentation." *AMC: Le Moniteur Architecture – Revue Mensuelle* 108 (2000): 94–100.
Pushkarev, Boris, with Photographs by Sandford Meech. "Yale Art Gallery and Design Center." *Perspecta* 3 (1955): 47–58.
Scully, Vincent. "Introduction." In *The Paintings and Sketches of Louis I. Kahn*, edited by Jan Hochstim, 15–17. New York: Rizzoli, 1991.
Scully, Vincent. "Louis I. Kahn and the Ruins of Rome." *Engineering & Science* (1993): 2–13.
Scully, Vincent. "Yale Center for British Art. Louis I. Kahn, Architecture." *Architectural Record* (1977): 95–104.
Smithson, Alison, and Peter, Smithson. "The Space Between." *Oppositions* 4 (1974): 75–78.
Solomon, Susan. *Louis I. Kahn's Trenton Jewish Community Center*. New York: Princeton Architectural Press, 2000.
Wurman, Richard Saul, and Eugene, Feldman, eds. *The Notebooks and Drawings of Louis I. Kahn*. Philadelphia: The Falcon Press (distributed by New York: George Wittenborn and Company), 1962.

2

DISPLACEMENTS

House II and House IV by Peter Eisenman

I

Manfredo Tafuri characterises Peter Eisenman's analysis of the Engineering Building at the University of Leicester by James Stirling and James Gowan as an exemplary approach to teasing out theoretical implications in late modern architecture.[1] According to Tafuri, Eisenman's analysis triggers the 'conceptual destruction' of a number of conventions. Tafuri suggests that at least three conventions are wrested apart and provisionally distanced due to Eisenman's effort. Solid volume is rendered as a paper-thin surface. As opposed to glass operating as transparent, fragile, and dematerialised, it functions as an opaque and solid prism. A literal void assumed to be created by the cantilevered struts supporting the body of the sheds actually functions as a conceptual solid.[2]

While Eisenman's essay and, in turn, Tafuri's evoke a number of themes of relevance to our work on conceptual objects, let us focus on two. The first released is exactly Tafuri's claim to discern in the Leicester building qualities discovered by Eisenman which upset or displace conventions. In so doing, architectural consequences cause us to pause and think. As discussed earlier in the opening chapter, Continuities, this is a sign for Hubert Damisch of a theoretical object in operation.

In a related theme, though more decidedly methodological, Eisenman conjectures that what is important in certain projects such as the Leicester Engineering Building is that they should be seen to be on the side of the critical and the polemical, and thus carrying the potential to reveal or catalyse other capacities and strains in architecture. According to Eisenman, such projects are, by their nature, different from those that are 'merely iconic.'[3] As an illustration of the differences between the critical and the iconic, Eisenman contrasts Stirling and Gowan's Leicester building with Paul Rudolph's Yale School of Art and Architecture, placing the latter on the side of the only iconic. As a consequence of placing the Yale School of Art and

DOI: 10.4324/9781003009641-4

34 Conceptual objects

Architecture on the side of the iconic and not the critical, argues Eisenman, the Rudolph project has no capacity to disrupt conventions.

This difference of the critical versus the iconic can serve as a point of departure to the following observations in which we consider a pair of projects by Eisenman, House II and House IV. We suggest both projects can be placed on the side of the critical. By locating these two projects on the side of the critical, we are suggesting that they have the capacity to displace convention. We continue, that is, a track of investigation pursued in Chapter 1 around Louis Kahn's project for De Vore House. In this and the earlier chapter, we adopt Damisch's idea of the theoretical object as one of several thematic trajectories that delimit the temperament at work in certain examples of late-twentieth-century architecture. In examining two projects from Eisenman's House series, the analysis undertakes a close reading of plan, section, and volume manipulations, considering design processes and elements, mechanisms, and real or virtual spatial effects.

Four devices or form conditions are taken as a starting point. The four conditions or rubrics concern plan dispositions, oscillating wall and column relationships, the virtual capture and simultaneous release of movement from volumes, and oblique over frontal emphasis and their conjunction around ideas of structure (frame, bay, skeleton) and spatial animation. Each of these rubrics is offered as one aspect of an architectural process rendered in works of architecture that we argue fall on the side of theoretical objects. The order is relative, and all four can be said to converge in unique space sensations or space conceptions.

Expanded and combined, in other words, these rubrics further yield design tactics or principles and a limited number of architectural form relationships, including compression (or collapse), dispersal (or distancing, whether in a linear or a centroidal or a pinwheel motion), and diagonality (or rotation).

For this foray, two houses provide material for the investigation. The two projects are House II (Hardwick, Vermont, 1969–1970) and House IV (Falls Village, Connecticut, 1970–1971). Eisenman's House II, also known as the Falk House, was designed for an academic couple on a gently sloping hundred-acre (forty-hectare) site in Vermont and completed in 1970. It was the topic of an extended narrative by Eisenman in *Five Architects*. A number of preparatory sketches, analytic diagrams, conceptual models, and photographs were reproduced in *Houses of Cards*, and descriptions and commentary can be found in monographs on Eisenman's work.[4]

The designs for House IV were developed in the same years for an unreported client. The project has been the object of more limited publication and commentary as compared to House II, which is not to suggest House IV embodies any less intensity. As one measure of the depth of exploration, the Peter Eisenman fonds at the Canadian Centre for Architecture, Montréal, contain some 232 drawings related to House IV in addition to holding a physical model commissioned in 2002 for an exhibition mounted at the Yale School of Architecture. In a monograph dedicated to the House series, House IV is documented in sketches, diagrams, model photographs, and partial images of manuscript pages, presumably for an unpublished essay on the house. House IV is the object of limited secondary commentary further considered later.[5]

The two house projects are discussed in what follows largely from a formal point of view. As published, and as described by Eisenman, both projects insist on formal appraisal. One might suppose House IV, which remained unbuilt and thus, in theory, more abstract, to more immediately call for such a position when compared to House II. As the analysis shows, however, House II equally calls for such a viewpoint. The two projects provide an appropriate set of conditions for comparative interrogation: of similar scale, though, as we discuss, rendering diverse qualities, the two houses sit within a lineage of experimental work carried out through small residential projects. Each continues to provoke reflection and comment some six decades after its conception, evidencing their ongoing enigmatic characters.

In addition to an overarching analysis chasing the trajectory of conceptual objects, three general propositions inform the following. The first proposition concerns architecture's form. It suggests that the range of spatial and temporal effects in any work of architecture results from specific combinations of elements, and that the number and nature of relations at any one moment are limited. This proposition suggests that various spatial systems, or styles, have their own combinations. Such a point of view, for example, can be found in that neoclassicist temperament that Colin Rowe discovered around the same period.[6]

The second proposition concerns the methodologies of design research and claims that studio- or practice-based research, as compared to traditional text-based methods, has a more plastic and intimate relation to the work. The process of research thus has an interpretive as well as an explicitly creative side.

A third correlative proposition is that there are a limited number of space systems, analytic methods, and generative strategies to deploy when describing works of architecture. It is proposed that they result, and differentiate themselves from one another, in the manner by which they reappraise the forms and functions attributed to key architectural elements.

Turning now to the analysis of the selected projects, it is worth recalling the four organising themes. The first concerns plan disposition and, in part, ground relationships. Which kinds of organisational form and idea characterise the overall functioning of the two plans? What are the differences? The second organising theme concerns column and wall or pier and plane oscillations, evident in both projects. As we will argue, this is explicit in the case of House II and more allusive in House IV. In both projects, the column/post undergoes transformations in orientation and a greater or lesser integration with the wall plane. In House II, multiple column/post-to-wall transformations occur. How might the differences among them be understood? What might an examination of how they function suggest about architecture's relation to space and time? Animation of space resulting from volume manipulation and diagonal over frontal emphasis provide additional thematic orientation.

II Analysis

Let us return to that late-1960s moment when Eisenman observed with some alarm that 'the importance of the plan as a conceptual device has been all but overlooked.'[7] Accepting Eisenman at his word, one might be justified in betting that in his own design work, redressing such concerns will be a front-and-centre preoccupation. Stated differently, one assumes given his concern over an apparent loss that Eisenman will be at pains to fully exploit the plan's potential as a concept apparatus. One may hypothesise, that is, that his own efforts will attempt to inject the plan, as the locus of knowledge in architecture, with value and a critical force sufficient to disrupt disciplinary conventions. To track down such effort is to interrogate the plan as a catalyst and vehicle for experimentation on certain primary architectural concepts in the Damischian sense. Let us now turn to House II and House IV with that frame established.

II.i House II

To begin, one observes precise dissonances in the House II floor plans, with the analysis revealing a uniformly activated field in which a number of architectural figures are tested. See Eisenman's sketches in Figure 2.1.

Ambiguity reigns throughout. One enters upper left, already on an oblique, and seemingly without the opportunity to pause and orient, one is immediately being pushed or squeezed out. Such movement never resolves the full-time play between compressions and extensions.

Horizontal walls potentially constrict such movement vectors, and piers perpendicular to them redirect energy fields outward through openings. The plan is neither primarily a nine-bay nor a sixteen-column grid structure, even though there are instances of both at work. A stable bay reading is blurred as a result of an internal phase shift to the upper left, or lower right, depending on the starting point. This in turn creates a constant oscillation between what is fixed and repeatable as regular frame elements. The plan promotes and at the same time resists a reading of erosion. The plan can be read, that is, as simultaneously additive (bays or modules adding or starting from the upper left as a point of generation) and subtractive (starting at the lower right, modules can be read to be cut away.

The major unbroken wall-line at the top of the plan stands out. It is reinforced by the slightly shorter and parallel wall-line just below. This sets up a strong, if ambiguous, horizontal force, ambiguous in that it inverts a more common configuration of bottom-to-top dissolution. Here, rather, things become increasingly dense as one's eye moves to the top of the plan. This temporary densification occurs at the same time as vertical stratifications are established, in part by the six small vertically oriented fin walls and at the same time by narrow openings or slots of space contrasted with larger fields or areas. As a result, there is, moving left to right, a pattern of alternating A (narrow) and B (wide) openings, yielding an A-B-A-B-B-A rhythm that reinforces this interpretation.

Displacements **37**

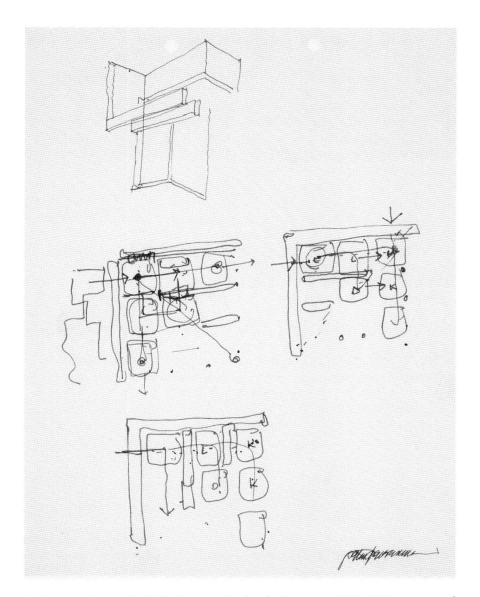

FIGURE 2.1 House II (Falk House), Hardwick Vermont, 1969–1970, conceptual sketches, Peter Eisenman, black ink on yellow paper 27.9 × 21.5 cm, DR1994:0130:015

Source: Peter Eisenman fonds, Collection Centre Canadien d'Architecture/Canadian Centre for Architecture, Montréal

These vertical stratifications start on the left with a slot of space pushed along by the vertical fins. There is equally a tension resulting from the horizontal wall-lines that divert the eye laterally. This system of vertical and horizontal oscillation is further complicated by an animation of the perimeter. There is intensification at the edge, especially in the upper right and lower left corners. This is contrasted with and contributes to a voiding of the centre.

To take a different tack, readings of shallow space stratification as a consequence are confronted with potential readings of deep space attributable to an ideal but never fully realised or felt nine-bay or nine-volume figure. Intimations of formal or visual depth are constantly retracted. There is, for example, a displacement or sidling movement starting with the upper left of the plan, with elements sliding along in echelon fashion toward the bottom right. The eye's movement is carried along by a momentum in the larger open spaces themselves, a movement leading to a reading of increased openings to the lower right of the plan. A rift of space is felt opening up, the ratcheted, lateral sliding of the visual field becoming only more determined as the eye travels into the middle of the plan and out again, reinforcing the interpretation of a voided centre. Contrary to a structure of stasis or an architectural model of stability, all is movement.

To come back to a convention noted earlier, there is at work a desire to find an ideal, regular grid in the plan. As with House IV, to be discussed later in this chapter, however, the field set-up is then concealed, or dissolved, so it is both potentially generative and neutral at the same time.

This survey of primary concepts that interpenetrate without dissolution or destruction of each other suggests there is some justification in reading the House II plan as a theoretical object following Damisch. Recall from the opening chapter, Continuities, Damisch's notion of primary concepts. Superpositioned, and eluding discursive reduction, such concepts constitute the architectural questions or problems the plan can be claimed to be working on. The House II plan, when examined closely, discharges architectural propositions about certain primary conditions. Eluding capture by historical and critical review, the plan works to construct and then destabilise architectural figures and field effects. Such figures necessarily remain in a state of ambiguity, suspended in constant tension, all qualities of the theoretical object proposed by Damisch.

Let us turn now to column/wall ambiguities. One way to formulate the question of the column in House II is to ask at what moment, or under what conditions, does the vertical frame become a column? Alternately, what does it take for the column to disappear and become part of a larger skeletal frame? Such questions are posed by House II, even though it appears that the frame was there from the beginning and evolved toward, in only very limited instances, a column. In House II, is it in fact the column in question, or is it more precisely a matter of panel- or pilaster-to-frame relations?

Another way to phrase the question of oscillations resulting from manipulation of columns and walls, or columns into walls: where does the wall become a plane, or do certain planes become elements of a larger structural frame? And to these would be added the question of style. Does the column's presence necessarily reveal a classical sentiment and the structural frame a modern one? And what of that supposed mannerist tendency, that variation on a stable language? Can we identify mere characteristics as evidence of traditional architectural instruments such as the reveal, the partial reveal, the false capital, the plinth, the shadow line, the pilaster: in other words, that whole world of mouldings? This would also direct one to take on Henry Cobb's characterisation of Eisenman as the inventor of a new kind of ornament. Discussing Eisenman's work some years after House II, Cobb writes: 'Eisenman's architecture results not from an idea of construction but from the construction of an idea. In this case, the idea being constructed is by nature systemic, systematic, rhythmical, dynamic – and hence inherently decorative or ornamental.'[8] As we have seen already in the earlier discussion of the dynamic state of affairs in House II, there is certainly a resonance with the effects and attitude discerned by Cobb.

Movement, resulting in part from space-volume distributions, is a third theme. Sketches by Eisenman support this term for both houses. In House II, sectional

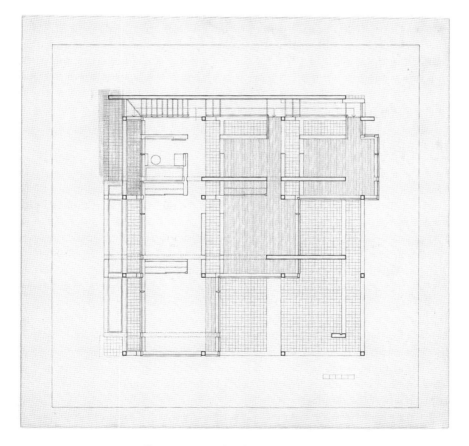

FIGURE 2.2 House II (Falk House), Hardwick Vermont, 1969–1970, upper floor plan, Peter Eisenman, reprographic copy 63.5 × 65 cm, DR1994:0130:291

Source: Peter Eisenman fonds, Collection Centre Canadien d'Architecture/Canadian Centre for Architecture, Montréal

40 Conceptual objects

relations emphatically record an echelon or spiral. See again Figure 2.1. The sketch studies and diagrams reveal a similar movement in House IV. Both projects rely on slots to transition between slipping, major volumes, as well as displacing any debt to a Domino sandwich world. Or are the slots, whether in section or plan, in reality, not gaps between but in fact elisions or cuts within a larger figure? Are the effects or consequences different, and, if so, what are the distinguishing spatial characteristics? Eisenman's proposed mock-up cover for *Casabella* suggests certain of these. See Figure 2.3.

A fourth rubric concerns an emphasis on oblique or diagonal conditions over frontal ones. Considered as preeminent in Chapter 3's analysis of John Hejduk's Diamond, as we see, in House IV and House II a resistance to frontal readings is at work. Such conditions of diagonality can be claimed to signal a temperament that resists a single, stable unity at the origin of the project. The multiplicity of form decision determinants as described by Eisenman in a series of thirty-five diagrams reinforces this reading.[9] When compared to House IV, as we will discuss in the next section, House II can be read perhaps as more stable, centralised, and balanced if one accepts a certain part-to-whole ambition. In a statement that accompanied the publication of House II in 1974, Eisenman, however, disrupts such an interpretation of a totalising aim in the design process, the goal, he writes, being to create a 'total structure of relationships.'[10] This could include a suite of variations on the nine-square grid as suggested in Figure 2.4.

II.i House IV

Let's start again with Tafuri. In thinking about the implications of Eisenman's work in the House projects, Tafuri believes it essential to recognise an ambition to displace a reliance on, or sole reference to, what is visible. The diagrammatic proliferations that accompany Eisenman's thinking and visualisations around House IV signal for Tafuri a strategy of 'multiplying frustrations to be imposed upon the visual approach.'[11]

This strategy of frustrating single readings of that which is visible is further complicated by intentional differences from historical elementarism and an implied residual reliance on dialectical relationships. Writing some years later about House IV, Eisenman is explicit about this. House IV was operating as a 'challenge to the hierarchical nature of configurational systems.'[12] Such a challenge could be further extended, according to Eisenman, to lead to disruptions of the very conceptual foundations bound to dialectical pairs and the prioritisation of one term over another. Such pairs include frontality over obliqueness, figure over ground, and the sequential over the simultaneous.[13]

Is there evidence that House IV functions this way? Do the plans, sectional drawings, and models elude discursive reduction, forcefully operating as a field of speculation and thus, as Damisch describes, is the result 'putting thought to work'[14] through specific figures and effects? And assuming a positive response to the latter, which architectural propositions and conditions are at stake in House IV?

Displacements **41**

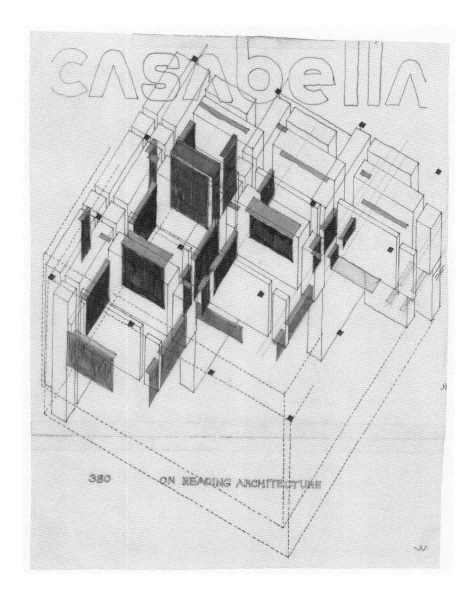

FIGURE 2.3 House II (Falk House), mock-up of a proposed cover for *Casabella* magazine, Peter Eisenman, ink and coloured ink on translucent paper 35 × 27.2 cm, DR1994:0130:301

Source: Peter Eisenman fonds, Collection Centre Canadien d'Architecture/Canadian Centre for Architecture, Montréal

42 Conceptual objects

A	B	A
B	C	B
A	B	A

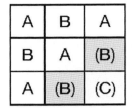 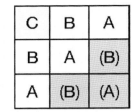

FIGURE 2.4 Nine square variations in House II

Source: diagram by the author

Looking closely, the plans of House IV are not characterised by cross-axial plaiding, nor Cubist directionality, nor elementarist floating dissolutions. See Figure 2.5. Plan manipulations are there to misdirect and deny any such direct interpretations. House IV is not characterised by those free-plan stratifications and centrifugal forces seen at work in Eisenman's House II. There is, that said, an initial desire to read the plan as a regular modulation of volume and plane: as surfaces ordered through an at-first-glance regular point grid-frame or cage. Closer attention quickly yields a more complex story.

The longer one studies the drawings, however, the more such assurances slip away. Accepting the challenge of a more complex reading, one starts to discern other effects, and certainly Eisenman himself felt more was at stake. More baldly than in House II, there are indications in the published diagrams and in the final stage of design development that somewhere in House IV is a four-square that becomes a nine-square scheme, which converts into a sixteen-column response, and then a series of pivoting volumes.

House IV is a box with tight, flattened edges pulled out. Openings and partitions provide a response to every other condition such that the grid and cage as potential neutral fields or backgrounds are never allowed to be read once and for all, leading to that overall ambiguity noted earlier.

Turning to the columns, one questions whether they can be read as columns, with all that implies of a supplement or ornament, or whether it is more accurate to see them as indices of a grid or field condition. The column-post is perhaps better read as an index or mark whose impact is traced by banding, never actually assuming corporeal presence. More like that absent column that Mies sketches for his interior study of the Barcelona Pavilion as revealed by Damisch.[15]

This might have been Eisenman's desire, accepting his description of the questions at play in the project. And these might be considered conceptual conveniences rather than physical ones, but their effect is undeniable as generated from a floor plan or axonometric interpreted as a thinking machine. Such an interpretation would situate House IV's posts and planes not as columns with a particular presence but as regular field markers, with the articulations of floor surfaces contributing to the establishment of a neutral field against which various elements, lines, shapes, and surfaces react as suggested. In this manner, they do

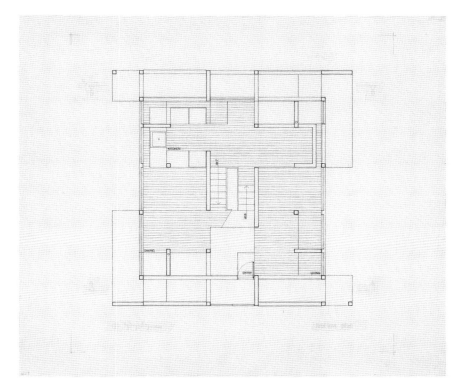

FIGURE 2.5 House IV, Falls Village, Connecticut, circa 1970–1971, first-level plan, Peter Eisenman, drawing in ink with transfer type and traces of graphite on translucent paper, 79 × 92 cm, DR1994:0132:333:007

Source: Peter Eisenman fonds, Collection Centre Canadien d'Architecture/Canadian Centre for Architecture, Montréal

not constitute a frame, a cage, or a three-dimensional bay system other than in a weak sense. See Figure 2.6.

Following Damisch, such a reading avoids the constraint of interpreting the plans as a generator of volumes. The system of volumes creates tensions or vibrations relative to adjacent elements; thus, they have an impact as singular events and not primarily as part of a larger unity. This is to continue a reading of layer-like stratifications independent of the interpretations of the three-dimensional volume I started with in relation to House II.

House IV suggests an exploration of the architectural-tectonic structure as a series of spatial units, or spatio-structural units as the main ordering element. However, it is not the case that any component – volume, column, wall, penetration – is primary. In the published diagrams, there is no centre; or if there is a centre, it has taken on the form of a hollowed volume generated by the switchback stair stepping up and down the midfield of the house.

44 Conceptual objects

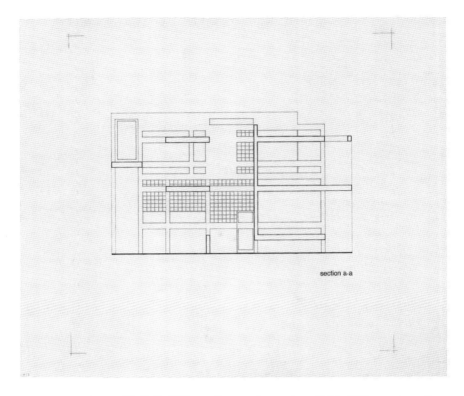

FIGURE 2.6 House IV, Falls Village, Connecticut, circa 1970–1971, section, Peter Eisenman, drawing in ink with transfer type and traces of graphite on translucent paper 79 × 92 cm, DR1994:0132:333:002

Source: Peter Eisenman fonds, Collection Centre Canadien d'Architecture/Canadian Centre for Architecture, Montréal

The scheme is emphatically haunted in the sense in which Damisch uses the word when writing about characteristics of architectural acts that function as theoretical objects. Haunted by all the iterations of those analytical diagrams. See Figure 2.7.

Confronted with the plan, one might ask if House IV functions within the parameters of typical composition formats. Is it critical of them? Does it introduce new instruments or effects? Or inflect old instruments and devices to create another kind of overall organisation?

The final stage drawings for House IV as published suggest a concern with planes, and a subdivided cubic frame, and volumes. Which kind of unit is it? There is an intertwining of articulated surfaces (not planes) and cages (not frames) and ultimately with volumes, with vertical surfaces recording implied trace conditions that might provide a clue to their provenance. There are apparent directions or biases in the otherwise supposedly neutral space, though it is hard to imagine any

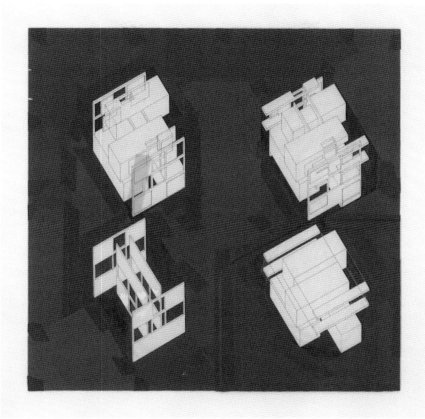

FIGURE 2.7 House IV, Falls Village, Connecticut 1970–1971, axonometrics, Peter Eisenman, mounted drawings in ink on paper 61 × 61 cm, DR1994:0132:193

Source: Peter Eisenman fonds, Collection Centre Canadien d'Architecture/Canadian Centre for Architecture, Montréal

space being neutral when one begins to examine the subtle inflections and agitations that always inhabit Eisenman's work.

The spatial units appear somewhat unsettled, maybe even randomly placed, responding to no apparent single compositional order. So, how might we describe the unity? House IV cannot be read as simply additive nor subtractive. It works to deflect any reading of centralisation or hierarchy or part-to-whole relation. There is only a part-to-part logic at work.

The first impression is that House IV can be read as a transformation or simple variation on the nine-square plan: it suggests an erosion or a transcription, a subtle variation, one consequence of which is that the centre is displaced and overlaid or interpenetrated with bars of space. Or perhaps it is more accurate to claim that the centre is transformed into a permanently absent promise. It is all movements and transformations from a four-square to a nine-square, twenty-seven-cube condition. Notice in particular the potential shifts of the centre.

A second interpretation is that background space, which normally might have resulted from plaiding, is moved to the perimeter and becomes figural. Or perhaps there are only figures of similar value and role and no ground, no background at all: everything is a figure. All three alternatives could be tested.

Bands of space at the top and bottom edges of the project fall out and cannot be clearly seen to contribute to forming or shaping a space. House IV can therefore be said to emphasise peripheral composition. This can be interpreted as an exploration of edge relations, further disrupting the possibility of tracing it back to a generating parti diagram. In the upper left of the upper-level plan, for instance, there is a stratification of the vertical elements, generally in a diagonal orientation, working to reinforce this, with the former centre pushed to either the lower left or the upper right of the project.

Oscillating column-and-wall or wall-to-scrim-to-pier-to-column relationships emerge as the second theme from the analysis of House IV. Such oscillations are evident in both House II and House IV. Are they of the same nature or made manifest from the same devices? Are they more clearly worked on in elevations or in sections? How might the differences be characterised?

Both projects contain evidence of ambiguities in column/wall readings and an engagement with the potential therein. These can range from a choice and use of different materials or implied materials in the coloured plexiglass model of House II to decisions on the layout or finish of similar materials. At first glance, this is explicit in the case of House II, more allusive in the case of House IV.

In House II, the column/post undergoes transformations in its orientation and in its integration with wall planes. In House IV, multiple post-to-pier-to-plane-to-wall variations are tested.

It is perhaps in House II that a more literal transcription of a system of column, wall, roof, or ceiling plane relationships is realised. House IV is an immaculate translation of the distinctions between the functions of support and enclosure. House II seems not to take these on or, perhaps more accurately, takes them on in an emphatically secondary and not primary manner. Support is assumed to be located in the skeleton frame so present as to constitute the thing itself, all else relegated to incident.

A spatio-structural unit perhaps was there at one point. However, it is impossible to pin down with any certainty. It is neither bay nor skeleton frame, and certainly not a Domino point column slab. Thus, the function of the pier is unclear, without easy precedent. The question about the roles of the column and wall as variations on support/skin relationships requires reformulation following the performance of House IV.

The order of the spatial unit (room, volume) in a free or open group plan versus the order of the skeleton frame could be an alternative formulation. Absent are the elements and relations that characterise International Style space. It is perhaps an example of a free group plan: the collective plan which manifests a 'this and this' or part-and-part relation suggested under the first rubric earlier.

To take things differently, the frame post of House IV tends to emphatically function to mark a place in the larger frame or skeleton system, whereas the frame or pier/plane in House IV plays a part in defining major volumes as an expression of, and simultaneously displacement toward, an underlying spatial idea. The presumed neutrality of the latter, however, is agitated by the sequence of shifts of other spatio-structural units and as a consequence of the specific relation to whatever occupies the position of infill as opposed to primary internal space and in whatever manner: gap versus alignment, transparent versus opaque.

In House II, the column is tied to a network of walls, screens, and beams that coalesce into a larger entity. The pier in House IV is more autonomous, its identity unique, and the walls, whether internal partitions or serving as the external enclosure, exist as mutations of a modern/International Style logic of point support and screen that retain their autonomy. House II suggests a sensibility which favours the continuous (even if complex and agitated) whole, and House IV a sensibility which favours multiple, separate entities.

Movement, especially in the form of echeloned volume arrangements, is the third theme or rubric. As suggested earlier, House II demonstrates sectional relations that emphatically record an echelon or spiral. A certain reading of the plan reveals a similar movement in House IV. Both projects rely on slots to transition between sliding rooms/volumes. A different interpretation is that the slots, whether in a section or the whole plan, are, in reality, not gaps between but elisions or cuts within a larger figure. Are the effects or consequences different in House IV, and if so, what are the distinguishing spatial characteristics?

The trajectory created by the disposition of volumetric elements puts space in motion.

In House IV, the following devices are at work: slipping, gaps, height differentials. The slippage of central volumes is a design decision that puts the whole into motion. The ground and next partial level up push to the upper left and lower right. On the upper platforms, volumes rotate 90 degrees relative to those below and are directed to the upper right and lower left with multi-storey scrims peeling away from the enclosed parts, reinforcing this bias.

To take another measure, House IV appears to display a condition of frontalisation established by the roughly symmetrical, and certainly balanced, distribution of the front five pavilions, with the entry on the middle all framed, in the plan at least, by the heavy line of the wall. A play of frontalisation and rotation is introduced through the increased height of the second unit and the drifting of the other units to the left and right or up and down relative to the wall. This play is further reinforced by a series of minor cross-axial moves which echelon or stagger along from left to right or right to left, depending on which is taken as the beginning element.

If the internal partitions in Eisenman's sketch plan are emphasised, however, there is evidence of a centripetal force that resembles certain classic International Style space episodes. Such a reading, if expanded, would focus on the internal

48 Conceptual objects

pinwheel or fugal movement that results from the manner in which light or movement slips away at the corner of the glass or cavity wall.

In House II, structural and spatial expression is more or less integral, even allowing for the duplication of structural frames as claimed by Eisenman. House IV maintains, if we accept that the spatial experience is that primarily between things, an independence of the two. A review of changing ceiling articulations demonstrates the difference. House II emphatically reveals the frame, with beams tied to columns or to shear walls, even if there are all those mannerist inflections which complicate the real. The ceiling in House II is more neutral, more bound to the individual spatio-structural cell to which it belongs, and in this it resolves or ignores the problems of frontality and centralisation that occupy House IV, which is not to imply a value to either, just a difference.

III Close

Tafari might again provide a clue as to how we think about these two architectural acts. Eisenman sets the stage in his short text that accompanies the publication of House III. In his comments, Eisenman refers to the relationship of an individual to a house as that of an intruder.[16] As Tafuri notes, 'the allusion to Brecht [in the title and text of Eisenman's article] is legitimate only if it refers to a technique of dislocating the spectator from his habitual codes.'[17] The burden thus is to develop a practice of displacement while retaining a semblance intention.

Let us compare the findings now having looked at House II and House IV. The problem of knowledge in architecture that adheres to House II and House IV, though revealing different problems, or where problems are placed in similar registers – as about the oblique, the absent centre, ambiguities among elements – is that the degree of emphasis is different.

The pattern rests generally on a balancing of pairs of terms or concepts and perceptions. Perhaps the temperament in these instances is not dissimilar to Alberti's 'butterfly mind,' to borrow a qualifier used by Michael Baxandall.[18] Baxandall calls up the term not as a kind of equivalent for what he himself characterises as a 'universal man.' Rather, it appears intended to qualify the architect's ability in his writing and projects to display in multiple, dispersed fields a 'productive deployment of a firm but transferable style of thought.'[19]

If, by implication, the suggestion is that House II and House IV equally and differently each display a kind of butterfly-like sensibility, this can be used to turn toward comparative observations on the two projects.

In this section, we close with a summary look at the two case studies and then add two final terms or themes, bifurcating again the itinerary in the spirit of opening up additional routes of investigation. Table 2.1 sets out, provisionally and in one possible way, the approach and problems, the materials, and the preliminary findings revealed in the analysis.

As a form of open-ended conclusion, the form relationships revealed in the analysis can be reviewed. Ambiguities in the two projects are manifest throughout.

TABLE 2.1 Comparative table: design principles or devices and findings comparing House II and House IV

Design conditions	House IV	House II
Ground plan disposition	Four-square modified	Nine-square variations
	Invisible idea of rotation	Single, clear volume
	Contraction versus expansion (centroidal versus centripetal)	Part-to-whole relationships
	Part-to-part relationship	
Column and wall ambiguities	Pier to wall	Skeleton
	Contiguous, contingent	Post/frame to pilaster to wall
	Pier to cavity wall to glass	
Simultaneity over sequence (or: virtual volumetric movements)	No single centre: or displaced centre	Perimeter emphasis
		Linear and spiral
	Sliding or slipping: echelon	Contained
Oblique over frontal	Rotation over frontalisation: ghost of the 45% rotation	

Source: table by the author

There is ambiguity in the overall plan distributions. The plans can be read as additive and as subtractive. Or more accurately, they are a record of erosion and of expansion/growth, a case of collapse as well as a case of dispersal. House IV is breaking apart, drifting out in a gentle, gradual centripetal way, and at the same time, the spatial units are coalescing into a coherent shape.

House II suggests it results from erosion from a pure state, and at the same time, it is an implosion; a multiplication or growth from a nine-square beginning, one diagonally expanding.

Another kind of ambiguity is available in the space system at work. Frampton sees in Eisenman's contemporaneous House I clear evidence of a picturesque rationalist sensibility overlaid on an analytically classical organisation.[20] And House IV might be said to create sensations both modern and primitive according to Rowe in his essay 'Neo-Classicism and Modern Architecture II.' Perhaps it is a residue of that Greek revival in the air. So, ambiguity of the space conception broadly could be another way to describe the effect. Rotation and frontalisation, oblique and axial are additional themes.

There is in addition an ambiguity of skin and structure readings in both. Only touched on here, but to be examined more in the future, is the relation to the site. House II is emphatically stereometric, a single mass (even if eroded or built up), sitting flat on the crest of its low hill. It does not yet begin to work the ground as certain of Eisenman's later projects, such as House X, will miraculously do. In terms of a response to the site, in House IV, the ground relationship is ambiguous: elevations are drawn as if there is a flat site, but the house is constantly stepping up from the entry over four levels.

The initial analysis complete, are there generalizable lessons, whether of substance or of method? The three terms of reference – plan disposition, column-to-wall relations, movement – have had more or less success as tools for critical analysis. The beginning assumption that the building's ground relation would be revelatory proved not to be the case. The rubric of column and wall provided a frame of reference, on the other hand, and proved valuable in highlighting fundamental differences. And the suggestion of a space system unique to each and expressed by volume movements in part is compelling as a way forward in a larger effort to understand the elements and devices at work in the processes of architectural design.

What is clear, finally, is that with all their subtle and sometimes brazen differences, and the range and nature of conditions they engage, House II and House IV engender a kind of instability or displacement. This displacement, enacted as a conventional relation from regular polarities, may lead one to characterise them as what Eisenman later advocated for as an 'other architecture,' one latent in certain strands of modernism. The two house projects maintain a resistance to simple interpretation, bearing along a strong trail of positive uncertainties, positive in their ability to provoke. And therein, perhaps, lay the power of their forms and ideas, and the ongoing ability of the plans after some six decades to still provoke, and some justification for locating each on the side of the theoretical object.

House II and House IV being surveyed, as a form of provisional conclusion, let me return to the opening propositions. The first asked which architectural problems are revealed by a close reading of the plans as an object of plastic experimentation in Eisenman's period projects.

In the case of House II, the analysis revealed a number of conditions, including compression and extension, oblique and diagonal force supplanting any desire or effect of frontality, echelon movement which contributes to the voiding of the centre, and shallow space over deep space. In the case of House IV, while certain of these same concepts are being worked on – compression and extension, deep and shallow space in particular – a number of other conditions are in play, resulting in a work toward an overall spatial warping generated from right-angled systems in particular that creates effects different from cross-axial and centrifugal ones. There is a continuous dialectic in House IV's volume-to-frame-to-plane/wall, between fact and implication, such that a tension between or within concepts exists, reinforcing a state of simultaneity that puts theory 'to the test' following Damisch. Perhaps it is fair to say that the plan wants it both ways and on several levels.

This first proposition was framed as a way toward demonstrating that the architectural plan can be the site for a kind of work knowledge in architecture. The plan, in other words, provides one realm in which plastic research can be undertaken. Adopting the terminology of Damisch, certain architectural plans can thus be claimed to operate as theoretical objects, revealing a set of primary concepts as a 'model for thought.'[21] Perhaps more distinctively, such architectural objects do a kind of work 'on' theory as thinking machines and thus can be said to make manifest theory in the making.

My second proposition was that the late 1960s are the endpoint of a period of decline – or at best of transition – the architect, critic, and historian losing sight of the plan, their attentions directed elsewhere: toward the city, toward the symbolic, and toward history, to name only the most evident concerns.

At least as regards theory, the proposition that the plan was in decline in practice would illustrate or provide evidence of theory in dissipation. To address this proposition, however, would require an extended engagement with a number of topics, their associated literatures, and manifestations not possible in this initial brief study. As a final, concluding observation, therefore, I offer three topics that seem most immediately at hand as lines for such future research around this proposition. The first concerns the axonometric. I suggest that the appearance and particular use of the axonometric early in the twentieth century starts to trigger a decline of the plan's importance in architectural knowledge. The second topic is a more extended development and application of Damisch's concept of the theoretical object, one that would examine more deeply the implications of the architectural object as a thinking machine according to Damisch's approach. To formulate this aspect differently, a subsequent project will need to research more rigorously the methodological power in Damisch's idea of the theoretical object and its potential deployment in the reading of architectural works in a more nuanced and deep manner than is possible in this chapter.

To claim that the discipline's passion for the plan lost its vigour is certainly too general a statement, even if there is some truth to it according to the proposition that architectural knowledge at that time moved, its primary manifestations shifting elsewhere. As a third topic, therefore, I believe we need to call for a reconsideration today of the plan's primacy in architectural education and as an object of deep historical scrutiny and theoretical speculation on projects from that fertile period of the late 1960s and early 1970s considered here through to the contemporary. In other words, bringing the study toward the present, I believe we need to inaugurate and promulgate in university studio teaching and scholarship a move from a critical stance vis-à-vis the plan to a generative one. A research project testing these will continue the line of questioning opened above into the plan as a locus of architectural knowledge.

Eisenman's ambition could be captured in part by reference to Damisch, to a work that transforms the object under consideration, introducing a swerve such that the object works differently. In a conversation with Yve-Alain Bois, Denis Hollier, and Rosalind Krauss, Damisch frames it succinctly: 'That's what I want to do, to succeed each time in displacing the objects slightly, and at that point they gain their function as theoretical objects.'[22] Damisch goes on to comment on the change his thinking on this has undergone, as if itself the product of theory's impact. Damisch continues: 'I started out with the idea of a theoretical object as something that would make doing theory an act of extrapolation; but more and

52 Conceptual objects

more I see it simply as a kind of deviation, as a displacement within which theory takes place.'[23]

Theory takes place within the theoretical object, according to Damisch. This could be another manner of characterising the effort of displacement that Eisenman achieves with the House II and House IV projects.

Notes

1 Manfredo Tafuri, "L'architecture dans le boudoir," in *The Sphere and the Labyrinth: Avant-Gardes and Architecture from Piranesi to the 1970s*, trans. Pellegrino d'Acierno and Robert Connolly (Cambridge, Mass.: The MIT Press, 1987), 271. Tafuri is referring to Eisenman's essay 'Real and English: The Destruction of the Box. I'. See note 3 for the full bibliographic reference to the latter.
2 Tafuri, "L'architecture dans le boudoir," 271.
3 Peter Eisenman, "Real and English: The Destruction of the Box. I," *Oppositions* 4 (1974): 7.
4 Descriptions of and commentary on House II and House IV can be found in Peter Eisenman, "Cardboard Architecture: House II," in *Five Architects: Eisenman, Graves, Gwathmey, Hejduk* (New York: George Wittenborn and Company, 1972), 24–31. Peter Eisenman, "Cardboard Architecture," *Casabella* 374 (1973): 17–31. Peter Eisenman, *Houses of Cards* (Oxford: Oxford University Press, 1987). P. Ciorra, *Peter Eisenman: Opere e progetti* (Milano: Electa, 1993).
5 House IV is partially documented in *Houses of Cards*. Oxford: Oxford University Press, 1987. See: Sketches 28–35, Diagrams 62–79, Models 102–107, Manuscripts 150–53, 157.
6 Colin Rowe, "Neo-'Classicism' and Modern Architecture II," *Oppositions* 1 (1973): 14–26.
7 Peter Eisenman, "Big Little Magazine: *Perspecta* 12 and the Future of the Architectural Past," *The Architectural Forum* 131(3) (1969): 75.
8 Henry N. Cobb, "A Note on the Criminology of Ornament: From Sullivan to Eisenman," in *Eleven Authors in Search of a Building: The Aronoff Center for Design and Art at the University of Cincinnati*, ed. Cynthia C. Davidson (New York: The Monacelli Press, 1996), 97.
9 Eisenman, *Houses of Cards*, 56–59.
10 Eisenman, "Cardboard Architecture: House II," 26.
11 Manfredo Tafuri, "Peter Eisenman: The Meditations of Icarus," in *Houses of Cards*, trans. Stephen Sartarelli (Oxford: Oxford University Press, 1987), 173, 175.
12 Peter Eisenman, "Misreading," in *Houses of Cards* (Oxford: Oxford University Press, 1987), 178.
13 Eisenman, "Misreading," 178.
14 Damisch, Hubert, "Against the Slope: Le Corbusier's La Tourette," in *Noah's Ark: Essays on Architecture*, ed. Anthony Vidler (Cambridge: The MIT Press, 2016), 204.
15 Hubert Damisch, "The Slightest Difference: Mies van der Rohe and the Reconstruction of the Barcelona Pavilion," in *Noah's Ark: Essays on Architecture*, ed. Anthony Vidler (Cambridge: The MIT Press, 2016), 129.
16 Peter Eisenman, "To Adolph Loos & Bertold Brecht," *Progressive Architecture* (1974): 92.
17 Manfredo Tafuri, 'European Graffiti.' Five x Five = Twenty-five," (translated by Victor Caliandro) *Oppositions* 5 (1976): 49.
18 Michael Baxandall, *Words for Pictures: Seven Papers on Renaissance Art and Criticism* (New Haven: Yale University Press, 2003), 28.
19 Baxandall, *Words for Pictures*, 29.
20 Kenneth Frampton, "Frontality vs. Rotation," in *Five Architects: Eisenman, Graves, Gwathmey, Hejduk, Meier* (New York: Wittenborn, 1972), 9–13.

21 Damisch, "The Space Between," 107.
22 Hubert Damisch with Yve-Alain Bois, Denis Hollier, Rosalind Krauss, "A Conversation with Hubert Damisch," 85 (1998), 11.
23 Damisch, "A Conversation with Hubert Damisch," 11.

Bibliography

Allen, Stan. "Trace Elements." In *Tracing Eisenman: Peter Eisenman Complete Works*, edited by Cynthia Davidson, 48–65. New York: Rizzoli International Publications Inc, 2006.
Baxandall, Michael. *Words for Pictures: Seven Papers on Renaissance Art and Criticism*. New Haven: Yale University Press, 2003.
Cobb, Henry N. "A Note on the Criminology of Ornament: From Sullivan to Eisenman." In *Eleven Authors in Search of a Building: The Aronoff Center for Design and Art at the University of Cincinnati*, edited by Cynthia C. Davidson, 94–97. New York: The Monacelli Press, 1996.
Damisch, Hubert. "Against the Slope: Le Corbusier's La Tourette." In *Noah's Ark: Essays on Architecture*, edited by Anthony Vidler (translated by Julie Rose), 176–211, endnotes 350–352. Cambridge: The MIT Press, 2016.
Damisch, Hubert. "The Slightest Difference: Mies van der Rohe and the Reconstruction of the Barcelona Pavilion." In *Noah's Ark: Essays on Architecture*, edited by Anthony Vidler, 212–228, endnotes 352–353. Cambridge: The MIT Press, 2016.
Damisch, Hubert, with Yve-Alain, Bois, Denis, Hollier, and Rosalind, Krauss. "A Conversation with Hubert Damisch." *October* 85 (Summer 1998): 3–17.
Eisenman, Peter. "Big Little Magazine: Perspecta 12 and the Future of the Architectural Past." *The Architectural Forum* 131(3) (1969): 74–75, 104.
Eisenman, Peter. "House II." In *Eisenman Architects: Selected and Current Works*, edited by Stephen Dobney, 24–29. Malgrave: The Images Publishing Group Pty Ltd, 1995.
Eisenman, Peter. "House IV, Falls Village, Connecticut, 1971." In *Tracing Eisenman: Peter Eisenman Complete Works*, edited by Cynthia Davidson, 44–47. New York: Rizzoli International Publications Inc, 2006.
Eisenman, Peter. "House IV." In *Eisenman Architects. Selected and Current Work*, edited by Stephen Dobney, 34–37. Malgrave: The Images Publishing Group Pty Ltd, 1995.
Eisenman, Peter. "Misreading." In *Houses of Cards*, 167–186. Oxford: Oxford University Press, 1987.
Eisenman, Peter. "Progetto per la House IV, Falls Village, Connecticut 1971." In *Peter Eisenman: Tutte le Opere*, edited by Pier Vittorio Aureli, Marco Biraghi and Franco Purini, 72–77. Milano: Mondadori Electa, 2007.
Eisenman, Peter. "Real and English: The Destruction of the Box. I." *Oppositions* 4 (1974): 5–34.
Eisenman, Peter. "To Adolph Loos & Bertold Brecht." *Progressive Architecture* (1974): 92.
Frampton, Kenneth. "Frontality vs. Rotation." In *Five Architects: Eisenman, Graves, Gwathmey, Hejduk, Meier*, 9–13. New York: George Wittenborn and Company, 1972.
"House II." *Eisenman Architects*. Accessed 15 March 2022. https://eisenmanarchitects.com/House-II-1970.
"House IV." *Eisenman Architects*. Accessed 15 March 2022. https://eisenmanarchitects.com/House-IV-1971.
Peter Eisenman Fonds, 1925–2008. "Falk House (House II)." *Canadian Centre for Architecture*, AP143.S4.D12 (Certain materials have been digitised and can be found on the CCA website). Accessed 12 March 2022. www.cca.qc.ca/en/archives/380476/peter-eisenman-fonds/387751/projects/388649/falk-house-house-ii.

Peter Eisenman Fonds, 1925–2008. "House IV, Falls Village, Connecticut (1970–1971)." *Canadian Centre for Architecture*, AP143.S4.D12 (Certain materials have been digitised and can be found on the CCA website). Accessed 12 March 2022. www.cca.qc.ca/en/archives/380476/peter-eisenman-fonds/387751/projects/389245/house-iv-falls-village-connecticut-1970-1971.

Rowe, Colin. "Neo-'Classicism' and Modern Architecture II." *Oppositions* 1 (1973): 14–26.

Tafuri, Manfredo. "'European Graffiti.' Five x Five = Twenty-five." (Translated by Victor Caliandro) *Oppositions* 5 (1976): 35–74.

Tafuri, Manfredo. "L'architecture dans le boudoir." In *The Sphere and the Labyrinth: Avant-Gardes and Architecture from Piranesi to the 1970s*, translated by Pellegrino d'Acierno and Robert Connolly, 267–290. Cambridge: The MIT Press, 1987.

Tafuri, Manfredo. "Peter Eisenman: Meditations of Icarus." In *Houses of Cards*, translated by Stephen Sartarelli, 167–187. Oxford: Oxford University Press, 1987.

3

OVERCOMING

Diamond Projects by John Hejduk

I

In November 1967, architect and educator John Hejduk exhibited a series of drawings and models in New York at the Architectural League. The work explored the architectural implications of the forty-five-degree rotation of bounding architectural elements relative to an orthogonal system and was the result of investigation into the problem starting as early as 1962.

Diamond House A, Diamond House B, and Diamond Museum C are the three developed projects in Hejduk's Diamond series. The Architectural League exhibition also included paintings on the same theme by Robert Slutzky. The Diamond Projects have been partially published, were referred to in writings by Hejduk at the time, and were the object of his retrospective considerations.[1]

The projects have received only limited consideration in secondary writing, though writers have almost uniformly commented on their significance. Key secondary writing includes Stan Allen's brief reference to the Diamonds as part of Hejduk's research on form and space relations that also includes for Allen the 1/2 and 3/4 Houses.[2] Over three dense pages, and in the context of a longer commentary on Hejduk's last work, K. Michael Hays discusses the so-called 'Diamond Thesis' text and the role of the Diamond Projects as contributing to the thinking and practice that created part of the momentum leading to Hejduk's Wall Houses.[3] In a chapter devoted to Hejduk's Wall Houses, Mark Linder discusses the Diamond Projects and reproduces a number of drawings included in, and a photograph of, the 1967 Architectural League exhibition discussed earlier.[4]

The Diamond Projects occupy a unique place in Hejduk's work. As he notes in an interview some twenty years after their formulation, Hejduk reflects on the sudden drift from the Nine-Square (Texas) series that happened around 1962. According to Hejduk, the Diamonds promulgated a shift, if not a full break, in his interests

DOI: 10.4324/9781003009641-5

and mode of apprehension. Here is Hejduk in an interview with Don Wall: 'Suddenly a shift occurred, a shift in the path and the Diamond Projects appeared.'[5]

The Diamonds follow his near decade-long work on the Nine-Square or Texas Houses, and the significant differences are described in what follows. The Diamonds are themselves followed by a number of shorter studies by Hejduk, including the 1/4, 1/2, and 3/4 Series among others, and, in due course, the Wall Houses.[6]

To take Hejduk at his word at the time, the three Diamond Projects arrived in part out of an ambition to explore the implications of 'the diamond canvases of Mondrian for architects of today.'[7] Following this description by Hejduk, therefore, their role might be justifiably thought to be primarily morphological, the projects exploring formal-spatial modifications and resulting possibilities in diamond configurations by means of columns (House A), planes (House B), and biomorphic shapes (Museum C) to make only the most reductive of interpretations. The variations resulting from manipulation of these three elements – columns, planes, biomorphic shapes – are the most immediately accessible and evident architectural motifs addressed in the Diamonds, as Hejduk himself suggests in his synoptic table diagramming of his work between 1955 and 1972.[8]

As we argue next, however, the impact and importance of the Diamond Projects is more than a search for new form relationships or a transmutation of architectural space concepts. In addition to these, the Diamond Projects can be read as an index of at least two other considerations. First, the Diamonds can be seen as an effort to overcome a number of architectural biases Hejduk traces to the Le Corbusier of Villa Garches and the Visual Arts Center at Harvard University (more commonly known today as the Carpenter Center for the Visual Arts).[9] In particular, as discussed in what follows, Hejduk tries to escape from the biases of frontality and the horizontal stratifications of space idealised in Le Corbusier's Domino diagram and traced by Hejduk to the Villa Garches. I suggest that in this, the Diamonds operate as theoretical objects in the way Hubert Damisch uses the term as set out in the opening chapter. Thus, the Diamonds operate so as to disrupt easy interpretation, causing one to pause and create a gap in time to give way for thought. Following Damisch, then, the theoretical object 'opens the way for reflection.'[10]

There is a second consideration underlying the analysis. The Diamond Projects can also be interpreted as manifestations of a specific sensibility about movement and time. While I examine the first consideration in detail, this latter aspect – that of a uniquely architectural notion of movement and time – is returned to in Chapters 6, 7, and 8. As a provisional observation, the temporality rendered in the Diamonds, I suggest, is time that is always already compressed. It is different from a time composed of a line of images or vignettes and thus is reliant neither on futures nor on pasts. Importantly, in terms of its potential for architecture, the temporality revealed or explored in the Diamond Projects is independent of movement. In this, it shares certain of the traits at work in, for example, Le Corbusier's Visual Arts Center, as discussed in Chapter 6.

Research for this chapter has benefited from work on unpublished materials held in the John Hejduk Archive at the Canadian Centre for Architecture, Montréal;

published interviews and writings of Hejduk; and secondary writings on Hejduk. The drawings form the primary analytic material. These are supplemented by key documents, including Hejduk's *Three Projects* text and his so-called 'Diamond Thesis' published to accompany the 1967 exhibition as noted earlier. Hejduk's meditation on Le Corbusier's just-opened Visual Arts Center, published in 1965 as an homage following Le Corbusier's death in August of the same year, provides additional clues to what is at stake. I also rely on interviews between Hejduk and Don Wall published in 1985 as part of *Mask of Medusa*, which catalogues the architect's work between 1947 and 1983. Secondary writings from the period when Hejduk was working on the Diamond Projects, and more recent scholarship, provide historical and critical context and additional frameworks for situating the material.

The first thing that is striking when looking at drawings of the three Diamonds is that the rotation of the bounding frame relative to a strictly horizontal-vertical orthogonal column grid generates a number of unique conditions. The new conditions or relationships of form brought into effect via the rotation have at least four major consequences. The first of these is what Hejduk characterises as peripheric tensions of the edge. In addition, field extensions are generated beyond the building volume that result in a sense of space expanding.[11] A third consequence is that rotation creates conditions which challenge potential bay readings by disrupting oppositions between frontal and oblique vectors, as everything in one sense is or has become diagonally engaged in a perimeter condition. A fourth consequence results from the fact that, generally unlike the preceding Nine-Square (Texas) house series, there are no site plans for the Diamond Projects, and thus the ground as distinct from the figure is not available as a difference. In other words, there is no outside, no house – site relationship.[12]

A fifth consequence is something like a 'hypotenuse moment,' as Hejduk characterises the densest effects produced in the Diamond Projects. I return later in the chapter and elaborate on what Hejduk is alluding to with this term.

II Analysis

In this part of the chapter, the three Diamond Projects are described, and architectural consequences surveyed. A thematic analysis then follows that argues that the projects operate to escape conventional qualification and thus align with key criteria of the theoretical object as described by Damisch.

II.i The projects

Diamond House A is a thirteen-column, ten-grid-line, square-bay plan. See Figure 3.1. Unlike in the Texas house investigations, bay manipulations are not a particularly useful way to characterise projects in the Diamond series, the number of regular four-sided bays being highly limited. In House A, for example, there are four full bays, eight three-fifths bays ringing the perimeter, and eight minor triangular bays at the points. Column or grid lines are counted both vertically and

58 Conceptual objects

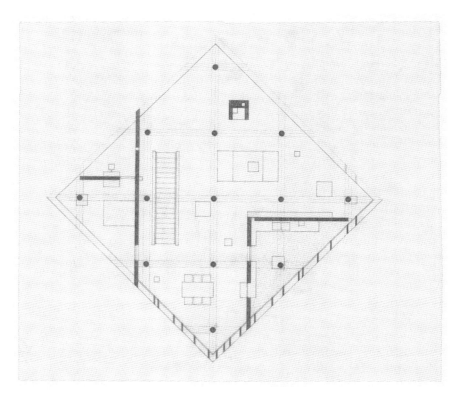

FIGURE 3.1 Diamond House A, 1963–1967, sketch plan with red columns, John Hejduk, drawing in graphite with coloured pencil on translucent paper 50.9 × 76.3 cm, DR1998:0060:002:003

Source: John Hejduk fonds, Collection Centre Canadien d'Architecture/Canadian Centre for Architecture, Montréal

horizontally. The columns are round, introducing what Hejduk claimed as a 'centrifugal force and multi-directional whirl' into the plan.[13]

Grid lines are inscribed in the floor plan as narrow bands, and there is a straight run stair in the second bay from the left. Elements such as fireplaces, furniture, and partitions generally abut the column/beam bands, though not consistently. Certain partitions on the second and third floors are located well off the grid. On the second and third levels, full floor-height brise soleil bars provide a continuous agitation of the light, to use Hejduk's characterisation of the effect. Here is Hejduk describing this intent: 'Well, the whole idea of the periphery in the Diamonds dealt with the fragmentation of light, you have to understand that.'[14]

The rhythm of brise soleils varies from floor to floor, and there is no evident method for placement of the brise soleil, with one exception. The bars on the grid-line extension to the perimeter are consistently doubled, and the glass is pushed out in these instances, including at the top and bottom points, to the

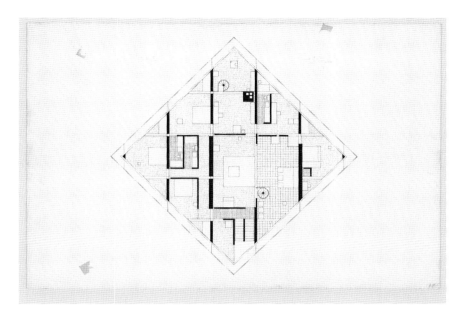

FIGURE 3.2 Diamond House B, 1963–1967, floor plan, John, ink over graphite on cardboard 50.9 × 76.3 cm, DR1998:0061:002:003

Source: John Hejduk fonds, Collection Centre Canadien d'Architecture/Canadian Centre for Architecture, Montréal

outside of the slab. This is most easily seen in model photographs and introduces a direction in the plans to the extent that left–right grids are not treated in the same manner either in the mid-bay positions or at their points.[15]

In Diamond House B, another four-level project, parallel rows of partitions replace the columns of House A. The partitions generally run vertically according to the plans as published. See Figure 3.2, which reproduces the second-floor plan.[16] Unlike in House A, the stairs have shifted: there is a switchback stair at the bottom and two spiral stairs framing the spine. Right-angled relations inside the diamond plan are constant until the final floor is reached and curved elements appear. Counting from point to point, this is a twelve-grid line, square-bay plan. Floor scoring continues as in House A: wall-width scores follow the regular bay pattern.

If House A was an exploration of the formal implications of right-angled conditions within a diamond configuration via columns or walls in shifting right-angled or oblique relationships, then House B tests the potential using walls alone. As discussed in what follows in relation to Diamond Museum C, the Diamonds also experiment on specific relations created by curvilinear walls and Hejduk's research into the architectural problem of ordering colours. On the former, listen to Hejduk's remarks in the 'Diamond Thesis': 'A curvilinear surface would have the effect of softening the experience and impact' as compared to the impact of 'confronting the diagonal with right-angled conditions.'[17]

60 Conceptual objects

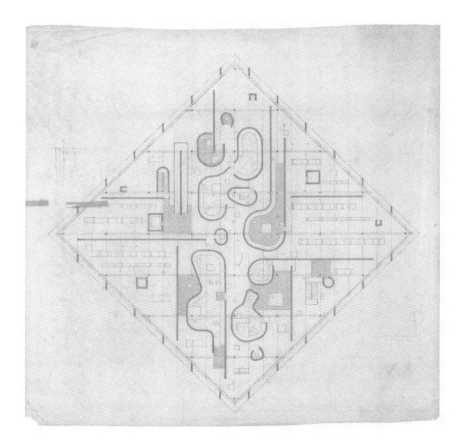

FIGURE 3.3 Diamond Museum C, 1963–1967, plan, John Hejduk, drawing in graphite on translucent paper 93 × 92 cm, DR1998:0062:003

Source: John Hejduk fonds, Collection Centre Canadien d'Architecture/Canadian Centre for Architecture, Montréal

As in House A, revealing a lingering tendency that might be described as cubistic, a direction as well as an eccentricity is introduced in House B by the placement and delineation of walls of different dimensions. Thicker walls are located on top-to-bottom grid lines three and five (counting left to right), establishing a dominant direction in organising spatial flow and a shifted centre onto grid line four. The perimeter agitation of light in House A that Hejduk found so troubling twenty years later is not present in House B.[18] A constant floor slab overhang continues, interrupted in this case only by glass blades extended along eight of the grid line extensions, all continuing the top–bottom alignment of the major internal walls and further reinforcing the direction.

Diamond Museum C begins again with a square bay, now in a larger eighteen grid line, forty-one round column configuration. See Figure 3.3. Like Diamond Houses A and B, a greater concentration in the vertical (bottom-to-top) alignment is palpable when reading the plans as published. All three vertical circulation elements – the switchback ramp and two switchback stairs – as well as the cluster of biomorphic-shaped walls are aligned in a bottom-to-top arrangement. As in House A and House B, the bottom-to-top bias is reinforced by perimeter brise soleil blade walls. The brise soleil blades are on a two-thirds grid-line rhythm that continues without interruption around the full diamond perimeter, aligning with every other grid line. The rows of display cases in Diamond Museum C are all on a horizontal left-to-right alignment. In this, they could be interpreted as following the general disposition of Piet Mondrian's last unfinished painting, *Victory Boogie-Woogie*.[19]

In its final state, *Victory Boogie-Woogie* has eight prominent horizontal rows of small colour swatch tapes. The display cases in Museum C roughly align in number with these. Other features shared by Museum C include the openness of all four points of the diamond field and the use of relatively large areas of neutral colour (open field) on the bottom-to-top spine. Major walls are more or less on a pinwheel configuration. Scoring of the plan on the column grid with variously spaced double lines follows a left-to-right pattern, reinforcing this directional bias. A second level of single-line floor scoring at right angles to this divides each bay into three vertical rectangles. This could be interpreted as introducing a cubistic gesture (directional) into a neo-plasticist (non-direction, square grid) realm.

Plan tensions are introduced and swing between a bias to the vertical and uniform extensive or explosive forces, not at the points but out to the edges of the diamond.

II.ii The situation

Having now an overview of key characteristics and drawings for each of the three developed projects, it is appropriate to look at the larger context. To understand the impact or potential of the Diamonds, it is helpful to review Hejduk's period writing and examine what was happening around him. To start, let us consider three moments. In the air and occupying Hejduk is the experience of Le Corbusier's Visual Arts Center, the specific suggestions and sensibilities of what Hejduk calls that 'last realist'[20] – the Mondrian of *Victory Boogie-Woogie* – and Colin Rowe and Robert Slutzky's explication of Villa Garches as an exemplar of flat space in their 'Transparency: Literal and Phenomenal' essay.

Certainly, this cluster of moments or events can be conjectured as a contributing vector to that shift in his thinking and practice. Hejduk's experience of the Visual Arts Center in 1965 and Le Corbusier's death in August of the same year no doubt are contributing forces. Hejduk's desire to get out from under or to go beyond a number of motifs or biases, including those located in the work of Mondrian and the Le Corbusier of Garches, is another vector. Such motifs include the limits of frontality, a lost centre, the Domino spatial idea, and a chronological or linear notion of time expressed in certain cases as privileging a narrative borne from an allegiance to the architectural promenade.

Perhaps these influences or traits are what, in the end, Hejduk endeavours to get beyond, to work outside architecturally. The Diamond Houses are privileged in Hejduk's interviews with Wall as the site of working outside certain Corbusian devices. A close review of subsequent project drawings from Hejduk's 1/4 Series, 1/2 Series, and Extension House, however, reveal lingering traces. As Hejduk himself states in an interview with Wall, the Diamond isometrics 'reminded me of Le Corbusier. So I had to get rid of that, by working it out, by exorcising the images. Corbusier, and then Mondrian in a way.'[21]

To further unpack the formal moves and motivations, consider the admonitions of a contemporary witness. Kenneth Frampton describes Hejduk during the Diamonds phase as an architect trapped, unable to adopt the 'multi-directional spatiality of the De Stijl or Suprematist movements,' 'unable to abandon . . . [an] emphasis on frontality.'[22]

There is evidence of these two conditions in the Diamonds' general reliance on the free plan, column-slab or wall-slab model, and all three projects are horizontally layered within a regular volume and thus are indebted to or rely on the Domino space concept. However, Hejduk was never aiming for, or concerned with, Frampton's Suprematist dissolutions and their associated multi-directional spatiality, convinced as he was at the time that the already dense two-dimensionality of architectural space was the only one he should pursue. This belief is in evidence when he writes at the time about architectural space's actual 'two-dimensionality.'[23]

Form relations, concepts of space, and perhaps, as I am proposing, notions of time are all being worked on here. At first blush, and as suggested earlier, two compositional devices are constantly explored in the Diamonds. The first is an expansion or exfoliation toward the periphery and beyond. The term 'exfoliation' is Frampton's, used to characterise the tensions in the periphery of the Diamond Projects.[24] A second form-space generation strategy is that leading to a condensation of space and mass toward an always voided centre. Hejduk, in an interview with Wall, states rather specifically this ambition and elevates it to a career-defining motive: 'All my houses have voided centers. . . . Maybe my contribution to architecture is the voided center.'[25]

This latter trait is worth expanding on and confirms a move in Hejduk's attention away from a trabeated logic of post-and-beam frames, of singular columnar surfaces, and of articulated roofs (clearly and methodically treated in the Nine-Square (Texas) series). Instead, the Diamonds reveal a move toward a ground-less architecture of round columns, freestanding partitions, and flat-slab floors and ceilings. In other words, a critical work on Le Corbusier's Domino world of column-slab construction is one that would fully engage with the implications and effects of two kinds of architectural freedoms, those of 'liberated space [and] liberated structure,' as Hejduk writes in a manuscript sheet from the period.[26] It will take a few more projects, a few more steps, to get to what he claims was that 'real break' of the Wall House.[27] However, certain problems explored in the Diamond configurations – voided centre, frontality, perimeter warps – are evident. In addition, there is perhaps an underlying dimension related to time. To track these conditions, I will start with the voided centre.

In House A, the centre is occupied by a round column. In House B, the centre is held by a shallow room bound by walls in shear. In Museum C, it is another round column that is placed at the centre of the floor, here marking a spring-point of pinwheeling elements. There is no tension; rather, there is a state of equilibrium where all the architectural energy has moved to the perimeter. This is consistent with the form studies underway. As documented in *Mask of Medusa*, and teased out in the interviews, at the time, Hejduk was trying to establish an architectural condition that made manifest a phenomenon of 'all-over kinetic equilibrium.' This is the same pendulum arc as he tried to realise the condition for a neutral container, the two together mimicking what he described as a Michelangelo effect. Listen to Hejduk: 'The effect is like in Michelangelo's architecture. At first there's a sense of a perfectly neutral condition. Then when you begin to penetrate, it becomes kinetic and dynamic.'[28]

In terms of frontality, here Hejduk is drawing to get over or to abandon the curious limits he sees in the Renaissance vision still evident in Le Corbusier's Garches.[29] In the Diamonds, he works through that reliance on frontality by at least two moves already touched on earlier: those of voiding the centre and charging the perimeter.

Linked to all these, and even if a first move, the forty-five-degree rotation of the bounding envelope allows him to move beyond the Le Corbusier of the Visual Arts Center and of Villa Garches. For when confronted with the receding or encompassing walls – depending on the observer's position, as is made clear in diagrams 8 and 9 of Hejduk's 'Diamond Thesis' – the projects are always ready to place the observer in an oblique state even without moving, as Hejduk discusses in *Three Projects*.

In the rotation, there is also generated a curious notion of time, one that Hejduk recognises as distinctive, and thus calling for a specific designation. He characterises the temporal state as a 'moment of the present.' Accepting Hejduk at his word, there is nothing fantastic or imaginary about it, and in this regard, we can think of Hejduk, like Mondrian, as a pure realist. This perhaps explains his unease at revisiting any of the Diamond Projects decades later, whether A, B, or C. For the state they capture is the 'flattest . . . quickest . . . fastest . . . most extended . . . most heightened.' These terms come out, are, it feels, drawn out, during his interviews with Wall. Here is Hejduk: 'The place where a perspective or diamond configuration on the horizontal plane flattens out and the focus moves to the lateral peripheral edges. . . . This is the moment of the hypotenuse of the diamond: it is here that you get the extreme condition, what I call the moment of the present.' Hejduk continues: 'It's here that you are confronted with the flattest condition. It's also the quickest condition, the fastest time wise in the sense that it's the most extended, the most heightened; at the same time, it's the most neutral, the most at repose.'[30]

Perhaps he really did work Le Corbusier out of his system, or was close to doing so, by 1967, the year of the Architectural League exhibition. As evidence, Hejduk appears to have overcome frontality in favour of the always oblique and moved beyond or away from a horizontal layering of regular volumes (the Domino model) for a flat-space world of constantly vibrating and animated planes. Certainly, from a certain point of view, the subsequent 1/4 series and 3/4 series bear out this interpretation.

This flat-space world is evident in the three Diamond Projects. House A places el and single-plane walls on the perimeter in a manner that torques the regular horizontal space volume. House B introduces double height volumes that cascade up or down the building and thus also disrupt a single horizontal space idea. Museum C achieves this by the intensity of plan figures such that the possible experience is as a section idea that goes beyond a simple horizontal layering.

64 Conceptual objects

What came next were projects that substantially varied the process of form employed in the Diamond Projects. Subsequent projects took on similar or related ideas and themes, replacing frontality, for example, with shear (3/4 Series, Extension House), the pinwheel (such as 1/4 House C, 1/4 House D), and the echelon (1/4 House B). Compressive space is taken even further, whether on the vertical (1/4 House A, Wall House 1) or the horizontal plane (Grandfather Wall House).[31]

Evidence of the explorations made possible by the efforts of the Diamond Projects can be seen in these and other developed projects. If in 1967, Hejduk has not yet fully overcome Le Corbusier's influence, he is on the way. Consider as evidence two drawings situated somewhere in that whirl of 1960s work on Nine-Square (Texas) House 5 (1958–1960), the Diamond series (1962–1967), the 1/4 Series (1967), and the 'Out of Time' (1965) and *Three Projects* (1967) texts.

In the John Hejduk Archive at the Canadian Centre for Architecture, on a sheet containing several plans, all in diamond configurations, the most developed disposes four round columns, thirty-six feet on centre, in a single square bay set inside the midpoints of bounding walls, with all other elements – partitions, fireplaces, and furniture – in right-angled relations.[32] See Figure 3.4. Internal partitions are arranged like a pinwheel, with the four arms at approximately similar nine, one, three, and five o'clock positions. Some of the effects of spatial warp, the elements and their relationships needed to get there, are being explored.

To take another example of what was made possible, consider what appears to be an early study for 1/4 House C. Having been set aside during the investigations into the diamond configurations, the ground has suddenly returned as a diamond-shaped site in this study.[33] Each quadrant bounded on one side by pinwheeling walls is occupied by a volume (rectangle, diamond, quarter circle, quarter square), and wall positions and fireplace elements are tested. In the developed 1/4 House C, the site remains, gripped by those four walls whose direction is one of the many ambiguities at work: are they moving into or out of that impossible centre, impossible because so compressed? Thus, other concerns come to the fore, other questions come into view, to be examined in the opening created by the Diamond Projects. Such concerns lead Hejduk to the 1/4, 1/2, and 3/4 Series, and what many see as the real break of the Wall Houses, as alluded to.

III

To conclude, and as an opening into themes further explored in Chapters 6, 7, and 8, I return to Gilles Deleuze's concept of a pure time in *Cinema 2* as discussed in the opening chapter. As Deleuze succinctly characterises it, there are certain conditions rendered in works of cinema – and by extension, I would claim, in certain readings of the Diamond Projects – such that one is plunged directly into an experience of time irrespective of a reliance on movement. As Deleuze stated, certain kinds of aesthetic works are constituted in such a way that 'we are plunged into time rather than crossing space.'[34]

FIGURE 3.4 Sketches for a fourth diamond house, 1963–1967, John Hejduk, drawing in graphite on translucent paper 60 × 84 cm, DR1998:0063:007

Source: John Hejduk fonds, Collection Centre Canadien d'Architecture/Canadian Centre for Architecture, Montréal

According to Deleuze, a reversal in the relation of movement and time can be discerned in certain works of art. In cinema, again according to Deleuze, the reversal of the movement – time relationship, affording time the capacity to manifest itself independent of motion – occurred after 1945. Deleuze's concept of direct time is one independent of movement, and he finds examples of this condition in films directed by Jean Renoir, Federico Fellini, and Orson Welles, among others.[35]

Is there similar evidence in Hejduk's Diamond Projects? Could a similar reversal be said to have occurred more generally in the realm of architecture, and if so, how would we recognise it? What kinds of devices would be at work to give rise to a pure time, one different from a past-present-future time, that purely empirical succession of things that, for example, the *promenade architectural* manifested in Le Corbusier's Visual Arts Center gives apparent expression to?

Though tentative, and calling for further development, I believe there is evidence of a concept of direct time at work in the three Diamond Projects, briefly considered here and with a partial interpretation sketched out. Returning to the opening questions, it can be claimed that two theses accompany the Diamond Projects of Hejduk: a thesis of simultaneity and a diagonal or diamond thesis. The thesis of simultaneity is claimed by Hejduk in his essay on the Visual Arts Center:

'The major thesis – the thesis of simultaneity.'[36] This first thesis announces a multi-planar, explosive world replacing a world of frontality and contained horizontal stratifications – the world, that is, of the Villa Garches and the Visual Arts Center. This thesis assumes there is an oblique, always-lateral spatial order endeavouring to supplant or at least get away from Renaissance frontality. The second thesis concerns the concept of a temporality characterised by a concept of direct time.

These two theses work in parallel on the problems of the observer in motion, and thus of time (the thesis of simultaneity) and of space (that collapsed, 'actual' two-dimensional space of the diamond). They are given further expression, explication, and exploration in the projects that follow the Diamond series and in Hejduk's writing. The thesis of simultaneity and of time independent of an observer in movement, for example, is explicit in the diagrams that Hejduk used to illustrate the history of space in architecture and give expression to the ideas in the 'Diamond Thesis.'[37]

Providing a kind of open unity to the form relations and spatial orders at issue – voided centre, peripheral tension, exploded field, volume transmuted into plane, and thus creating the conditions for flat space to appear – Hejduk's specific sensibility translated through the Diamonds is that dimension which ensures a single whole is never completely given.

In this regard, the refusal to relate part to whole and a resistance to any claim to unity confirm the Diamonds' alignment with the criteria of a theoretical object. As produced by the Diamond Projects, diagonal time has the strange power to affirm parts that do not make a whole in space, nor form a succession in time. Time is exactly the diagonal collapsing all possible spaces made possible as a result of those two freedoms that Hejduk found in Le Corbusier, those of liberated space and of liberated structure. The Diamond Projects therefore can be read as rendering certain characteristics of a theoretical object, and in this, they constitute an appropriate interpretive category alongside the formal-spatial ones emphasised by Hejduk.

Notes

1 Partial publication by Hejduk of the Diamond Projects can be found in the following: John Hejduk, *Three Projects* (New York: The Cooper Union School of Art and Architecture, 1969), a set of loose plates. John Hejduk, "Deux projets," *L'Architecture d'aujourd'hui* 163 (1972): 43–45, limited to Houses A and B. John Hejduk, "Out of Time and into Space," *A+U (Architecture and Urbanism)* 53 (1975), including photographs of the 1967 exhibition. John Hejduk, "Frame 3 1963–1967 Diamond House A, Diamond House B, Diamond Museum C," in *Mask of Medusa: Works 1947–1983*, ed. Kim Shkapich (New York: Rizzoli International, 1985), 241–251, containing all three projects and some sketches. An anonymous brief commentary and four drawings of House A are published as "John Hejduk," *Architectural Design* 55(3–4) (1985): 66–67.
2 Stan Allen, "Nothing but Architecture," In *Hejduk's Chronotope*, ed. K. Michael Hays (New York: Princeton Architectural Press, 1996), 90.
3 K. Michael Hays, *Sanctuaries: The Last Works of John Hejduk. Selections from the John Hejduk Archive of the Canadian Centre for Architecture, Montreal & the Menil Collection, Houston* (New York: Whitney Museum of American Art, distributed by Harry N. Abrams, Inc., 2002), s.p.

4 Mark Linder, *Nothing Less than Literal: Architecture after Minimalism* (Cambridge: The MIT Press, 2004), 173–203.
5 John Hejduk, "Interviews with Don Wall," in *Mask of Medusa: Works 1947–1983*, ed. Kim Shkapich (New York: Rizzoli International, 1985), 34.
6 For the Nine-Square (Texas) houses, see Kenneth Frampton, ed., *7 Houses: January 22 to February 16, 1980* (New York: Institute for Architecture and Urban Studies, 1979). Partial publication of the 1/4, 1/2, 3/4 series is most readily accessible in *Mask of Medusa*.
7 The citation is from Hejduk's so-called 'Diamond Thesis'. The 'Diamond Thesis', as George Sadek and Hejduk describe the text in their prefacing paragraphs to the *Three Projects* set of plates, has been published at least three times. In 1969 it appeared in *Three Projects*. In 1972 it appeared in French translation in an article titled "Deux projets" where, in addition to the nine diagrams of the 1969 publication, the 'Diamond Thesis' is also illustrated by plans and isometric projections of Houses A and B but not Museum C (Hejduk, "Deux projets," 44). And finally, the 'Diamond Thesis' is published in *Mask of Medusa* as noted earlier. In this last, where it is labelled 'Introduction to Diamond catalogue', the order of early paragraphs is modified relative to the two previous publications, and diagrams eight and nine, external and internal to the diamond respectively, do not include the position of the observer, which is marked in the two earlier versions. Hays suggests that the 'Diamond Thesis' text was in existence as early as 1963 (Hays, *Hejduk's Chronotope*, s.p.). Page references to Hejduk's text will be to the last and most accessible publication, that in *Mask of Medusa*. To avoid confusion with references to other texts in *Mask of Medusa* – the interviews with Don Wall, for example, and the "Out of Time and into Space" essay discussed elsewhere in this chapter – these endnotes will adopt the standard convention of author, Hejduk, followed by "Diamond Thesis" and the relevant page number, thus in this instance: Hejduk, "Diamond Thesis," 48. For an insightful and nimble chapter on Hejduk's Wall Houses, which also includes observations on the Diamond Projects, Mark Linder refers to slight variations in Hejduk's 'Diamond Thesis' text as printed on exhibition panels in the 1967 Architectural League show compared to later published versions. See Linder, *Nothing Less than Literal*, 269 note 16.
8 See Hejduk, *Mask of Medusa*, 285. This hand-drawn table is also included in "John Hejduk," *A+U* 53 (1975): 73–146, 134.
9 The Visual Arts Center is what Hejduk, and Le Corbusier in the *Oeuvre complete/Complete Works*, call what is more commonly known today as the Carpenter Center for the Visual Arts. Hejduk's essay "Out of Time and into Space" was first published in 1965 as "Hors du temps dans l'espace " in *L'Architecture d'aujourd'hui*. A longer version was published in 1975 in *A+U*. This last version is the one used in *Mask of Medusa* and referenced in this chapter as Hejduk, "Out of Time and into Space" followed by the page number from the version published in *Mask of Medusa*.
10 Hubert Damisch, "Against the Slope: Le Corbusier's La Tourette," in *Noah's Ark: Essays on Architecture*, ed. Anthony Vidler (Cambridge: The MIT Press, 2016), 178. The essay was first published in *Log* 4 (2005), 29–48, trans. Julie Rose. All references in what follows are to the publication in *Noah's Ark*.
11 Hejduk, "Interview with Don Wall," 90.
12 There is no site plan for Hejduk's Nine-Square (Texas) House 7. The Nine-Square series is most fully documented in *John Hejduk: 7 Houses*, ed. Kenneth Frampton (New York: The Institute for Architecture and Urban Studies, 1980). Peter Eisenman's essay in this exhibition catalogue miraculously evokes the architectural thinking at work in, and animates the differences among, the Nine-Square projects. See Eisenman, "In My Father's House Are Many Mansions," In *John Hejduk: 7 Houses*, ed. Kenneth Frampton (New York: The Institute for Architecture and Urban Studies, 1980).
13 Hejduk, "Out of Time and into Space," 73.
14 Hejduk, "Interview with Don Wall," 135.
15 For model photographs of Diamond House A, see Hejduk, *Mask of Medusa*, 244–245. A good photograph of the House A upper floor model is also reproduced in Manfredo

Tafuri, "'American Graffiti': Five × Five = Twenty-five," trans. Victor Caliandro, *Oppositions* 5 (1976): 39.
16 The numbering of floor plans follows the North American convention Hejduk used, with the ground floor typically referred to as the first floor, the floor about the ground floor referred to as the second floor, and so on.
17 Hejduk, "Diamond Thesis," 49.
18 'The fracturing of light in an apparently simple program is maddening,' Hejduk, "Interview with John Wall," *Mask of Medusa*, 135.
19 Victory Boogie-Woogie has been extensively published.
20 Hejduk, "Interview with John Wall," *Mask of Medusa*, 128.
21 Hejduk, "Interview with John Wall," *Mask of Medusa*, 36.
22 Kenneth Frampton, "John Hejduk and the Cult of Humanism," *A+U (Architecture and)* 53 (1975): 142.
23 Hejduk, "Diamond Thesis," *Mask of Medusa*, 49.
24 Frampton, "John Hejduk and the Cult of Humanism," 141.
25 Hejduk, "Interview with Don Wall," *Mask of Medusa*, 131.
26 Hejduk, annotations on a sheet of unpublished sketches for Diamond House B, Collection Centre Canadien d'Architecture/Canadian Centre for Architecture, John Hejduk fonds 145, Series 2: Professional Work, File 15: Diamond Houses, Sub-file 4: Miscellaneous Diamond House Sketches, drawing DR1998_0063_005.
27 Hejduk, "Interview with Don Wall," *Mask of Medusa*, 36.
28 Hejduk, "Interview with Don Wall," *Mask of Medusa*, 90. On the phrase 'kinetic equilibrium', see also Hejduk, "Interview with Don Wall," *Mask of Medusa*, 52.
29 Hejduk, "Diamond Thesis," *Mask of Medusa*, 48.
30 Hejduk, "Interview with Don Wall," *Mask of Medusa*, 90.
31 See Hejduk, *Mask of Medusa*, 255, 260, 259, 263, 266, 293.
32 Canadian Centre for Architecture, John Hejduk Archive/Fonds 145, Sub-file 4: Miscellaneous Diamond House Sketches, drawing DR1998_0063_007.
33 Canadian Centre for Architecture, John Hejduk Archive/Fonds 145, Sub-file 4: Miscellaneous Diamond House Sketches, drawing dr1998_0071_006. This drawing is reproduced in *Mask of Medusa* in a sequence of 1/4 House projects. See *Mask of Medusa*, 264.
34 Gilles Deleuze, *Cinema 2: The Time-Image*, trans. Hugh Tomlinson and Robert Galeta (Minneapolis: University of Minnesota Press, 1989), xii
35 Deleuze, *Cinema 2: The Time Image*, xii.
36 Hejduk, "Out of Time and Into Space," *Mask of Medusa*, 71.
37 Hejduk, "Diamond Thesis," *Mask of Medusa*, 49, diagram 7 in particular.

Bibliography

Allen, Stan. "Nothing But Architecture." In *Hejduk's Chronotope*, edited by K. Michael Hays, 78–96. New York: Princeton Architectural Press, 1996.
Anonymous. "John Hejduk." *Architectural Design* 55(3–4) (1985): 66–67.
Bois, Yve-Alain. "A Picturesque Stroll around 'Clara-Clara'." *October* 29 (1984): 32–62.
Constantin, Eleni. "John Hejduk: Constructing in Two Dimensions." *Architectural Record* 167(4) (1980): 111–116.
Deleuze, Gilles. *Cinema 2: The Time-Image*. (Translated by Hugh Tomlinson and Robert Galeta). Minneapolis: University of Minnesota Press, 1989.
Eisenman, Peter. "In My Father's House Are Many Mansions." In *John Hejduk: 7 Houses*, edited by Kenneth Frampton, 8–20. New York: The Institute for Architecture and Urban Studies, 1980.
Frampton, Kenneth, ed. *John Hejduk: 7 Houses*. New York: The Institute for Architecture and Urban Studies, 1980.

Frampton, Kenneth. "John Hejduk and the Cult of Humanism." *A+U (Architecture and Urbanism)* 53 (1975): 141–142.
Hays, K. Michael, ed. *Hejduk's Chronotope*. New York: Princeton Architectural Press, 1996.
Hays, K. Michael. *Sanctuaries: The Last Works of John Hejduk. Selections from the John Hejduk Archive of the Canadian Centre for Architecture, Montreal & the Menil Collection, Houston.* New York: Whitney Museum of American Art (distributed by Harry N. Abrams, Inc), 2002.
Hejduk, John. "Deux projets." *L'Architecture d'aujourd'hui* 163 (1972): 43–45.
Hejduk, John, "Hors du temps dans l'espace." *L'Architecture d'aujourd'hui* 122 (1965): xxi–xxiii.
Hejduk, John. "Interview with Don Wall." In *Mask of Medusa: Works 1947–1983*, edited by Kim Shkapich (interspersed throughout). New York: Rizzoli International, 1985.
Hejduk, John. "Introduction to the Diamond Catalogue [the so-called 'Diamond Thesis']." In *Mask of Medusa: Works 1947–1983*, edited by Kim Shkapich, 48–49. New York: Rizzoli International, 1985.
Hejduk, John. *Mask of Medusa: Works 1947–1983*. (edited by Kim Shkapich). New York: Rizzoli International, 1985.
Hejduk, John. "Out of Time and into Space." *A+U (Architecture and Urbanism)* 53 (1975): 2, 4, 24, illustrations 147–54.
Hejduk, John. "Out of Time and Into Space." In *Mask of Medusa: Works 1947–1983*, edited by Kim Shkapich, 71–75. New York: Rizzoli International, 1985.
Hejduk, John. *Three Projects*. New York: The Cooper Union School of Art and Architecture, 1969.
Hejduk, John, and David, Shapiro. "John Hejduk or the Architect Who Drew Angels." *A+U (Architecture and Urbanism)* 244 (1991): 59–65.
Linder, Mark. *Nothing Less than Literal: Architecture after Minimalism*. Cambridge: The MIT Press, 2004.
Pommer, Richard. "Architecture Structures for the Imagination." *Art in America* 66(2) (1978): 75–79.
Rowe, Colin, and Robert, Slutzky. "Transparency: Literal and Phenomenal." *Perspecta* 8 (1963): 45–54.
Tafuri, Manfredo. "'American Graffiti': Five x Five = Twenty-five." (Translated by Victor Caliandro) *Oppositions* 5 (1976): 35–74.

TRAJECTORY II
Sensation

4
ANIMATE MATTER
Bryn Mawr College Dormitory by Louis Kahn

I

Let us start with two of Louis Kahn's closest commentators. Vincent Scully, writing some thirty years after the design and construction of Kahn's Bryn Mawr College Dormitory, is moved to acknowledge a kind of violence in Kahn's mature works. Scully finds a number of the architectural projects mute and 'devoid of gesture.' It is in this apparent absence of posture that Scully discerns a latent violence.

Here is Scully: 'Kahn's buildings, the very distillation of the twentieth century's later years . . . are wholly devoid of gesture, as if beyond that, or of a different breed. Their violence is latent, potential, precisely because they do not gesture or seem to strike any attitude at all.'[1] If there is an immanent risk of a display of frustration, of an angry burst so palpable that Scully is pulled up and feels compelled to comment, to what ends might it have been directed?

In an effort to answer this question, let us turn to another close observer of Kahn. In an homage published in the May 1974 issue of *Progressive Architecture* shortly after Kahn's death, Romaldo Giurgola accompanies his words with a photograph of Kahn. Kahn is captured standing on the landing of a stair in the central building of the Bryn Mawr College Dormitory group. The photographer has set the camera lens front on relative to the stair landing, and the image as published is cropped to frame symmetrically the stair and surrounding elements. The architect, however, is tilted off axis and twisted slightly to his right.[2] It is not unlike so many of the published photographs of Kahn: hands clasped, body tilted, propelled forward as if in constant motion, and scanning the distance as if hopeful and anticipating a favourable change of wind. Or perhaps it's simpler, and he's looking for an acquaintance or some sign to assure him that all the momentum and the energy he has worked to instill his project with is for the good, and more or less in the right direction.

DOI: 10.4324/9781003009641-7

In Giurgola's text, this impatient temperament is recalled and is used to broadly characterise Kahn's practice and teaching. For Giurgola, Kahn's work displays a sentiment different from both the classic and the modern, the former placed on the side of static enclosures, the latter on the side of dissolution and atmospherics.[3] A few years later, Giurgola, writing with Pamille Berg, returns to the Bryn Mawr dormitory building. At some distance from Kahn's sudden death, and the mourning process perhaps worked through, the Bryn Mawr project is turned to again by Giurgola, on this occasion to illustrate what he argues is Kahn's constant concern with connections on the one hand and the physical nature of light shaped by architectural devices on the other. This is an architecture that maintains the separate character of elements over an underlying whole. It is for Giurgola an architecture that transforms the structure of space by commanding an ever-changing, living, and idiosyncratic light over a uniform and 'all-pervasive' one.[4]

Let us stay with Kahn at Bryn Mawr College where he was commissioned to provide a dormitory for approximately 130 students. The brief also included a reception hall, social areas, a dining hall, administrative facilities, and other service spaces. The location for the building was on a narrow south-facing site on the edge of the college campus. The central functional problem for Kahn was the grouping in an appropriate manner of a large number of dorm rooms with the larger common facilities. Joseph Rykwert notes that the design development process was a slow one.[5]

Bryn Mawr was begun in a fertile and fervent period in Kahn's practice. It was undertaken alongside the First Unitarian Church (Rochester), the project for the United States Consulate in Luanda, and the Salk Institute for Biological Studies (La Jolla), all started in 1959. The Richards Medical Research Laboratories (Philadelphia, 1957–1961) and the Tribune Review Printing Press (Greensburg, 1958–1961) were nearing completion when Kahn received the commission for Bryn Mawr and aspects of their design problématiques find an echo in the dormitory project. Bryn Mawr predates the Philips Academy Library (Exeter, 1967–72) in which the spatial unit (the reading carrel in the library project) and the open corner (a device used at Bryn Mawr) are further tested. Philips Academy Library also continues the building within a building concept, a distinguishing feature of Bryn Mawr as discussed in what follows.

The plan by Bryn Mawr went through multiple variations starting in May 1960 and was largely settled into the version now known by December 1961. Final design development and working drawings would take another eighteen months to complete to allow bidding in mid-1963, and another twenty-four months for the construction phase to building hand over in May 1965.

The Bryn Mawr project has been the object of extensive secondary and critical commentary, and the history and project development chronicled in a number of sources. Heinz Ronner and Sharad Jhaveri's *Louis I. Kahn – Complete Work 1935–1974* provide a useful compilation of key process drawings, many of which will be referenced in what follows.[6] The archival work on architect and client correspondence in Michael J. Lewis's project history is another useful starting point.[7]

Though Bryn Mawr was just beginning construction documents at the time of publication, Scully's *Louis I. Kahn* is a standard early monograph and provides a further good historical overview and interpretation up to that point.[8] There is a brief specific reference to Bryn Mawr, and Scully publishes a design development plan that is soon after abandoned following decisive changes at this moment in the three-rotated square option's evolution.[9] Key plan changes followed which led to the final version. It is relevant to our analysis to highlight the changes.

The shared bathrooms are brought into the squares to frame in part the main double-height spaces as opposed to separating them. This allowed the three squares to overlap and thus strengthen the diagonal, on-the-corner circulation and displays one solution for the 'space within a space' strategy. The octagonal geometry of the dorm rooms is abandoned for the adopted interlocking Ts plan. In addition, the geometry of the bounding walls to each of the main rooms change from circles to squares.

The Louis I. Kahn Archive. Personal Drawings: The Completely Illustrated Catalogue of the Drawings in the Louis I. Kahn Collection contains nineteen drawings of Bryn Mawr, eleven of which are a graphic analysis of the brief or components of the brief. There are also a few plan diagrams and only one overall plan from the early phase of design.[10] Drawing 565.15 is a site plan sketch, reproduced by Rykwert and Robert McCarter, which summarizes many of the key features. There is also a large elevation study (565.18) perhaps used by Kahn in the client presentation referred to by Lewis and I don't believe otherwise published elsewhere. The elevation shows a number of features not pursued in the final project: keyhole windows on the top two dorm room floors, large unit glazing on the entry floor, no crenellations, and, while not specific, it's possible, given its rendering style, the contemporary studies for the Meeting House at Salk, and the absence of other indications in the drawing, that Kahn thought of it as all concrete.

Other key published sources on the project that we will return to in what follows include Maria Bottero's insightful "Organic and Rational Morphology in Louis Kahn,"[11] Romaldo Giurgola and Jaimini Mehta's monograph *Louis I. Kahn*,[12] David Brownlee and David De Long's magisterial exhibition catalogue, *Louis I. Kahn: In the Realm of Architecture*,[13] and Robert McCarter's *Louis I Kahn*[14] mentioned previously to highlight only a select set of studies.

Kenneth Frampton provides an insightful analysis of certain aspects in nineteenth-century academic education which might have influenced Kahn. These are used earlier in Chapter 1 to broaden our analysis of Kahn's De Vore House.[15] Frampton concludes with a statement that adds to other interpretations on the sources of Kahn's manner of working. Different from Scully, Frampton argues that Kahn's work relays without synthesis the American organicism of Sullivan and Wright along with the European rationalism of Ledoux and Boullee. Not a lineage that can be understood from a strictly Beaux-Arts and International Style heritage, nor says Frampton, 'the Greco-Gothic notion of structure as the essential mediator of light.'[16] It is a temperament still to be qualified.

II Analysis

To move now to an analysis of the project from the lens of sensation, there are two organizing questions which are considered sequentially in what follows. The first: of the series of formal design moves made by Kahn at Bryn Mawr, what devices and which compositional strategies are at work? Which shapes create the conditions of possibility for this architecture, and what kinds of physical relations characterise it? What spatial and plastic effects are realized? The second organising question asks how the notion of active matter might be informed by, or inform, the analysis? Which traits of a life force, if any, might be actively working in the building?

As in previous chapters, we are interested not primarily in isolating the history of, or proposing a meaning in, the building but rather with identifying a range of composition devices and formal decisions and their possible architectural effects in a significant built work by one of late-twentieth-century architecture's most transformative figures. We do this by examining select building conditions as expressed through the medium or vehicle of plans, sections, volumes, and elevations. These in turn are postulated to render instances of a project more on the side of sensation than ideation and thus a contribution to addressing that absence in architecture of a discourse on sensation. This is to return to a gap according identified by Colin Rowe and discussed in the opening chapter, 'Continuities.'

II.i Plan

As almost all commentators have observed, the central architectural problem facing Kahn at Bryn Mawr coincided to a large degree with the organizational problem. It was one largely studied in plan.[17] As suggested in what follows, however, the impact of the design decisions is felt in the volumes, whether those shaped and made active externally or those internally charged. The design challenge, in part, was to resolve the circulation and operational relationships between three large common public spaces – dining room, entry hall, lounge – and the much smaller and more numerous spaces of the individual student dorm rooms.

Giurgola and Mehta, in a chapter on five constants in the work of Kahn, suggest the fifth constant is that of connections, and Bryn Mawr is used as one example to illustrate this idea. The authors also speak of the spatial intensity in the building which resulted from the decision to rotate the squares.[18]

Kahn's response thus, in part, was to search for an 'architecture of connections.'[19] In place of an architecture of isolation and separation, Kahn's approach to the plan relied on formal design moves which include rotation, slippage, and a building overlapping a void strategy. Prior to examining these, I will consider the plan variations studied by Kahn.

The published material reveals that multiple plan arrangements were studied by Kahn. Certain of these design studies are reproduced in Ronner and Jhaveri as drawings BCD.7, BCD.11, BCD.6, BCD.24 in *Complete Works 1935–1974*.[20] The drawings, when examined together, show Kahn experimenting with combinations that range from what might be described as a classical, axially ordered organization to a group form which produces multiple, ambiguous readings. As Lewis notes based on a review of project and client archives, and as Ronner and Jhaveri document, parallel design efforts to those of Kahn in early project stages were undertaken by Anne Tyng. Tyng explored options based on polygonal modules as the generator of plan and volume. Without denying the merit in further consideration of that line of formal exploration, this chapter only considers the line of research followed by Kahn.[21]

In BCD.7, we see a "T" arrangement of four courtyards or large rooms, three at the top, one at the bottom, each wrapped by bars of rectangular dorm rooms. In BCD.11, two distinct areas in a linear arrangement are created with major public rooms on one side and dorm rooms on the other in an "H" arrangement. The dorm rooms are interlocking "L"s, arranged in an echelon pattern, the two areas symmetrically bound by an entrance lounge. In BCD.6, the public rooms are again distinct from the dorm rooms, the latter now clustered in two rows of four units (the rooms now rotated "L"s), with the public rooms together and sited as the binding element at the bottom of the "U"-shaped plan. BCD.24 tests a single large rotated square or diamond plan with interlocking octagonal dorm rooms wrapping a rotated cruciform-shaped cluster of the larger public rooms.

These and other studies accompanied Kahn as he worked toward the adopted solution, a linear arrangement of three rotated squares which operate as diamonds, joined at the corners, with interlocking and flipping "T"-shaped dorm rooms wrapping double-height public spaces. See Figure 4.1 for the final plan. The building is sited perpendicular to an axial approach from campus and follows the slope, with a two-story elevation on the campus and a three-story elevation on the opposite side.

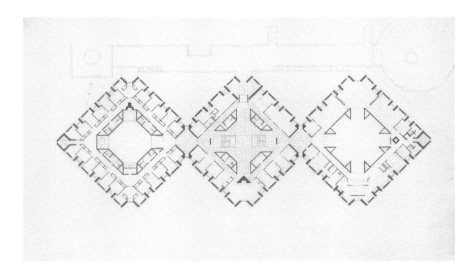

FIGURE 4.1 Bryn Mawr College Dormitory, floor plan, Louis I. Kahn

Source: Louis I. Kahn Collection, University of Pennsylvania and the Pennsylvania Historical and Museum Commission

Having arrived at a site plan and overall building disposition, Kahn then undertakes a series of design refinements in plan, in the volumetric treatment and layout of the main public rooms as noted, in the shapes and dispositions of dorm rooms and support spaces, as well as in refinements in patterns of entry and circulation.

A key plan move introduced by Kahn is the use of diagonal or corner entries for the large public rooms. This condition is created in part when the main plan elements are rotated 45 degrees off of the campus axis and the three-diamond plan is adopted. Brownlee and De Long claim that the diagonality of the Bryn Mawr plan, along with the monumentality of the internal stairs in the middle volume and other elements, ensconce the project within a classical sensibility of the most stable kind. 'The diagonality of the [Bryn Mawr] Erdman [Hall] design,' they write, 'allowed Kahn to achieve classical balance without the artificiality inherent in conventional axial planning.'[22] A close look at the plan does reveal a reliance on axial planning from this perspective. However, the building, as built and experienced, is anything but stable and suggests a different interpretation of the temperament at work is merited. Perhaps the latent violence discerned by Scully all those years later, as referenced at the beginning of this chapter, was a record of Kahn's ambition explicit or not to instill a sense of urgency into the project.

The forty-five-degree rotation of the main volumes off their starting orthogonal alignment transforms the individual parallelepipeds from squares to diamonds. Entry into and passage between the three occurs on their corners or points and results in one entering within what can only be described as an already-spiralling system. This condition was even more pronounced when the internal public room walls were still on their starting north/south alignment.[23]

Perhaps some of the consequent enigmatic vitality of the project is caused by this surprising violation, not to say the violence that comes out of joining rotated squares on their corners. Not that it is easily perceptible. As Scully notes: 'You would never realize when you look at them that they are in fact three rigid squares joined the way all of us were taught you never could possibly join things – just at their points.'[24]

A further consequence resulting from rotation of the three masses at Bryn Mawr is that one feels to be always moving obliquely, almost never in a frontal condition. This is documented clearly in photographs of the three main common rooms. There is almost no stable condition of frontal approach, and this relationship occurs immediately at the main entry on the campus side point of the middle diamond. Perhaps the photograph of Kahn published by Giurgola as referenced early in this chapter can be taken as a further witness to this quality.

The main entry hall in this case appears to be already sliding away, the framing external and bounding internal walls ostensibly freely turning in a gentle rotation this way and that. The resulting oblique lines of force are reinforced and at the same time redirected on entering the hall by the major architectural elements: stairs, ceiling plane grill and light hoods, fireplaces. Importantly, these architectural elements do generally retain the original alignment, that is, are rotated 45 degrees off the bounding walls of the respective diamond. In views of the entrance hall, for example, the parallax effect created, and the ambiguous character of the space which results is palpable. Maria Bottero provides a set of contemporary photographs that convey these properties.[25]

This can be considered an instance in the use of a strategy of simultaneity in plan. It was a move in some manner present in most studied options and fully exploited in the final plan. One consequence of adopting a strategy of simultaneity, or overlap, is that the dormitory building is an affair of ambiguous shapes (in plan) and walls (in elevation). Different from an elementarist strategy of isolation, of freely disposed and clear figures, there is a blurring of any originating geometry and a resistance to any sense of the room as module. The resulting plan is neither a diamond nor a square – though both are present at different moments – and the effects are strongly felt volumetrically and in elevation as will be discussed in what follows. In this regard, the effect is different from an additive strategy (1 + 1+). Things merge and flow, but in a manner different from the continuity of the free plan. Something else is going on. As another possible clue as to what is at stake, Scully comments on a similar arrangement in Buffalo. Scully discusses this state in the Unitarian Church at Buffalo where 'the individual spaces remain discrete, that don't move into the other, they remain cubical and very separate.'[26]

The overlap device introduces a dynamism into the otherwise static elementarist beginning to the larger formal composition. In a talk given to students at Bryn Mawr, Kahn gives a succinct formulation of his transformation of an elementarist approach. The problem, he said, was 'to distinguish each space, each room as a single entity, not just a series of partitions.'[27]

II.ii Entry hall

It is easy to imagine Kahn wandering in Rome among the Renaissance palaces and experiencing the Roman ruins with Frank Brown while at the American Academy in Rome.[28] Rome is not a city of the perimeter block, nor the modern city of slabs and towers. Kahn's city is one populated by August Choisy's mass and void buildings and etched with Henri Labrouste's taut, flat language of walls. It is a city of singular presences and of what Bottero characterised as 'the discontinuous and the non-homogeneous.' Here is the full citation of Bottero: 'The arches, squares, cylinders, skylights, exedra and symmetrical axes which spring from this architecture in ever richer and more complex ways, give rise, once they are realized, to fragile and powerful simulacra of the discontinuous and the non-homogeneous, of what is ours and at the same time what is not. The clean-cut surfaces of the walls are slim diaphragms, the flexible and unconventional use of which creates a continuous interplay of light and shade – highly refined and complex filters of the energy field of light.'[29]

A part of the quality of Rome is recalled in the internal common rooms at Bryn Mawr. A number of formal devices are used to achieve the plastic and spatial effects that result, and many are at work in the entry hall. See Figure 4.2.

80 Sensation

FIGURE 4.2 Bryn Mawr College Dormitory, photograph of entry hall, Louis I. Kahn

Source: Louis I. Kahn Collection, University of Pennsylvania and the Pennsylvania Historical and Museum Commission

The interior common spaces at Bryn Mawr have a contained energy: not dramatic, but constant. In the common rooms, for example, one senses a downward pressure, a weight only provisionally held off, or contained by, the continuity and assumed stability of the deeply coffered ceiling. These are echoed by the dark-coloured floors and then released by the large scaled light hoods that pull up and release any horizontally directed lines of force and extend their reach.

Such a reading reinforces a sense that at Bryn Mawr, Kahn was not primarily infatuated by spatial voids and Piranesian effects but with physical entities (recalling the Roman ruins) in space. As Bottero and Scully have noted, it is more Giotto than Piranesi. Specifically referring to Bryn Mawr, Scully writes: 'Such is the quality Kahn achieves at those places . . . which are like the spaces of Giotto – an environment just big enough for human beings to be noble and grave in.'[30]

In this regard, Bryn Mawr is an interim episode before the larger scale and more complex efforts in Ahmedabad and Dhaka. And only a fragment of what was imagined for the Meeting House of the Salk Institute to which it would have shared certain qualities as Kent Larson has illustrated and to which we turn our attention in Chapter 7.[31]

Consider the balcony over the door and the framed fireplace stack above, with what seem to be canted stairs in the foreground, a repetition of the approach on the point of the rotated square. The stacking of these stave off any closed order, any cumulative or pyramidal arrangement. In their place, there arises an order of enigma and ambiguity, not lucidity. This interpretation is reinforced by the treatment of the entry wall. Apparently mobile, bent, and twisted, these concrete walls generate multiple readings due in part to the effects of natural light washing the walls which pass beyond. The walls themselves, because they do not close the room but extend up toward without however reaching, the large light hoods disrupt and thus resist any single reading.

The walls appear, in other words, to overlap as one moves about the space, reinforcing the initial parallax effect. The eye is deflected constantly. The location and detailing of the stairs in the hall extends this quality. They are effectively adrift, not bound or tightly held. Kahn's building is alive, animate, and he introduced into the entry hall a vitality that is contrary to the stable, ponderous fact of it all.

Kahn's use of light hoods in Bryn Mawr contributes to this spatial impact. Thick, swirling volumes formed out of thin planes, vibrating and forced into motion in part by the light hoods, sliding by like the march of columns in Kahn's photograph of the Colosseum.[32] The volumetric dimension shares nothing, however, with the ancient world. For Kahn accompanies it all by a twentieth-century tautness, a thinness of planes, a vitality that introduces an animation into the work that's specific to his modernist training and sensibility as discussed in Chapter 1 in relation to the project for the De Vore House. Looking at Larson's 3D photo realistic computer models of unbuilt works of Kahn, the Meeting House of the Salk Institute, in design development at the same time as Bryn Mawr, is especially relevant. Thinking about that specifically modernist debt to Le Corbusier, Scully observes out that Kahn's walls are not thick but thin, taut, 'like those of Le Corbusier.'[33] Architectural matter is rendered animate.

The corners of each of the three mass volumes dissolve, and the light pulls one's eye out of the room, around corners, in a manner different from that achieved in the just-completed First Unitarian Church in Rochester. It is perhaps useful to compare the two.

At Rochester, the light boxes face inward, continue the closed corner walls of the meeting room, and the focus is on the contained space and cruciform ceiling. At Bryn Mawr, the design solution differs: the light hoods face outward and are set 45 degrees off the room alignment.

At Rochester, light is directed inward, the focus contained, and largely horizontal. At Bryn Mawr, the corners are open, light and shade slide across the disengaged bounding double-height walls as well as give glimpses of the sky beyond. The light hoods themselves, rotated as noted, spring out of the coffered ceiling and not from any wall. At Bryn Mawr, the focus is outward, the eye directed upward, enhancing that oblique movement already found in the plan arrangements. The effect is even stronger due to the staggered disposition of large elements in plan and section. As noted, the rotated chimney stack on the upper floor which confronts one on entering the middle volume is an example of this. Light washes around it and adds to the overall effect of disengagement and drifting.

The buildings at Bryn Mawr clearly articulate the structural and functional characteristics of the parts: individual dorm rooms surrounding three major common uses. They also embody a full drama of material forces, of building materials and light, in which the observer can physically participate. The complex intersections in plan and massing in the entry hall are not, however, disposed in a picturesque manner. Different from modernism's free plan, a version of a Beaux-Arts discipline of poché (structure/light) is at work.

In this sense, the space of the entry hall is not perceived as a firm shape. It occupies a kind of interstitial condition to borrow a turn of phrase from Peter Eisenman.[34] It is a consequence of the overlapping squares, rotated doors and light hoods, thrusting stairs, and diagonal circulation.

II.iii Building fabric

Bottera provides a forceful description of Kahn's state of mind in these years when she writes: 'The more intelligent and pertinent the use of design and appropriate the choice, perfect the technique of execution and detail, meticulous the expression of all the static forces involved, the more the measurable enters the realm of the immeasurable.'[35] This can provide an opening into considerations of the elevations.

Scully sensed that ability called out by Bottera in describing Bryn Mawr some years later. Thinking about the force of the project, Scully emphasizes the vibrancy of the walls. Not a façade, nor an elevation, the scheme is alive for Scully. Restlessly sitting near the crest of a hill but somehow not quite cresting it, the dormitory appears to be crouching there. The assembly of slate and concrete and glass induces Scully the historian to exclaim, as if caught off guard by the building's force, that the walls are 'really quite fluid . . . plastic, and full of life.'[36] See Figure 4.3.

For Scully and others, Bryn Mawr produces a kind of vibration, a kind of movement, despite the, at first glance, stability of the complex. Let us now consider the evidence of this in the disposition and detailing of the external walls. The factors are multiple, though a number of specific design moves and effects stand out: open corners, horizontal and vertical plaiding, flush detailing, an open-bay rhythm. Other factors could be considered; however, our reading is limited, as noted in the beginning, to an analysis of devices and their plastic effects as a contribution to tracking a proposition about the trajectory of sensation in late-twentieth-century architecture.

Back at Bryn Mawr, and sticking with the terms of reference, the external has, in part, to do with the folding and unfolding envelope, to Kahn's disinterest in the skeleton frame. In a different degree, it also has to do with the detailing of the slate and glass. All of these are recorded as variations on a sensibility of strategies and devices developed or refined elsewhere. Rochester, and in part the Tribune Review Publishing Company Building, developed the articulated, deep external wall. At Rochester, the glass is set deeply back; in the Tribune Review building,

Animate matter **83**

FIGURE 4.3 Bryn Mawr College Dormitory, photograph of exterior detail, Louis I. Kahn

Source: Louis I. Kahn Collection, University of Pennsylvania and the Pennsylvania Historical and Museum Commission

like Richards Medical, it's upfront, unrelieved. The Yale Center for British Art will see Kahn reach some reconciliation with glass, which he tried to ignore at Exeter and which is perfunctory at Bryn Mawr. Here also, at Bryn Mawr, it is the non-frame system of infill panels, of solid and glass, and, importantly, the striping by horizontal and vertical members, delineated by stone, concrete, and glass that is important.

The building is constructed of reinforced concrete frame, cinder block walls, with exterior slate cladding, and interior plaster. Large unit fixed and operable glazing, stainless steel (drip sills, hand rails), and oak doors complete the major material elements of the building. Different from the brick of both Richards Medical and Rochester, Bryn Mawr uses slate in two- and three-division panels, in both horizontal and vertical orientations. Rykwert notes that brick was not allowed on the campus, and so it is likely that Kahn was required by the client to use slate. Lewis suggests in his footnote, based on a reading of trustee transcripts, that they did not want to have any exposed concrete. It is possible Kahn was thinking of concrete in preparing that 'hastily' prepared elevation presentation drawing.[37]

84 Sensation

The decision to stop short the bounding walls and not close any of the corners of the three diamonds creates an effect of sliding or drift, reinforcing the sense of life in motion already identified in the examination of the plan and entry hall. This strategy is continued even at the eastern and western stair towers which are located at two of the twelve corners.[38] The effect of this formal move can also be felt in the entry as discussed. The walls cant away, and the entry itself is some distance in from the building face. In the Philips Library at Exeter, which starts design shortly after completion of Bryn Mawr, this strategy of the open corner is used again, though the effect is different, more monumental because of the greater height of the building, generally planar nature, and single material of the external building envelope.

Returning to Bryn Mawr, one feels that the cladding is distended to the bursting point at the corners. They can be read as walls being forced apart by some interior pressure, or simply adrift. Kahn uses a specific device consistently to reinforce this reading: the wall always 'bursts' or opens up at the corners. This is true at the four returns of the overlapping volumes, at the six external corners, and at the extreme east and west ends where one might have anticipated closure. Or is it to the apparent folding and unfolding which is the most constant, palpable, and recurrent effect, that of the walls marching in and out? See Figure 4.4.

FIGURE 4.4 Bryn Mawr College Dormitory, photograph of exterior, Louis I. Kahn

Source: Louis I. Kahn Collection, University of Pennsylvania and the Pennsylvania Historical and Museum Commission

The fact that the walls dissolve at the top of each of the wide bay verticals to create a crenelation effect reinforces a sense of disengagement as opposed to closure. I have already alluded to this reading in reference to the relation between the freestanding walls in the entry hall and what might be anticipated as a hard, rationalist geometry borne out of the squares. This sensation is equally felt in the external views of the building, or buildings. A plural reading is produced in part by the faceting of the wall.

This is not an architecture of prismatic volumes as the shape of the building is highly ambiguous. It is not possible to grasp a formal whole, a single form, from the exterior. It is not clear whether there is a separate building projecting from behind the one immediately in front of us in other words, or whether and in what manner they are linked. Of equal impact is the absence of a continuous edge or profile to tie it all together. We are confronted instead with what appear to be independent volumes, intense in their rhythmic insistence, but ultimately marked by what feels like disconnected vertical members, and a dense, complex, moving silhouette of many parts. The size, cranked orientation, and detailing of the light hoods and stair towers contribute to the energetic instability and variety.

The vertical precast concrete elements do not so much serve to reveal and bind together closed volumes as to isolate a cluster of shallow masses standing freely about. Despite the similar alignments of the median horizontal members, the full-height faceting and strong vertical modelling continuously interrupt a single reading.

The design of the building envelope follows neither allegorical or structural precepts. The building envelope is not quite a screen, or a curtain wall, nor a frame with infill. With its incessant thrusting and receding and simply detailed qualities all in a vertical plane – albeit an agitated plane, with its push and pull – it puts Kahn's building, as Scully notes, in a tradition of Tuscan palazzo. It is a line of investigation by Kahn that achieves an evermore solid resolution to that later achieved in the Yale Center for British Art as suggested.[39]

There are no strictly classical elements, no columns with capitals and bases, no mouldings – other than the shallow drip sills at the windows. The building makes no specific gesture to the ground, is not fixed to the earth. There is no plinth, no rustication, no *piano nobile* to identify the ground floor from things above. Everything is flat, blunt, final, hard. As discussed at the start of this chapter, perhaps that is what Scully identified in calling out the building as without gesture.

The precast vertical members appear not to pull upward, nor to be in compression. They simply stand there, perhaps a bit thin but certainly not fragile even if ending rather abruptly as there is no cornice to work up to and only the slightest capping. Scully sees a change in thinking as recorded in the drawing, 'a new kind of probity of the physical mass, if I may use that word, of the drawing itself. It is the working out of a deeply structural material sense in the character of the drawing.'[40] He goes on in a way that perhaps has relevance to Bryn Mawr and the external envelope, in his discussion of Labrouste again, and of the Bibliothèque Sainte Geneviève.

He writes about the wall and expression in a formula that was perhaps uncorrected in the text: 'It began of course with the expression, in the wall, of the space, and of the structure that makes it. Such expression has been familiar to modern architecture recently [this is written in 1976] in the work of Kahn, which derives in part from that Beaux-Arts idea.'[41] If not specifically pointing to Bryn Mawr, the turn of phrase is apt.

As suggested earlier, really, the elevation is not about the frame nor really about a façade. At Bryn Mawr, it is about the plane, the vertical surface, the wall, and light washing across and around. Kahn talked about constructing light, and his large, free-hand elevation study emphasizes the qualities and impacts of reflected light, shade, and shadow sought in the building.[42] In this sense, the work on the external walls continues that of the internal ones.

There is some tension between the contained glass and slate panels and the plaiding of minor horizontal and dominant vertical members. The building volume is expressed as such with a physical purpose, one emphasized by the continuity of the horizontal members banding the alternating slate and glass panels.

As noted earlier, there is a tautness in the surface that is different from compression or suspension. The wall is held together: things could be slipping away, pulling away, yet between the members, a physical drama of compression, tension, and vertical continuity is made physically manifest and providing further justification to qualifying the sensibility behind it as on the side of sensation over idea.

The clean-cut surfaces of the walls are slim diaphragms, the flexible and unconventional use of which creates continuous interplay of light and shade. The raking photographs in Bottero and in Brownlee and De Long reveal this in a striking way.[43] It could be said that Kahn was concerned with the power of forces that move through all the building materials and, at the same time and in that vein, was determined to make such forces comprehensible. From the framework in this part of the book and to reiterate, this would support placing Bryn Mawr on the side of sensation.

Due to the extreme flatness of the junction between the slate panels and the concrete members, and their slight variations, the slate slabs give the sensation of moving: they appear to be alternately receding, then moving forward from their framing. The treatment of the members work to resist the anticipated wholeness by not combining in any cumulative manner.

The detailing reinforces this effect, in one sense denying the material's specific conventional sensual qualities. Glass and slate in the same plane blur the qualities of each: slate is given no revealed thickness and seems brittle. Glass appears always gray, hard, thick. This detailing differs from that at Rochester where the glass is deeply recessed but shares some features of the Tribune Review, Richards Medical Research, and Philips Exeter Library. Scully and Michael Cadwell see a kind of prophetic achievement at the Yale Center for British Arts and Studies where Kahn's handling of the glass culminates a line of research that started at Richards and Tribune Review and was refined at Bryn Mawr to recall earlier observations in this line.

Further supporting this reading, Kahn's deployment of the precast concrete members resists any structural or geometric reading. The major vertical elements do not lead one to the other in a closed system; rather, these members remain isolated, self-referential, abstract. There is a sense that the major vertical units are set in motion and have been captured in a moment's rest. There is a curious power of potential movement, a rippling that comes across certainly in Kahn's elevation rendering. A potential movement exactly because, in part, the building is not so grounded, and one can imagine the building pulling itself up by the precast piers and gingerly stepping away.

This manner of articulating building mass is different to the order of a single platonic volume, module-generated, or that produced by an independent but linked building mass. In these cases, the whole would have been bound together, tied together in a perceptual whole. Each part would have related to a general law. As built, Kahn's Bryn Mawr displays an altogether other point of view toward massing and bulk.

It is characterized by infinite variations (in the multiple readings of building volume), of connections (in the resolution of the general organizational problem as an overlapping three-diamond shape), and movement (in the abstract, non-contour lines of the external concrete members and vertical folded bays).

The bay rhythm furthers this effect. The projection and recession is laid out in a formally incomplete A | B | A | B | A | B | C pattern. This three-large-bay rhythm is consistent for eight of the building's twelve faces. On the four faces bracketing the east and west ends, the rhythm is modified to accommodate the stair tower and becomes a part four-bay A | B | A | B | A | B | A | D rhythm.

This reinforces the other elements and an overall effect, the fabric of Bryn Mawr stretching almost to the point of dilation. The piers leap or push forward and upward to achieve a relatively tense and tightly stretched envelope. There is a sense that the building, if not already lumbering down the hill or up onto the lawn, will start to do so shortly to recall a previous characterisation.

III

The analysis suggests that Kahn's building does illustrate some aspects of the notion of active or animate matter. The call for a concept of architecture in which material relationships are created such that events are allowed to emerge, shapes to vary, and materials to act as if animated is given a retrospective possible response in Bryn Mawr. Perhaps the realist sensibility, like that of Kahn at Bryn Mawr, thus proposes an alternative to that late modern free plan, curtain wall, prismatic volume dogma which Kahn worked so hard to get away from. In Chapter 1, this practice of resistance was argued to be at work already nascent in Kahn's development of De Vore House.

As we argue, there is at Bryn Mawr a splendid vitality through which the whole building seems to stir and dilate. And this sensation is created out of the plan manipulation as much in the internal volumetric treatment and elevations. The resulting effects, ones that Scully characterised as Giotto like without further elaboration,[44] are not overwhelming. The beauty is of another kind. In this, Kahn's building could be seen to provide through architectural means one manifestation of the realist alternate sensibility.

There is an insistence in Bryn Mawr's plan and elevation toward discontinuity and non-homogeneity which makes it open to exchange, to fulfilling that relay role of an active materiality. The various early plan options and the building as realized do demonstrate an internal animation, though in the specific disposition of the entry hall, there is also an upward and outward aspect to it.

The oblique throughout, resulting in non-frontal conditions and diagonal (becoming spiral) movements could be said to instill in the building the capacity for the singular event. The building fabric is quietly but insistently agitated and animated from within. A consequence perhaps of its crystalline, blunt, prosaic nature, it is all potential and future-looking as Scully suggests in the citation which opens this essay.

In developing this argument, a number of strands – thematic, technical, methodological – have emerged and merit further investigation. Two such topics relate to the primary focus of this essay, that of the architecture of Louis Kahn, and its potential lessons for a contemporary modernist practice.

Kahn bemoaned the loss of architectural knowledge in relation to the manipulation of light and the full range of conditions and differences – shade, shadow, reflected light – that were part of his training but which, by the late 1960s, he believed were no longer available to those around him.[45] Of relevance to Bryn Mawr, for example, is the idea of a 'pocketed' plan, the generating part of structure – a wall, a pier. Kahn is quoted as saying: 'I learned the difference between the hollow wall and the solid wall. . . . I made the wall a container instead of a solid.'[46]

Further research could include comparing the positions of Jacques Lucan and Eisenman on Kahn's use of poché. I think Lucan, despite the thoroughness and elegant utility of his thinking, misses a point when he contrasts the reading of Kahn by Eisenman and that of Scully. Both concede that Kahn's is a return to certain precepts or devices whose formulation can best be understood when placed in the context of his Beaux-Arts training. Quoting Eisenman: 'In essence Kahn proposes a condition of almost pre-modern architecture; a return to the structure as the order and definition of the spatial unit' as different from another condition.[47] In subsequent essays that touch on Kahn, the context and reach of Eisenman's analysis is elaborated. See for example "In My Father's House Are Many Mansions" and "The Futility of Objects: Decomposition and the Processes of Differentiation."[48]

As others have shown, the formula structure/light is embedded in Kahn's idea of poché. A better understanding of Kahn's design methods, especially as regards plan development, might explore the Beaux-Arts tradition in relation to light and test options for a contemporary mass/void architecture.

At Bryn Mawr, much of the impact and ongoing force of the building some sixty years after conception is due to the building envelope. The origins and diverse evolutions of the modernist façade, the subject of work by Alan Colquhoun, could provide one springboard for more detailed research in this area. In an expanded examination, for example, one could spring from Colquhoun's proposal to track the origins and development of the façade in modern architecture according to two lines: one emphasizing the identify of elevation and use and having its formal and philosophical references in artistic movements as diverse as Expressionism, Futurism, De Stijl, and Constructivism. Another line or trend according to Colquhoun is concerned with the technical and aesthetic evolution of the façade beyond its nineteenth-century trajectory and finding its support in l'Esprit Nouveau and Neue Sachlichkeit progenitors.[49] Kahn's Bryn Mawr falls into the second line most easily.

Zaera-Polo has developed a categorization of building envelopes that acknowledges a building's multiple and other conflicting roles, and his work should be confronted in formulating further lines of inquiry in this area. Perhaps two parallel efforts, bound together by work with façade engineers on current technologies. Such efforts would further spur the vital potential of Bryn Mawr College Dormitory.

Notes

1 Vincent Scully, "Introduction," in David Brownlee and David De Long, *Louis I. Kahn. In the Realm of Architecture* (New York: The Museum of Contemporary Art, Los Angeles: Rizzoli, 1991), 12–14, 12.
2 Romaldo Giurgola, "Louis I. Kahn, 1901–1974," *Progressive Architecture* 5 (1974): 4.
3 Giurgola, "Louis I. Kahn," 4.
4 Romaldo Giurgola with Pamille I. Berg, "Louis I. Kahn," in *Macmillan Encyclopedia of Architects*, Volume 2, ed. Adolf K. Placzek (New York: The Free Press, 1982), 542, 544.
5 Joseph Rykwert, *Louis Kahn*, new photography by Roberto Schezen (New York: Harry N. Abrams, Inc., Publishers, 2001), 100.
6 Heinz Ronner and Sharad Jhaveri, *Louis I. Kahn – Complete Work 1935–1974*, 2nd revised and enlarged edition (Basel: Birkhäuser, 1987), 162–169.
7 Michael J. Lewis, "Eleanor Donnelley Erdman Hall, Bryn Mawr College," in David Brownlee and David De Long, eds., Louis I. Kahn: In the Realm of Architecture (New York: Rizzoli, Los Angeles: The Museum of Contemporary Art, 1991), 352–357. As noted in an earlier chapter, the 1991 publication cited here is the first, full version that accompanied a major retrospective exhibition on Kahn's work initially mounted at the Museum of Contemporary Art, Los Angeles. A second, condensed version, with the same title was published in 1997 by Thames and Hudson, London, and Universal Publishing, New York. Both versions have been used in the preparation of this chapter. To avoid confusion, in relevant notes the publication year will be included and the designation "condensed" when referring to the 1997 version and "full" to the 1991 version.
8 Vincent Scully, *Louis I. Kahn* (New York, George Braziller, 1962).
9 Scully, *Louis I. Kahn*, 39, 117.
10 Louis I. Kahn, *The Louis I. Kahn Archive. Personal Drawings: The Completely Illustrated Catalogue of the Drawings in the Louis I. Kahn Collection* (New York & London, Garland Publishing, Inc., 1987), Volume 2. Buildings and Projects, 1959–1961. "Erdman Hall, Dormitories for Bryn Mawr College, Bryn Mawr, Pa.", 164–171.
11 Maria Bottero, "Organic and Rational Morphology in Louis Kahn," *Zodiac* 17 (1967): 48–53, English translation, 240–245.
12 Romaldo Giurgola and Jaimini Mehta, *Louis I. Kahn* (Westview Press, Boulder, Colorado, 1975).

13 David Brownlee and David De Long, eds., *Louis I. Kahn: In the Realm of Architecture* (New York: Rizzoli, 1991
14 Robert McCarter, *Louis I Kahn* (London: Phaidon, 2005).
15 Kenneth Frampton, "Louis Kahn and the French Connection," *Oppositions* 22 (1980): 20–53.
16 Frampton, "Louis Kahn and the French Connection," 51.
17 In Ronner and Jhaveri, *Complete Work*, of the forty-seven drawings reproduced, thirty-seven are plan studies.
18 Giurgola and Mehta, Louis I. Kahn, 23–26, see their reference to Richards Medical Research Laboratories, the Fisher House, and the Congregation of the Dominican Sisters to discuss this specific quality. See also See Brownlee and De Long, Louis I. Kahn. In the Realm of Architecture, condensed version 1997, 151, and Ronner and Jhaveri, Complete Work, 163.
19 Brownlee and De Long, *Louis I. Kahn. In the Realm of Architecture*, full version 1991, 151.
20 Ronner and Jhaveri, *Complete Work*, 162–165. For the purposes of consistency with one of the major secondary sources, and to avoid reference to multiple books which reproduce some but generally not all four, I use the three-letter project code and drawing/illustration numbering system used throughout *Complete Work*, thus BCD standing as the acronym for Bryn Mawr College Dormitory.
21 Lewis, "Eleanor Donnelley Erdman Hall, Bryn Mawr College", 353.
22 Brownlee and De Long, *Louis I. Kahn. In the Realm of Architecture*, compressed version 1997, 153–154.
23 See for example the plan sketch in *The Louis Kahn Archive. Personal Drawings* 2, drawing 565.17, 171.
24 Scully, "Work of Louis Kahn and His Method," 294.
25 See Bottero, "Organic and Rational Morphology," photos 10 through 20 of the entry hall, living room, and dining room.
26 Scully, "Works of Louis Kahn and His Method," 294.
27 "Kahn Asserts Architect's Duty is to Make Institutions Great," *The College News* 47 (1961), page 1 as recorded in Lewis, "Eleanor Donnelley Erdman Hall, Bryn Mawr College," 353.
28 Frank Brown (1908–1988), a prominent archaeologist, taught classics at Yale and in addition to numerous publications on specific digs, published *Roman Architecture* (New York: George Braziller, 1961). Brown was at the American Academy in Rome when Kahn was there in 1950–1951. Scully frequently alludes to the impact of Brown and the Rome experience on Kahn's life and work. See Scully, *Louis I. Kahn*, 17–18; Vincent Scully, "Louis I. Kahn and the Ruins of Rome," in Neil Levine, ed., *Vincent Scully Modern Architecture and Other Essays* (Princeton: Princeton University Press, 2003), 298–319.
29 Bottero, "Organic and Rational Morphology in Louis Kahn," 244–245.
30 Scully, "Works of Louis Kahn and His Method," 294.
31 See Larson's miraculous computer model constructions of the Meeting House. Kent Larson, *Louis I. Kahn: Unbuilt Masterworks* (New York: The Monacelli Press, 2000), 48–77.
32 Larson, *Louis I. Kahn: Unbuilt Masterworks*, 10.
33 Vincent Scully, "Foreword," in Kent Larson, *Louis I. Kahn: Unbuilt Masterworks* (New York: The Monacelli Press, 2000), 7–9, note 1 page 230, see especially page 8.
34 Peter Eisenman, "Real and English: The Destruction of the Box. I," *Oppositions* 4 (1974): 9. Eisenman, while not here referring to Bryn Mawr – he references elsewhere De Vore, Adler, Trenton Bath Houses, Richards Medical Research and includes an early plan for Rochester –, makes useful and dense comments about Kahn's use of inherited elements (plaided grid, poché).
35 Bottero, "Organic and Rational Morphology in Louis Kahn," 245.
36 Kahn, "Work of Louis Kahn and His Method," 294.
37 See Lewis, "Eleanor Donnelley Erdman Hall, Bryn Mawr College," 356.

38 For a particularly clear photo of this condition see McCarter, *Louis I Kahn*, 230.
39 Scully describes Bryn Mawr's façade as a 'Tuscan Romaneque kind of pre-Brunelleschi surface that is very elegant indeed.' Vincent Scully, "Works of Louis Kahn and His Method," in *A+U, Special Issue Louis Kahn* (1975), 294.
40 Vincent Scully, "Extemporaneous remarks – Forum: The Beaux-Arts Exhibition, 22 January 1976," in K. Michael Hays, ed., *Oppositions Reader. Selected Readings from A Journal for Ideas and Criticism in Architecture 1973–1984* (New York, Princeton Architectural Press, 1998)**,** 679.
41 Scully, "Extemporaneous remarks," 680.
42 Kahn, *The Louis I. Kahn Archive. Personal Drawings*. Volume 2, see the large elevation study, 565.18, 171.
43 Bottero, "Organic and Rational Morphology in Louis Kahn," photos 3–9. Brownlee and De Long, *Louis I. Kahn: In the Realm of Architecture*, full version 1991, 206–209.
44 Vincent Scully, *American Architecture and Urbanism* (London, Thames and Hudson, 1969), 218.
45 Kahn, L. (1974). "On Beaux-Arts Training." *The Architectural Review* vol CLV no 928 (1974): 332. An undated interview given to William H. Jordy, Kahn discusses three aspects of the beaux-arts training: the esquisse, poché, shades and shadow. 'The Beaux-Arts system included lessons in shades and shadows. These exercises made us aware of light, of shade, of shadow, or reflected light. They gave us an unquestionable feeling of the inseparability of light and building, and the fact that we could construct light. They taught us to differentiate shade from shadow. Today shade and shadow are often confused as the same thing. They aren't.' Louis Kahn cited in William H. Jordy, "Kimbell Art Museum, Fort Worth, Texas, Library, Philips Exeter Academy, Exeter, New Hampshire." *The Architectural Review* CLV(928) (1974): 332.
46 Kahn cited in William H Jordy, "Criticism: Kimbell Art Museum, Fort Worth, Texas, Library, Philips Exeter Academy, Exeter, New Hampshire," *The Architectural Review* CLV(928) (1974): 332.
47 Eisenman, "Real and English," 9.
48 Both articles are collected in Peter Eisenman, *Inside Out Selected Writings 1963–1988* (New Haven: Yale University Press, 2004), 121–130, 169–188 respectively.
49 See: Alan Colquhoun, "Die Fassade in ihren modernen Varianten," *Werk, Bauen + Wohnen* 12 (2005): 12–20. I am indebted to essays by Alejandro Zaera-Polo for the reference to Colquhoun. Alejandro Zaera-Polo. "The Politics of The Envelope." *Log* 13–14 (2008): 193–207. "The Politics of the Envelope, Part II." *Log* 16 (2009): 97–132.

Bibliography

Bottero, Maria. "Organic and Rational Morphology in Louis Kahn." *Zodiac* 17 (1967): 48–53, English translation, 240–245.

Brownlee, David, and David, De Long, eds. *Louis I. Kahn: In the Realm of Architecture*. London/New York: Thames and Hudson and Universal Publishing, 1997 (abridged and condensed version of the 1991 publication with the same title).

Brownlee, David, and David, De Long, eds. *Louis I. Kahn: In the Realm of Architecture*. New York: Rizzoli and Los Angeles: The Museum of Contemporary Art, 1991.

Colquhoun, Alan. "Die Fassade in ihren modernen Varianten." *Werk, Bauen + Wohnen* 12 (2005): 12–20.

Eisenman, Peter. "Real and English: The Destruction of the Box. I." *Oppositions* 4 (1974): 5–34.

Frampton, Kenneth. "Louis Kahn and the French Connection." *Oppositions* 22 (1980): 20–53.

Giurgola, Romaldo. "Louis I. Kahn, 1901–1974." *Progressive Architecture* 5 (1974): 4–5.

Giurgola, Romaldo, and Jaimini, Mehta. *Louis I. Kahn*. Boulder: Westview Press, 1975.

Giurgola, Romaldo, with Pamille, Berg. "Louis I. Kahn." In *Macmillan Encyclopedia of Architects* (Volume 2), edited by Adolf K. Placzek, 537–546. New York: The Free Press, 1982.

Jordy, William H. "Criticism: Kimbell Art Museum, Fort Worth, Texas, Library, Philips Exeter Academy, Exeter, New Hampshire." *The Architectural Review* 928 (1974): 330–336.

Khan, Louis I. *The Louis I. Kahn Archive. Personal Drawings: The Completely Illustrated Catalogue of the Drawings in the Louis I. Kahn Collection* (Volume 2 Buildings and Projects, 1959–1961, Erdman Hall, Dormitories for Bryn Mawr College, Bryn Mawr, Pa., 164–171). New York: Garland Publishing, Inc., 1987.

Larson, Kent. *Louis I. Kahn: Unbuilt Masterworks*. New York: The Monacelli Press, 2000.

Lewis, Michael J. "Eleanor Donnelley Erdman Hall, Bryn Mawr College." In *Louis I. Kahn: In the Realm of Architecture*, edited by David Brownlee and David De Long, 352–357. New York: Rizzoli, 1991.

McCarter, Robert. *Louis I Kahn*. London: Phaidon, 2005.

Ronner, Heinz, and Sharad, Jhaveri. *Louis I. Kahn – Complete Work 1935–1974*. (2nd revised and enlarged edition). Basel: Birkhäuser, 1987.

Rykwert, Joseph. *Louis Kahn, with New Photography by Roberto Schezen*. New York: Harry N. Abrams, Inc., Publishers, 2001.

Scully, Vincent. *American Architecture and Urbanism*. London: Thames and Hudson, 1969.

Scully, Vincent. "Extemporaneous Remarks – Forum: The Beaux-Arts Exhibition, 22 January 1976." In *Oppositions Reader. Selected Readings from A Journal for Ideas and Criticism in Architecture 1973–1984*, edited by K. Michael Hays, 679–680. New York: Princeton Architectural Press, 1998.

Scully, Vincent. "Introduction." In *Louis I. Kahn. In the Realm of Architecture*, edited by David Brownlee and David De Long, 12–14. New York/Los Angeles: The Museum of Contemporary Art, and Rizzoli, 1991.

Scully, Vincent. *Louis I. Kahn*. New York: George Braziller, 1962.

Scully, Vincent. "Work of Louis Kahn and His Method." *A+U (Architecture and Urbanism): Extra Edition – Louis I. Kahn* (1975): 287–300.

5

ELASTIC SPACE

I. M. Pei's approach to form-space generation

I

In 1960, after 12 years leading the in-house architecture office at Webb & Knapp, Inc., architect I. M. Pei decided it was time to open his own office, albeit initially within Webb & Knapp. Operating as I. M. Pei & Partners and supported by the broad range of potential clients Pei encountered with William Zeckendorf while at Webb & Knapp, the firm grew from its privileged start to become one of the most respected and successful New York practices over the subsequent decades.

A few years earlier, in 1955, historian, politician, and theorist Giulio Carlo Argan published what might appear to be a curious essay to introduce in relation to Pei. It can be argued, however, that Argan was transmitting ideas which were current and palpable at the time and that are now useful in contributing to a fuller understanding of the origin and significance of Pei's work. The title of Argan's essay 'The Importance of Sammicheli in the Formation of Palladio' does not hint at the theoretical leap and transformational power that Argan claims to have discovered in Palladio. According to Argan, the leap occurs between perspective interpretations of architectural form and what Argan comes to call non-perspectival (*aprospettico*) or elastic (*elastica*) conceptions of space.[1] It is this distinction, this putting forward of an elastic conception of space, that places Pei's thinking on the side of sensation.

In the 'Formation of Palladio' paper, Argan provides a close examination of spatial concepts and strategies of form disposition at work in Palladio. Argan argues that Palladio has a way of conceiving architectural form that departs from the classical point of view. The latter is marked by what Argan calls 'the traditional perspective concept' of space.[2] Palladio's non-perspectival or elastic concept of space has its origin, suggests Argan, in the military architecture of Sammicheli. In developing

DOI: 10.4324/9781003009641-8

his argument, Argan sets out to reveal the architectural qualities that evidence his claim. He then describes their consequences for the general theorisation of architectural form and space, which is the main object of his essay.

Argan's interrogation identifies a number of key themes and that of sensation in particular. What is of interest to our purposes are the specific morphological implications and conceptual qualities contained in Argan's categorisation of the two ways of conceiving space and their potential for theorising, designing, and interpreting works of architecture.

An indication of the relevance to an examination of a prioritisation of sensation over thought in Argan's categorisation of two manners for conceiving space — the more conventional perspectival on the one hand and the non-perspectival on the other — can be found in the shift he identifies in Palladio. Argan claims that Palladio's newness can be found in the latter's establishment of 'a new viewpoint in architectural theory . . . [one in which a new relationship is] established between building and environment, new because it is . . . completely non-perspective.'[3] 'The building, for Palladio', continues Argan, 'does not sum up or represent the space [as in classical theories], it exists within it, and the space, which is no longer thought of as structure . . . counts as pure phenomenal reality, as a sensed and shifting assemblage of effects of light and atmosphere.'[4]

This idea of built form is one that is no longer always already within a space and in an a priori relationship. Rather, architectural space and, in turn, form is now considered a product of a 'sensed and shifting' assemblage of other phenomena. This is an important swerve by Palladio and a feature that Argan applies to a building on its own as much as to a larger complex of open space and built form.

For Argan, classical architecture's perspectival conception of space achieves unity through abstract proportional associations. An a priori geometric structure is assumed to be a precondition — one bounded and made tangible through the continuity of the wall plane. This is in contradistinction to a non-perspectival or an elastic conception of space, which is understood as a physically discontinuous realm. Non-perspectival unity is a posteriori and perceptual, relying on a body's movement and on the ground plane rather than on a wall. The latter is thus potentially capable of infinite extension in its swerve from the vertical surface to the ground plane.

One way of seeing architectural form leads most readily to an ensemble of homogeneous relationships. This is how Argan qualifies a conventional perspectival conception of form and space. A different cast of mind finds architecture's manifestation in heterogeneous states. A perspective conception of space, for Argan, leads to a system of parts in favour of a larger whole with spatial units, such as rooms, as well as linking elements attached one to the other via perspective connections in a striated plan. Palladio's non-perspectival idea of space, differently, propels spatial units to the surface — in plan, although more powerfully in certain projects in section and elevation – with parts never coalescing into a single unity. In such a non-perspectival point of view, spatial units follow a logic of 'unrelatedness or absoluteness among singular forms,'[5] continues Argan, finding one expression for instance in Palladio's en suite plan disposition.

It is worth citing Argan at length to begin to further understand the context and implications of these formulations. Argan writes: 'Our contention is that Palladio is not only is [sic] turning away consciously from the perspective interpretation of architectural form but is also deliberately disconnecting and disintegrating it, to produce, out of the destruction of all a priori relationships, the quality of unrelatedness or absoluteness in the individual forms.'[6]

Here, Argan further broadens, without development or further explanation, the formal-spatial reach of the difference he claims for the Palladian leap. This characterisation of Palladio's potential impact is one that includes rendering architecture into what one might call a blurred state. It is an a posteriori nonresolution, although only a temporary one for Argan, given that parts never coalesce and remain, for him, suspended in a state of disintegration. To push the latent implications in Argan's essay even further is to suggest that Palladio could actually motivate the disintegration of form as a consequence of the absolute independence of building parts.

Table 5.1 attempts to summarise the distinguishing conceptual and formal properties contained in Argan's dense prose and set out aspects of the underlying sensibilities aligned with what he argues are these two ways of conceiving architectural space. Acknowledging that such differences are never pure or final and before turning to the work of Pei, Table 5.1 can thus also serve as a chart of key elements and themes contained in Argan's text. These are further developed later and are illustrated speculatively in certain of Pei's statements and projects.

An underlying theme of this book concerns possible modes for conceiving and shaping architectural space from the lens of sensation over thought as a too-little-explored quality of certain late-twentieth-century works of architecture. To follow this approach, we looked in Chapter 4 at Kahn's Bryn Mawr College Dormitory. In this chapter, and with Argan's proposed characterisation of a temperament that favours non-perspectival or elastic space now in place, a number of questions can be asked. Which concepts of space are at work in the projects? What differences in strategy and effect are revealed in the three projects, and do they align with Pei's stated ambition to create an architecture of movement formed by multiple viewpoints? More pointed is the question: do the projects realise different kinds of space, and, if so, is one better aligned to theories of sight or sensation?

Three propositions underlie the larger research ambitions considered in this chapter. In order to extend Argan's categories and to introduce the first proposition, it can be claimed that an architectural temperament on the side of a perspectival conception of space is aligned with notions of the painterly plane and an

96 Sensation

TABLE 5.1 Conceptual and formal aspects of a perspective concept of space versus an elastic conception of space

CONCEPTUAL ASPECTS	Space is structured	Space sensed amid a shifting assemblage of light and atmosphere effects
	Space as geometric structure or grid	Space as datum or field
	Transitional conditions abound	Elements are confronted one to another with no transition
	Realised in the continuity of the wall plane at the horizon	Rendered as a ground of undulating levels
	Homogeneous configurations in a closed form	Heterogeneous dispositions in an open configuration
	Architectural form generated by a space concept	Singular spaces generated by architectural forms
	PERSPECTIVE CONCEPT OF SPACE (economy of sight)	**ELASTIC CONCEPT OF SPACE** (strategy of sensation)
FORMAL PARAMETERS AND DEVICES	A form generation process with a bias toward isolation and hierarchy	A strategy of assemblage with a preference for blurring and enfolding
	Rooms are distributed in a striated plan	Rooms are arranged in en suite patterns of interstitial space
	Spatial units are attached via perspective connections, generally plan based	Spatial units are propelled to the surface in plan and elevation
	A system of parts in favour of a larger whole	Parts never coalesce into a whole, retaining their independence
	Logical relationships established with exterior conditions	Significance is largely internal according to a logic of absoluteness
	Form relationships exist a priori	Relationships among forms are settled a posteriori

Source: table by the author

economy of sight. Moreover, it is suggested, again based on Argan, that a sensibility that is attracted to the values and effects of an elastic conception of space with its attendant conceptual and formal implications is one bracketed by theories of assemblage understood as the rendering sensible of forces in a strategy of sensation. While Argan does not explicitly develop the sight-versus-sensation dialectic, it is nascent in his essay.

    Secondly, it is postulated that each of the following terms and their associated descriptors refers to a different architectural sensibility in late-twentieth-century discourse. In other words, it is suggested that an analysis of projects according to the pair of terms "perspectival" versus "non-perspectival" and their concomitant traits may contribute to revealing aspects of mid- and late-twentieth-century architectural culture too little considered or not sufficiently visible to date.

Using traces of each of the terms "perspectival" versus "non-perspectival" in the thinking and work of Pei, it is conjectured finally that foregrounding their differences can contribute to an understanding the formal and conceptual stakes in his work still awaiting analysis and, in turn, future deployment. Stated differently, if, for the purpose of this paper, we accept the interpretive lens of a perspectival concept of space versus an elastic conception of space transcribed provisionally as a polarity of sight versus sensation as described, then there are heuristic and generative potentialities that may come out as a result of an examination of Pei's mindset when conceiving architectural form.

In order to test these propositions, we consider, in what follows, three projects from different periods of Pei's career. The projects selected for this chapter mark the 1960s, 1970s, and 1980s, which were central decades of Pei's professional life. The Everson Museum of Art (Syracuse, 1961–1968), marking the 1960s, is frequently and not unreasonably claimed by commentators and also by Pei himself to be a breakthrough project. The National Gallery of Art East Building (Washington D.C., 1968–1978) follows and explores, as indeed Pei argues, fundamentally different concerns and makes manifest a different idea of space. Meyerson Symphony Center (Dallas, 1982–1989) standing for the decade of the 1980s, again reveals different preoccupations and devices, emphatically introducing other spatial themes that Pei continued to explore in the late decades of his professional life, while still bearing a trace, it is argued, of a bias to sensation over thought.

In a chapter of this length, much is abandoned or left aside for later consideration. It is thus perhaps useful, before moving to case studies, to point out what is not under consideration. This paper does not review Pei's Mile High Center (Denver) and the problem of simultaneity it raises – a problem which could reasonably be claimed serves as another candidate on the side of logic of sensation. We do not examine this early project, in other words, as an illustration of what Colin Rowe describes as Pei's mannerist skills, accepting instead as reasonable a demonstration given by Rowe and Robert Slutzky's confrontation of Pei's Mile High Center and Giacomo da Vignola's Villa Farnese in Caprarola to argue the point.[7]

Also, there is no investigation of a recurrent and important turn by Pei to structure or geometry as form generators. Evident in projects as important as the Bank of China Tower (Hong Kong, 1982–1989), Jacob K. Javits Convention Center (New York, 1979–1986), and the Miho Museum (Shiga, Japan, 1991–1997) and aligned with the expression of geometric determinants and structural ideas and their impure deployments, this would be another appropriate thematic frame for interrogating Pei's manner of imagining form and space.

For further clarification, in this chapter, no attempt is made to integrally articulate the range of potential relationships between Argan the taxonomer of concepts of space and Pei the practitioner. Rather, we more narrowly isolate the idea couple, called up by Argan, of a non-perspectival (*aprospettico*) or elastic (*elastica*) conception

98 Sensation

of space, and start to use these terms to cast a light on one aspect of Pei's work as a way of extending the logic of Argan's claim to see if and how one might apply a non-perspectival interpretation of architectural form. In other words, here, the much more modest and limited notion of Pei's approach to form – space generation is seen as revealing aspects of a specific architectural sensibility – one rendered in a narrow interpretation of the kind of visual and spatial values, stated or implicit, at work.

Pei provides an appropriate candidate for this study. He is relevant today in part because of the renewed professional and scholarly interest in his work that emerged during the 2017 centenary celebration of his birth. His work continues to merit sustained and systematic research. The donation by Pei of his personal and professional papers to the US Library of Congress will support this effort in future years.[8] There is also some logic to the chronological overlap and thematic alignments with Argan that this chapter hopes to suggest.

A brief note on source materials: research on this chapter relied selectively on over 15 years of published interviews with Pei contained in key monographic studies. The interviews date from the mid-1980s through the 1990s and include those with Carter Wiseman, Janet Adams Strong and Philip Jodidio, and Gero von Boehm, published in 1990, 1998, and 2000 respectively.[9] Project information is from these publications and supplemented with data and documents contained on the Pei Cobb Freed & Partners office website.[10] The website contains a large volume of relevant information, including summary project histories, photographs, and drawings for key projects since the firm's founding.

As regards authorship, at its founding in 1960, I. M. Pei & Associates was a medium-sized New York firm with 70 employees. The company grew to some 350 at the time of the Grand Louvre project in the 1980s. As is common with firms working on large-scale, complex, architectural-urban projects, principal design and administration responsibilities were divided across different partners and associates, with individual architects given responsibility for detailed design investigation, design development, documentation, and construction administration of key aspects. In the three projects discussed later, Pei is identified in office records and in the *Complete Works* as a design principal; and, in what follows, I only refer to Pei, although I do not wish to diminish the contributions of the many individuals and entities who collaborated with him on projects.[11]

II Analysis

In this section, observations are made around three projects in light of the framework set out previously and through the lens of the shorthand opposition of sensation to sight. Comments are limited to published statements and project documents as evidence of the space aesthetic or sensibility on display and following the categorisation of ways of conceiving space done by Argan.

II.i Everson Museum of Art

Historians, commentators, and Pei himself often cite the Everson Museum of Art as a breakthrough or a beginning project. In terms of chronology and brief type, it is a departure. It was the first of Pei's major cultural projects. Located on the edge of Downtown Syracuse, which, at the time, had no significant collection to house, the project was intended to launch the revitalisation of the area into a cultural precinct. The project, according to project histories, had a slow gestation primarily for financial reasons.[12]

As a way of evaluating the project, let us consider two aspects. The first is an apparent detachment of the ceiling plane over the central atrium. This is visible in the concept sketch and is a clear feature of the building as built. A second is the organisational decision to adopt a pinwheel plan – one that extends centrifugally from the sculpture court into the large site via sunken courtyards, low terracing, and selective planting. In the absence of an art collection at the time of the building's commissioning, it can be described as a self-referential, autonomous gesture.

This manipulation of the ground, it can be argued, gives presence and extends, given the relatively modest footprint, the building's hold on the site.

For the purposes of this study, however, it is Pei's claim that the design was influenced by his interest in Cubism that drew our first attention: 'I admit that some of my work was influenced by Cubism, such as . . . the Everson Museum.'[13] Beyond his many references in interviews to Cubistic influences in his thinking, should we take Pei at his word, and if so, what are the distinguishing design principles and devices evident in the Everson Museum of Art? On which side of the Arganian polarity, if any, does the project fall?

The rendering of the interior sculpture court provides a point of departure (see Figure 5.1). The separation of volumes and the use of light sleeves or skylight bands in plans and sections results in more than an apparent vertical corkscrew-like sliding of the building's interior, which is a move that duplicates the centrifugal motions of the pinwheel plan. It perhaps shares qualities of that embrace of autonomy that Argan identified in his essay on Palladio. The project's specific state of 'unrelatedness or absoluteness in the individual forms,'[14] to echo Argan, is emphatically suggested in published renderings from the period. This is perhaps more insistent in elevation and section than in plan when looking at presentation renderings from the time of the project's development.[15]

When asked about Everson in an interview some 30 years after its construction and in support of this view, Pei sketched not the plan, as he so often did, but the elevation, highlighting the importance of the four gallery hoods and other museum elements extending out into the site.[16] The four gallery hoods pinwheel out from the double-height internal sculpture court, isolated and absolute in their material presence according to the period's photographs and as suggested in the presentation rendering. Too easily might one claim that they illustrate Argan's 'mere

100 Sensation

FIGURE 5.1 Everson Museum of Art, Syracuse, rendering of the interior sculpture court, I. M. Pei

Source: courtesy Pei Cobb Freed & Partners

manufacture'[17] building form and that its setting was conceived as 'completely non-perspective,' with space conceived as a 'pure phenomenal reality as [that is] a sensed and shifting assemblage of the effects of light and atmosphere.'[18] Photographs of the just-completed project support the building's achievement of this state as did a sketch by Pei in that late interview.[19] See Figure 5.2.

This use of specific tower forms at Everson is also aligned, according to Pei in conversation with Gero von Boehm, with the manner in which Cézanne creates a painting, although this is hard to defend. Here is Pei discussing this point with von Boehm: 'Mesa Verdes could have come out of a Cézanne painting, with its cubistic form. The National Center for Atmospheric Research [in Boulder] is a piece of cubistic work. I visited it recently and I found the approach was correct even though the architecture was a bit immature.'[20]

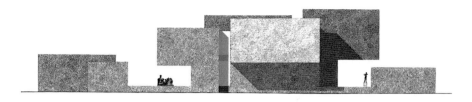

FIGURE 5.2 Everson Museum of Art, Syracuse, sketch of external massing, I. M. Pei
Source: courtesy Pei Cobb Freed & Partners

The extended views afforded to it and the charged natural setting may have provided the National Center for Atmospheric Research (Boulder, Colorado, 1961–1967), which came immediately before the Everson Museum of Art, additional potential to achieve such ambitions.

Perhaps the separated hooded towers, each differing from the other, at the National Center for Atmospheric Research do establish a kind of shifting assemblage of absolute objects. Although not flattened as in a Cézanne painting, it can be interpreted as a group form, one given to similarly charging the air with effects of light and atmosphere. By all accounts, Everson was located in a marginal site with little to either recommend it or provide clues to respond to. The Everson Museum of Art, even with its modest setting, however, is equally telling of Pei's particular mode of apprehension. Pei's sensitivity to the urban setting, honed out of years spent working with Zeckendorf, criss-crossing the country in search of viable urban renewal projects, can be reasonably conjectured to have contributed to these qualities.

II.ii National Gallery of Art East Building

The commission for the National Gallery of Art East Building was given to Pei in 1968, and the decade-long project occupied his office for much of the 1970s. Occupying a rhomboid-shaped site on the National Mall in Washington D. C., the building is an extension to the National Gallery of Art, providing contemporary exhibition, administration, conservation, museum storage facilities, public amenities, and a study centre. The extension more than doubled the available exhibition space, adding 56,000 m^2 (600,000 ft^2) to the original 42,000 m^2 (450,000 ft^2) building.

In an interview with Janet Adams Strong some 20 years after the project's completion, Pei emphasised up front a certain idea of space when talking about the

102 Sensation

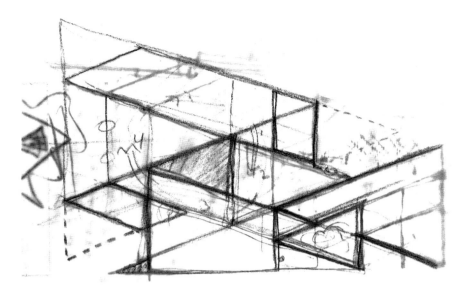

FIGURE 5.3   National Gallery of Art East Building, Washington D. C., early concept sketch plan, I. M. Pei

Source: courtesy Pei Cobb Freed & Partners

East Building: 'The introduction of an additional vanishing point . . . allowed me to move beyond Mies and [the] limited spatial possibilities of an orthogonal grid – which is not to say we were better architects but only that we were able to build upon what had gone before.'[21]

The appearance of the diagonal in Pei's early sketch may seem an obligatory response to site conditions (see Figure 5.2). According to historians, previous studies for this site over the decades had all assumed a small rectangular building as an appropriate response to an addition to the original building.[22] As he discusses in interviews with von Boehm, however, Pei's initial response was to resist the triangle. As he describes it, Pei sought to 'overcome' the triangle. Pei states: 'The site [for the East Wing] is a triangle. In the beginning I felt very uneasy about it. I felt that there was a restriction which I was obliged to overcome.'[23]

So there is also at stake, perhaps, a tale of overcoming. Rather than it being the triangle which is finally overcome, however, perhaps it is the limitations Pei came to feel in a single point perspective and the orthogonal grid of Everson that most distinguishes the East Building. This proposition can be made in relation to Pei's shifting aesthetic temperament and in narrow reaction to the orthogonal grid of Mies van der Rohe, so greatly studied by young Pei.

Evidence of overcoming an obligation to Mies and the liberation Pei found through the triangular grid in a third vanishing point can be seen at various stages of the East Building project. This, in turn, suggests that Argan's elastic conception of space may be at work.

There are many formal aspects one could focus on when examining the East Building: the development and character of the flexible museum pod-towers, diamond-shaped and modelled and extruded into elongated hexagons; the internal void around which the study centre was formed; and the ambitions to manipulate light while avoiding shadows when developing detailed designs for the atrium skylight. For the purposes of this chapter and as a contribution to reflections on the presence of valorisation of sensation in late twentieth-century architectural culture, select aspects can be foregrounded. One of the most telling, this includes the embrace by Pei of multi-point perspective, captured for instance in Steve Oles' 1969 rendering of the view from the entry.[24] Furthermore, Pei reinforces a bias to this temperament: 'I knew that if I could only bring the extra vanishing point into play, I could create more exciting spaces.'[25] What did Pei mean by referring to an extra vanishing point?

A sequence of three renderings during the East Wing's development phase dated to 1969, 1970, and 1971 can contribute to telling the story of Pei's thinking about this space. The dynamic swirl of space pulling up movement from the low-level connector to the main entry and into the atrium garden is clearly felt in Oles' renderings. Reproduced in *Complete Works*, one can imagine that this illustrator was pushed by Pei to visualise the resultant space as dynamic. This ambition was more fully crystallised when the decision was made to open up the ceiling via skylights, departing fully from the Everson Museum of Art and also perhaps Cubist aesthetic.[26]

The decision to change the ceiling from the deep coffered concrete explored in the early design phase to a triangulated glass and steel space frame as a recommended approach fundamentally changed the atmosphere of the project and pushed the character of the atrium space in a different direction from the Everson Museum of Art. The shift can be attributed in part to an ambition to experiment with a triangular grid and exploit the expressive power of those three vanishing points, which, as Pei had noted in an earlier interview, marks an approach differing from the orthogonal grid organising the early museum. Ezra Stoller's photography of the atrium reveals some of the qualities sought. See Figure 5.4.

Here again, Pei, in an interview with von Boehm, speaks directly of this aspect in relation to the East Wing: 'Most buildings are designed with an orthogonal grid that has only two vanishing points. A triangular grid on the other hand has three. It was this lesson that taught me to turn the constraint of the triangle into an asset.'[27]

Another clue as to the nature of what is going on is found in Pei's interest in the work of and collaborations with artists such as Miro, Henry Moore, and Dubuffet. Each of these had work which was abstract in a way that allowed it to be upscaled; more precisely, Pei's interest was in work that was scaleless – work that could be

104 Sensation

FIGURE 5.4 National Gallery of Art East Building, Washington D. C., photograph of atrium from 1978. Architect: I. M. Pei, Sculptor: Alexander Calder

Source: 1PP.025 © Ezra Stoller/Esto

enlarged to charge the urban scale space. As Pei noted in a late interview with Fumihiko Maki: 'Once you denature, once you become abstract, scale becomes different . . . I was interested in this problem . . . in the idea of having scaleless sculpture. . . . So after Picasso [used on the campus of New York University], Henry Moore. Moore's figures are abstract. They can be enlarged. Dubuffet. And one more, Miro.'[28]

II.iii Morton H. Meyerson Symphony Center or from two to three to infinite

The search for an architect for the Meyerson Symphony Center was started as early as 1980, shortly after the National Gallery of Art East Building's completion. According to office records, Pei was awarded the commission in 1981. As in the Everson Museum of Art, the Meyerson Symphony Center was intended to revitalise an emerging arts district, in this case on the edge of Downtown Dallas. The project began in 1989, coinciding with Pei's withdrawal from the practice he had founded. The change was intended to allow him to focus on small-scale projects without the pressures of the large office. Differing from almost every other project attributed to Pei as lead designer, the Meyerson Symphony Center had a second architect, Russell Johnson of Artec, engaged independently by the client and responsible for the design of the main performance space and, in fact, hired prior to Pei's being brought on board. Others have written on the disquiet and what some have suggested as somewhat compromised relations between the acoustic ambitions of Johnson and the sensual and spatial ones of Pei.[29]

On this last ambition, we come immediately to the relevance of Meyerson to our investigation into cases where sensation is privileged in late twentieth-century architecture. Here is Pei on the use of curved shapes: 'The curvature in Dallas makes the space more fluid and sensuous.'[30]

For the purposes of this section of the book, it is Pei's conception of space in the project's development that is of interest. 'I knew that if . . . I could explore curved surfaces with their infinite number of vanishing points, I could create even more exciting spaces. '[31] This statement by Pei, published a little over a decade after the Meyerson Symphony Center's completion, neatly encapsulates the desired attributes, at least retrospectively, for the architect. It is made within a defensible context if one reflects on the architect's experience in a series of projects that experiment with curved surfaces during these years.

Such projects include the Choate Rosemary Hall Science Center (Wallingford, Connecticut, 1985–1989), the Creative Artists Agency (Los Angeles, 1986–1989), and the German History Museum (Berlin, 1996–2003).

Whatever the sequence or influence, the Meyerson Symphony Center signals another singular approach to conceiving built form and space – one that departs far from the static, one-point perspective Pei so often dismissed in interviews as early as Everson and which has been previously discussed. The three-point perspective put into motion – thanks in part to the triangulations and the resulting triangular grid of the East Building – is clearly not enough for the Dallas project. Pei's way of thinking about space at that time led to a further differentiation in comparison to early projects, and, in consequence, further refinements to the architectural sensibility underneath can be claimed.

The passage in Meyerson Symphony Center can be said to be from the two vanishing points in Everson's flattened Cézanne-like space to an exploitation of three vanishing points via the triangular grid in the East Building. In working on

106 Sensation

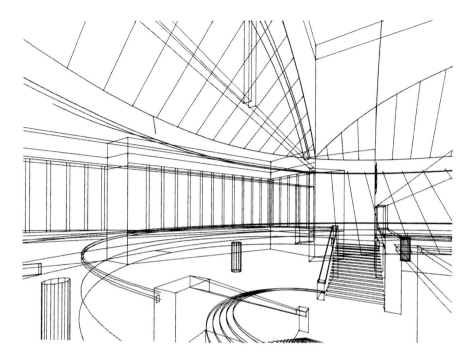

FIGURE 5.5   Morton H. Meyerson Symphony Center, Dallas, computer model study of the lobby, I. M. Pei

Source: courtesy Pei Cobb Freed & Partners

Meyerson, Pei discovers the excitement of working with curved surfaces and an infinite number of vanishing points with all the consequent impacts on the experience of the space. Here is Pei reflecting on the consequence of this regarding the Meyerson Symphony Center: 'You cannot look and understand it [the lobby of the Meyerson Symphony Center]. You have to walk and, as the space unfolds, you're drawn.'[32]

For the purposes of this chapter and returning to Pei's comments that opened this section, observations are limited to the major entry lobby for which Pei had most control. A survey reveals a number of key features. A preoccupation with curved surfaces and their infinite vanishing points may be the purest realisation of Argan's elastic space conception. Oles' published study drawings evidence the direction, visual lines, and velocity of this reading, now transitioned from the East Building's hand-drafted views to Pei's first use of computer-aided drawings, according to office records[33] (see Figure 5.5). A more emphatic concern with the creation of a shifting assemblage of effects of light and atmosphere also brings Argan back into play. Furthermore, in returning Argan back into the debate, the Meyerson Symphony Center does appear to share some of those elastic space qualities and values (see Table 5.1 again). Space at Meyerson is here manipulated into a shifting assemblage of light effects, dispersed in a heterogeneous disposition – the result of a strategy of dissociation and assemblage with a bias to blur edges over a process favouring isolation and hierarchy.

Perhaps most provocatively, and as Pei himself suggests, the Meyerson Symphony Center operates according to another idea of space – one facilitated by computer-aided drawing. It is neither Cubist nor Neo-plasticist; it is neither perspectival nor simply elastic. It is, at a glance and recognising the need for further elaborations, both beyond sight and exceeding sensation. Perhaps his description of the result as producing undulations is about right. As he said in an interview at the time, 'This building is our attempt to explore the possibility of undulating spaces. It is not exactly like the Baroque, but nonetheless it achieves much of the same purpose.'[34] Perhaps in it is a variation of a form-space idea yet to be fully examined.

III

In a way, the form-space possibilities of Meyerson were always there – at least since 1978, if we accept the date on a portrait of Pei in front of *Compass Rose*, which is a large 1974 acrylic by Al Held (1928–2005). The painting hung for many years in Pei's Madison Avenue office.

The importance to Pei of *Compass Rose* can be demonstrated both from its use in commissioned portraits and as part of Pei's personal art collection. One of the more telling commissioned portraits of Pei shows the architect in his then Madison Avenue office seated in front of Held's painting. Held's 1974 *Compass Rose* is a large canvas (96 × 144 in. (243.8 × 365.8 cm)) and was in Pei's possession until the end of his life. Several portraits of Pei with *Compass Rose* exist, including those dated 1978, 1980, 1982, and 1990. The last was used for the 1990 slip cover to Carter Wiseman's *I. M. Pei: A Profile in American Architecture*.[35]

Always cropped in portraits I have, to date, been able to locate, it may be useful to examine the painting and compare it to another by Held – *Solar Wind I* (1973, 114 × 114 in. (289.5 × 289.5 cm)) – and conjecture as to what Pei's selection of the one over the other, assuming both were for sale, might tell us about the architect's sensibilities and ambitions at that time.

Looking at a 1974 photograph of the two canvases hanging in Held's studio and published at one point in time on the Al Held Foundation website, the differences are striking. Furthermore, the epigraph that opens this section (it is from an interview with Pei in which the architect is retrospectively musing over his interests at the conclusion of the East Building) raises perhaps a distinguishing trait of this third moment – one additionally different from the orthogonal grid of Everson and Mies van der Rohe.

A different pairing and one perhaps more aligned with the distance and difference between Everson and Meyerson would be to confront Held's *B/W XVI* (acrylic on canvas, 1968, 144 × 168 in. (365.7 × 426.7 cm)) seen hanging in the central atrium in published photos which appear to be at the opening of Everson[36] with *Compass Rose*. The earlier project and painting might be on the side of an assemblage of discrete orthogonal shapes piled one on the other and gravity palpable. The later project and painting reveal a completely different space idea at work, with a curved surface that has been freed from any limits of orthogonality – centripetal in an outward whoosh: shorthand for differences in temperament. The other painting, *Solar Wind I* (1973) is – while equally expansive in its organisation – controlled and limited by, or at least subject to, interpretations which reference an orthogonal grid and their 'limited spatial possibilities.'[37]

Out of this consideration, and having assembled and framed the elements of this study, it is possible to return to the opening propositions.

It is evident that no single concept of space is present in the three projects considered. There is, however, evidence, depending on the element considered, of a bias toward one kind of sensibility or another. On balance, it allows us to identify Pei as displaying a bias for sensation over thought. The shorthand translation of perspectival space practices, on one hand, versus what Argan named non-perspectival or elastic conceptions of space into tendencies toward sight and sensation, on the other, was only proposed in a general way and could be further developed and nuanced. Whether these elements have a specific value in relation to late-twentieth-century practice and discourse is also yet to be properly tested. There does seem to be resonance between these elements and Pei's work, especially in the case of the National Gallery of Art East Building and the Meyerson Symphony Center. There also appears to be merit in a further interrogation of Pei's embrace of the dynamic richness in a multi-point perspective, generally, the triangular grid, and the infinite number of vanishing points he found in curved surfaces, in particular.

Meyerson Symphony Center's exploration of curved surfaces and infinite vanishing points, in other words, might be said to escape Argan and his focus on a non-perspectival swerve in our reading of Palladio. This seems clear. If not an evolution – Pei himself positions its provenance squarely with German Baroque as noted earlier – then it does require a third concept of space that can be provisionally called scenographic. This is to adopt Pei's own characterisation of the necessary cast of mind as depending on the need for one to walk to unfold or draw in the building space.[38] It is also consistent with Argan's description of an aspect of Palladio's way of seeing architectural form, on one hand, and manner of conceiving the problem of space, on the other.

Space, in the hands and mind of Palladio, is no longer conceived as existing a priori but comes into being as a 'product'[39] of relationships that require movement or time as a duration to set up. Listen again to Argan's excited description of a sensibility that imagines architecture 'as pure phenomenal reality, as a sensed and shifting assemblage of effects of light and atmosphere.'[40]

Another theme to be explored is Pei's relation to scalelessness. As alluded to earlier, in a late interview with Fumihiko Maki, Pei commented on a kind of methodology that is scaleless, one that requires non-architectural elements to be 'denatured.' Once denatured and truly abstract (without scale), 'scale becomes different.'[41]

There is, therefore, and as a form of provisional conclusion, a heuristic and generative utility realised in extending forward Argan's categorisations of a perspective concept of space and an elastic conception of space as an interpretive lens in relation to the projects considered. This conclusion is also a contribution to the study of architecture's recent past and its contemporary expressions. More specifically, there is a return to an opening proposition of Pei's work as a contribution to thinking critically about a still-to-be-exploited trajectory which favours sensation over thought, one deserving further elaboration.

Notes

1 Giulio Carlo Argan, "L'importanza del Sammicheli nella formazione del Palladio," in *Venezia e l'Europa. Atti del XVIII Congresso Internazionale di storia dell'arte, Venezia 12–18 settembre 1955*. (Venezia: Casa editrice arte Veneta, 1955), 387–389. An English translation is published in 1970 as: "The Importance of Sammicheli in the Formation of Palladio," *Renaissance Art*, ed. Gilbert Creighton (New York: Harper & Row Publishers, 1970), 172–179. In notes that follow on, page references are given firstly to the English translation followed by the Italian in italics.
2 Argan, "Formation of Palladio," 175/*388*.
3 Argan, "Formation of Palladio," 173–4/*387*.
4 Argan, "Formation of Palladio," 174/*387*.
5 Argan, "Formation of Palladio," 175/*388* translation modified.
6 Argan, "Formation of Palladio," 175/388.
7 Colin Rowe and Robert Slutzky, "Transparency: Literal and Phenomenal, Part II," first published in *Perspecta* 13–14 (1971), 287–301, reprinted with introductory comments in Colin Rowe, *As I Was Saying: Recollections and Miscellaneous Essays, Volume One, Texas, Pre-Texas, Cambridge* (Cambridge: The MIT Press, 1996), 77–83.
8 For information see: I. M. Pei papers, 1920–2016. Accessed 23–03–2022, https://catalog.loc.gov/vwebv/search?searchCode=LCCN&searchArg=mm%2096083787&searchType=1&permalink=y
9 Carter Wiseman, *I.M. Pei: A Profile in American Architecture* (New York: Harry N. Abrams, Inc., 1990). Gero von Boehm, *Conversations with I.M. Pei: Light is the Key* (New York: Prestel Verlag, 2000). Philip Jodidio and Janet Adams Strong, *I.M. Pei Complete Works* (New York: Rizzoli International Publications, Inc., 2008.
10 Pei Cobb Freed & Partners Architects LLP office website: www.pcf-p.com/.
11 See Jodidio and Strong, *Complete Works*, 354 and 359 for an overview respectively of Pei's role generally in the practice and in Meyerson specifically
12 Bruno Suner, *Ieoh Ming Pei* (Paris: Fernand Hazan, 1988), 58.
13 Pei cited in Boehm, *Conversations*, 45.
14 Argan, "Formation of Palladio," 175/*388*.
15 See the pencil rendering of the elevation reproduced in Boehm, *Conversations*, 46.
16 The sketch is reproduced on the office website, accessed 04–07–2022, www.pcf-p.com/projects/everson-museum-of-art/.
17 Argan, "Formation of Palladio," 174/*387*.
18 Argan, "Formation of Palladio," 174/*387*.
19 See Jodidio and Strong, *Complete Works*, 86–91, and project documents on the office website, accessed 04–07–2022, www.pcf-p.com/projects/everson-museum-of-art/.
20 Pei, cited in von Boehm, *Conversations*, 61.
21 Pei interview with Strong, 26–09–1996, in Jodidio and Strong, *Complete Works*, 146.
22 Jodidio and Strong, *Complete Works*, 134.
23 Pei cited in von Boehm, *Conversations*, 67.
24 See Jodidio and Strong, *Complete Works*, 138.
25 Pei in discussion with Strong, 26–09–1996, cited in Jodidio and Strong, *Complete Works*, 136.
26 Jodidio and Strong, *Complete Works*, 138, second rendering from November 1970.
27 Pei cited in von Boehm, *Conversations*, 68.
28 I. M. Pei from an interview with Fumihiko Maki in "I. M. Pei – Words for the Future," *A+U (Architecture and Urbanism) – Special Issue* 1 (2008): 101.
29 Wiseman, *I.M. Pei*, 270.

30 Pei in an interview with Strong of 26–09–1996, cited in Jodidio and Strong, *Complete Works*, 191.
31 Pei discussing the East Building, interview with Strong, 26–09–1996, cited in Jodidio and Strong, *Complete Works*, 146.
32 Pei cited in Jodidio and Strong, *Complete Works*, 191.
33 Jodidio and Strong discuss this in *Complete Works*, 191.
34 I.M. Pei cited in Michael Cannell, *I.M. Pei: Mandarin of Modernism* (New York: Carol Southern Books, 1995), 356. Originally given by Pei as an address, YMHA, New York, 29 November 1983.
35 *Compass Rose* was recently auctioned off by Christie's as part of The Collection of Eileen and I.M. Pei and can be seen here: Accessed 11–05–2022, www.christies.com/en/lot/lot-6233904
36 A particularly clear photograph of the Held painting hanging in the Everson Museum of Art can be found in *A+U (Architecture and Urbanism)–Special Issue* 1 (2008): 87.
37 Pei in conversation with Strong, cited in Jodidio and Strong, *Complete Works*, 146.
38 Pei interview with Strong, 26–09–1996, in Jodidio and Strong, *Complete Works*, 191.
39 Argan, "Formation of Palladio," 175/*388*.
40 Argan, "Formation of Palladio," 174/*387*.
41 Pei, "Words for the Future," 100.

Bibliography

Argan, Giulio Carlo. "L'importanza del Sammicheli nella formazione del Palladio." In *Venezia e l'Europa. Atti del XVIII Congresso Internazionale di storia dell'arte, Venezia 12–18 settembre 1955*, 387–389. Venezia: Casa editrice arte Veneta, 1955.

Argan, Giulio Carlo. "The Importance of Sammicheli in the Formation of Palladio." In *Renaissance Art*, edited by Creighton Gilbert, 172–179. New York: Harper & Row Publishers, 1970.

Cannell, Michael. *I. M. Pei: Mandarin of Modernism*. New York: Carol Southern Books, 1995.

Jodidio, Philip, and Janet Adams, Strong. *I. M. Pei Complete Works*. New York: Rizzoli International Publications, Inc., 2008.

Pei, I.M, interviewed by Fumihiko, Maki. "I. M. Pei – Words for the Future." *A+U (Architecture and Urbanism) – Special Issue* 1 (2008): 60–113.

Rowe, Colin, and Robert, Slutzky. "Transparency: Literal and Phenomenal, Part II." *Perspecta* 13–14 (1971): 287–301.

Suner, Bruno. *Ieoh Ming Pei*. Paris: Fernand Hazan, 1988.

von Boehm, Gero. *Conversations with I. M. Pei: Light is the Key*. New York: Prestel Verlag, 2000.

Wiseman, Carter. *I. M. Pei: A Profile in American Architecture*. New York: Harry N. Abrams, Inc., 1990.

TRAJECTORY III
Time

6
DIAGONALITIES
Visual Arts Center by Le Corbusier

I

In the opening chapter, three trajectories were proposed as thematic lines for revisiting and perhaps seeing things differently in certain works of late-twentieth-century architecture. The first section of the book then considered instances of architecture operating in a state of what Hubert Damisch calls conceptual objects. The plan as a conceptual device, whether vertical or horizontal, with or without a thickness, was used as a lens for examining De Vore House by Louis Kahn, House II and House IV by Peter Eisenman, and the Diamond Projects of John Hejduk. The second section analysed the polarity of sensation versus thought and considered attributes of architectural works that might be claimed to favour the sensible over the intellect. The miraculous effects of Kahn's Bryn Mawr College Dormitory provided a case study, and a small number of projects across I. M. Pei's career were considered as privileging elastic space as an aspect of how an architecture of sensation might function.

In this final trajectory, we consider the problem of architecture's relationship to time and of temporality more generally.

This chapter is organized into three parts: the first sets out the generating propositions, materials of study, and the approach. Part two proffers an analysis of Le Corbusier's Visual Arts Center according to four terms: diagonals, expressive volume, ambiguities, and a voided centre. Part three returns to the proposition of an architectural concept of time, responds to the opening questions, and outlines future areas of research as a form of conclusion.

I.i Propositions

In his 1965 essay on Le Corbusier's just-opened Visual Arts Center, published as a homage following Le Corbusier's death in August of the same year, John Hejduk conjectures that the Visual Arts Center generates a cut in time. Differing from a notion of time conceived as linear and progressive and as implied in the title of his essay, for Hejduk, the building creates architectural conditions that are 'out of time.'[1] This insistence on the building's capacity to engender a time out of joint – one that is liberated, according to Hejduk, from movement and structure – implies a specific kind of architectural temporality. It also highlights a too-little-explored aspect of modernist architecture commonly discussed in terms of formal and spatial characteristics.

Taking Hejduk at his word, a number of general questions are raised. How are buildings and projects composed such that time is confronted? Is there a specifically modernist concept of time – a modernist mode for the creation and expression of time? Just as there are different space concepts, are there different architectural concepts of time, and, if so, how do they work and what are their distinguishing characteristics?

Another way to formulate the question is this: is Hejduk finding evidence of a liberation of time from movement? Is it a liberation similar to that which Gilles Deleuze discerns in certain post-1945 works of art and cinema such that pure time is made palpable and architectural – plastic qualities are released independent of movement? As already considered in the opening chapter, Deleuze's idea of this kind of time can be summarily framed in his characterisation of works in which 'time . . . increasingly appears for itself.'[2]

Two propositions – simultaneously thematic, methodological, and conceptual – provide a preliminary framework for responding to these questions. The first proposition is that there is a largely untheorised temporality created in certain modernist works of architecture and those of Le Corbusier in particular. The second proposition is that this temporality can be characterised as one that is neither bound to a vision in motion nor one that requires a body's movement to gain presence. In certain works of late-twentieth-century architecture, rather, there is a condition of vibration and energy already contained or produced by a building independent of movement. Time, to take Deleuze's implied formula, has 'gone creative,'[3] and this condition perhaps resembles or renders physical a concept of direct time in the realm of architecture.

To begin to investigate these propositions, let us examine a building that overtly engages movement and, thus, by implication, imbeds or releases a concept of time. The Visual Arts Center (Cambridge, Massachusetts, 1960–1964), also known as the Carpenter Center for the Visual Arts, is an important project in Le Corbusier's late period and provides material for analysis.[4] The Visual Arts Center's apparent reliance on circulation for its coming into being is tested by focusing on other devices, strategies, and formal effects. Both on the surface and perhaps in reality, it treats the spiral, the diagonal, and the torqued perceptions produced as generators of singular effects, ones which are perhaps bound to rendering or recording a concept of time.

In the Visual Arts Center, I suggest we are confronted by forms of simultaneity and conditions of time as overlapping durations. The temporality rendered in the Visual Arts Center is an always already-compressed time – one different from that which is composed of a line of images or vignettes and thus is reliant neither on futures nor on pasts. This state is a consequence, in part, of compressions and releases which work to create folds in or give thickness to a kind of temporality potential in architecture and which is labelled, for the purposes of this chapter, diagonal time or a state of diagonality. This condition is named diagonal time to differentiate it from a linear past-present-future time and a purely empirical succession of things.

I.ii Approach

To begin to frame an approach to the concept of a temporality specific to certain works of modernist architecture, let us return to the notion of direct time as theorised by Gilles Deleuze and deployed most fully in his *Cinema 2: The Time Image*. In *Cinema 2*, as discussed in the opening chapter, Deleuze proposes that in some mid-twentieth-century films and works of fine art, a new relationship of movement and time is made visible. Time is no longer subordinate to movement, he writes, and a reversal occurs such that 'time ceases to be the measurement of normal movement [but, instead,], it increasingly appears for itself.'[5]

Though it requires further elaboration in subsequent studies, I believe a phenomenon similar to that which Deleuze discerns in the realm of philosophy, cinema, and certain works of painting and sculpture can be claimed for architecture. An examination of projects that release or make concrete a Deleuzian direct time – one not bound to a *promenade architecturale* from the point of view of time – may, in turn, reveal a range of formal moves and composition devices at work along with their resultant formal-spatial effects. An analysis of the Visual Arts Center is used to explore this idea.

The Visual Arts Center freeze stops a moment in time and thus illustrates an architectural concept of direct time by means of a number of devices and strategies. Four such aspects are briefly explored: oblique and transverse form relationships, ambiguity in figure/ground relationships, expressive volumes, and voided centres that create intensity independent of animating factors.

I.iii Scholarly context and structure

In the *Oeuvre complète* presentation of the project, Le Corbusier highlights the autobiographical role of the Visual Arts Center. It is, he writes, a 'demonstration of Le Corbusier's theories.'[6] He emphasises five such theories or devices: the interpenetration of internal and external space, the use of rough concrete (*béton brut*), the ramp as an organising device, the free plan, and the use of brise-soleil. The Visual Arts Center differs from Le Corbusier's focus on these formal and spatial devices and is consistent with our exploration of the trajectory of time. I believe the Visual Arts Center can be read as a display of, if not a turn, in his thinking, then a shift – one marked by a specific temporal bias and whose potential for practice and theory has yet to be examined in depth.

Taking primarily visual materials as the object of study, let us start with observations on approximate configurations aligned with the four aspects proposed earlier to guide the effort. We then move to identify their specificity in order to test how certain motives and effects might be generalized into architectural strategies that work directly on time. In so doing, I hope to begin to identify the formal and temporal attitudes underlying the Visual Arts Center and their potential extension as an interpretive and creative category. In this way, I endeavour to follow what Colin Rowe characterized as a Wölflinian style of 'critical workout.'[7]

I work using published drawings and photographs – both recent and dating from the time of the building's completion – writings of Le Corbusier, and secondary writings. I have benefited, as do all scholars working on this building project, from the archival and critical-historical efforts of William Curtis as well as those of Alan Colquhoun, Eduard Sekler, Peter Serenyi, and Stanislaus von Moos. These scholars provide important accounts of the building's genesis and design history, speculate on Le Corbusier's intentions, and interpret the role of the building in Le Corbusier's lifework.

Von Moos discusses, for example, aspects of the project to highlight Le Corbusier's typological design method and the metaphoric nature of certain forms.[8] Sekler's analysis focuses on the provenance of forms and spatial ideals and the relation of Le Corbusier's painting to his architectural practice. Curtis highlights, in his important survey that was recently published in an expanded second edition, formal inventions, transformations of established elements, and a condensation of spatial ideas; but he does not specifically discuss temporality.[9] In terms of method, and although he does not directly discuss the Visual Arts Center, Alan Colquhoun provides an exemplary and elegantly spare approach to Le Corbusier's late period work; and I have benefited from his comparative approach.[10] Peter Eisenman's *Ten Canonical Buildings* provides a methodological framework for the present essay – one whose depth and breadth of interrogation a longer study of the Visual Arts Center should attempt to approach.[11]

Far from attempting to establish the origins of forms or ideas – either within the work individually or within the context of a trajectory of Le Corbusier's work – I focus on the relatively modest aim of conjecturing on how Visual Art Center works on time, attempting to identify and catalogue the devices and formal moves used as well as the consequent architectural effects from the point of view of time.

Drawings of the building in the design development phase published in *Le Corbusier at Work* and of the structure as built constitute primary analytic materials supported by visits to the building. They complement the drawings published in the *Oeuvre complète 1957–1965 Volume VII*, which records an interim phase in the design process. The latter, for example, show an internal horseshoe ramp connecting levels 2 and 3 that was abandoned. Secondary writings from the period and more recent scholarship on Le Corbusier provide a historical and critical context. Floor plans are named according to the convention of the *Oeuvre complète*. Thus the ground floor is the ground level, the next floor up is level one, and so on.

Throughout, I use the name of the building as it is given in the *Oeuvre complète* and as referenced by Le Corbusier in project correspondence published in *Le Corbusier at Work*, namely, Visual Arts Center. Drawings from Le Corbusier's office carry the office's characteristic three-character project name shorthand, in this case VAC-BOS, which stands for Visual Arts Center, Boston; and thus the naming convention used here is consistent with the practice of the 35 Rue de Sèvres office. This differs from the more common practice of referring to the building as the Carpenter Center for the Visual Arts.

II Analysis

As suggested earlier, an examination of the project reveals at least four formal devices or composition strategies in play. These are diagonal and transverse planning, volumes treated as expressive space, ambiguities in figure-ground relationships, and an absent or voided centre. Each device is, in some manner, rendered in the Visual Arts Center and goes beyond or differs from other formal-spatial conditions and motifs in Le Corbusier's work.

Diagonal and transverse planning moves away from Le Corbusier's emphatic bias to frontality and cross-axial planning. Expressive volumes realised in lung-like figures disrupt a purely domino, flat plate, and free column reading. Ambiguities abound in the project, and there is a blurring of figure-ground relations in favour of a mannered manipulation of contour and surface resulting in figure-figure readings. A dominant centre is absent, and such an absence calls out for perhaps – most emphatically – an interpretation of the project's impact as engendering a specific kind of temporality.

II.i Diagonals or going beyond frontality

One of the first things that strikes you when visiting the Visual Arts Center or when examining its drawings or photographs is the rotation of the building relative to the bounding orthogonal field of streets and buildings. There are at least two major consequences resulting from this rotation: peripheric tensions of edges are created, and field extensions beyond the building volume engender an expanding space condition as suggested in the site plan (see Figure 6.1).

Rotation also creates conditions which challenge potential bay readings and disrupt frontal and cross-axial factors as everything in one sense is or becomes diagonally engaged in a perimeter condition. In the Visual Arts Center, oblique and transverse moves are at work throughout. Diagonal motions off the parallel streets of Prescott and Quincy initiate this condition. The level-one and level-two studios continue this non-frontal theme with what appears to be a spiralling and echeloned cascade along the outer edge of the lung-shaped spaces.

The plans as published in the *Oeuvre complète* show a U-shaped ramp connecting levels two and three of the Visual Arts Center in a clockwise spiral moving up the building, which, if built, would have continued and intensified the external ramp's

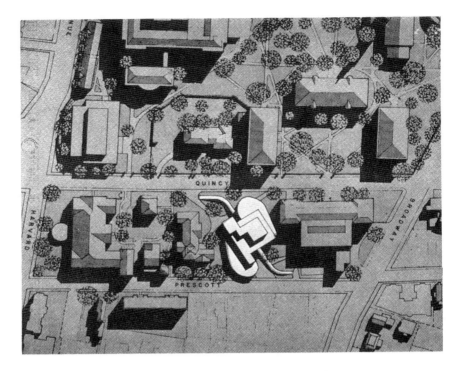

FIGURE 6.1   Visual Arts Center, Cambridge, site plan, Le Corbusier

Source: © Le Corbusier, ADAGP/Copyright Agency, 2022

momentum upward or, alternately, have contributed to a corkscrew motion downward from the rooftop apartment and garden.

Frontal views are difficult to achieve. Instead, three-quarter views are favoured in publications. Peripheral composition is sought over centralization, and interpenetration favoured over separation. Thus, the Visual Arts Center can be seen to be centrifugally ordered, though not purely. It is, in part, channelled and vertically stacked at the same time that it is self-bifurcating and horizontally distributed. This bifurcation might be characterised as creating a diptych condition as an examination of sketches and the Quincy Street elevation reveal.

Out of these relations, a fairly constant diagonal condition can be claimed to exist. A review of the plans reveals a disposition different from the enfilade (room to room) plan and the poché (served and servant) plan. This is the case in certain floors of an open plan (levels one and two, for example) and in others a free plan (level three). The building favours transverse over cross-axial or longitudinal arrangements, although, as with other readings, there is an ambiguity at work in relation to the larger site and campus setting.

One enters on the oblique and continually slides in either a counter-clockwise or clockwise motion up the building. This had already been revealed in the 1

April 1960 sketch and the building-as-movement reinforced as desirable by President Pusey, according to Le Corbusier's sketchbook notes of mid-June 1960.[12] The movement continues back down again, sliding always on the edge and compressed by the looming, bulbous volume of either the painting or the sculpture studio to one side. The building is layered by open letter 'Ls' cut by the flattened Z-shaped circulation ramp slipping along the edges in a sideling manner. Studio spaces are thrust forward in part in a burst of centrifugal energy, and there is the implied promise of future vertical extension. With some imagination, conversely, the building can be read as folding over itself in an almost Boolean movement – as if the ramp were holding down a vertically moving force and preventing the building from elevating further off the ground.

This can be considered another aspect of Le Corbusier going beyond frontality, and Kenneth Frampton provides a clue as to what is at stake. To further unpack the formal moves and motivations of this aspect, consider Frampton's description of modernist architecture during these years. He says they are trapped by frontality, are unable to adopt the 'multi-directional spatiality of the De Stijl or Suprematist movements,' and 'unable to abandon . . . [an] emphasis on frontality.'[13] There is evidence of this bias in the Center's reliance on the free plan, column-slab or thin plane to wall-slab model that is horizontally layered within a central regular volume and thus indebted to or relying on a Domino space concept.

II.iii Free volumes or expressive space

The central rotated square volume of the Visual Arts Center whose trace disappears at points can be said to contain two states. In one state, a horizontal space is formed flat and is bound as such by an extended floor and ceiling planes, illustrating a domino diagram. A second agitated state is manufactured as a line in motion by the ramp that bisects the built form. If one extends the description and abstracts the reading, then one can generalize the differences between these two: planes enclose horizontal space – the line of the ramp elaborates and energises space in its pull and push and torsion; while planes bring volumes into presence, thus providing emphasis, dissipating lines and leading the eye away from a static, single field focus of the effect which removes firm boundaries so that a new reality can be created.

We can perhaps say that the building disposes the two studio volumes so as to engender a dynamic space beyond Domino's limits to produce what can be characterised as expressive space. A view from Prescott Street gives a hint of this. This idea is supported by a previously unpublished elevation study by Curtis of the Prescott Street elevation. The drawing is from a January 1961 development phase and clearly shows the role of the two studio volumes relative to the central one.[14] The demands of expressive space can be considered an evolution of Le Corbusier's free plan into a free section – one animated by organ events and object types and which might only later be rationalised in terms of site, structure, desired compositional effect, or operational need, if at all. This sensitivity might extend to a divergence and toward continuity, on one hand, and toward separation or different kinds of continuity where continuity is understood as a unity of space and structure, on the other hand.

In the separation of supporting point columns and functional partitions, structure does not define space but punctuates it as photographs of the studio spaces, in particular, demonstrate. Look again at the site planning as providing additional evidence (see Figure 6.1). The Visual Arts Center occupies a relatively flat urban site and, to a certain extent, creates its own topography. A consequence of the volume disposition is the use of overlap and strategies of central compression and peripheral dispersion in the pursuit of an architectural idea.

This line of analysis might suggest that VAC is about movement of volumes and, despite appearances, is not primarily an illustration of the *promenade architecturale*. This might imply a temporal ambition and concept – even if of an ambiguous intent – that differs from one aligned with a primarily empirical (chronological) idea of time, which is subordinate to movement. This is to suggest a sensibility motivated by a time that is not simply (or ever) linear and faithful to a-this then that, a past then present, a before and after. In the Visual Arts Center, rather, we are never satiated by space whose nature can be justified solely by the generation of movement as the ramp's role is constantly denied or deferred. Frustrated, the ramp is never allowed to arrive fully. There is no culmination.

We observe, then, in the Visual Arts Center an intensification of local spatial event states that exist with a simultaneous horizontal and vertical emphasis in the junction split between level one and two. Those mandolin or lung-shaped organs of the two studios, vertically staggered, put in motion a spiralling disposition that edges along their Georgian neighbours. Site elements are organised such that a force, or multiple forces, are shaped and temporarily focused only to be quickly dispersed outward so that even in the absence of a peripatetic eye, there is still a vibration produced; thus recording perhaps a pure time independent of any reliance on motion or movement to bring it forth.

If perhaps it is too early to state a preliminary finding, one might thus far be justified in claiming that the Visual Arts Center works equally on concepts of space and on problems of time, though the relationship to time is unclear at this stage. Another way to characterise this state might be as a mannerist use of certain shapes and devices – those that have accompanied Le Corbusier since the beginning and which differ from other late buildings. In the Millowners' Association Building (Ahmedabad, 1954) – a precedent for the Visual Arts Center in certain elements – the ramp runs straight on, landing frontally at the entry while the lung-like main hall and meeting rooms remain inboard.[15] In the Congress Hall in Strasbourg (unbuilt, 1964),[16] and as others have noticed, the organs are also contained whereas at the Visual Arts Center they burst out, gripping vice-like, the squared volume though not in a centrifugal manner and resulting in ambiguous free organs perceived as partial figures.

II.iii Opacities

Thus far, our analysis of the Visual Arts Center from the point of view of an architectural notion of time has explored two aspects: that of diagonal and transverse relationships engendered by site rotation and that of external and internal volumes rendered expressive – the consequences, in part, of free-plan and free-section ideas. In general, as has been suggested, the overall architectural condition generated is one of inexactitudes and of opacities. The building as read is conceived around diagonal movements with functional spaces disposed either as coincident with circulation or as appendages to lines of circulation which bifurcate a volume in rotation, creating what might be characterised as a diptych state. This move disrupts or goes beyond an interpretation of frontality.

These traits are neither mutually exclusive nor interdependent but are offered as terms in provisional suspension to allow their reintegration in a future proposition about architectural time.

A third tactic to be developed concerns additional ambiguities or object/field and figure/ground conditions. The Visual Arts Center cannot be fully absorbed from without. The value of wholeness – the ideal of being able to stand at some point and receive a palpable impression of the whole – is specifically not an aim. Even the bird's-eye-view sketch from April 1961 only partially outlines some elements but does not yield the complexity of resultant conditions. The development of focus is a somewhat arbitrary and, for Le Corbusier, intentionally ambiguous proceeding: a potential single, central focus is consistently broken up, while concentration in one point is never sought or gained. Consider the external views which struggle to find a stable viewpoint.

So, while this is perhaps too easy a parallel and things are evidently subtler, can we say that when read at the scale of the site, the Visual Arts Center is all figure and no ground and, when read internally at the scale of the building, all field and no object? In other words, one is here confronted with a constant architectural state of background intensities; or, to give it an alternative formulation, it is all figure-on-figure with no evident relief that a point of focus or difference might provide.

This is surely one response, in part, to the fact that in the Visual Arts Center, the site and project brief required intensive development as elaborate external deployments were not fully possible within the more or less set and limiting boundaries. Inversion or intensification in the place of extension was done: more fluid at studio levels one and two were fluid, while the ground and upper floors were concentrated, being bound by floor and ceiling plates and directed horizontally, especially if you study the sliding or staggered distribution of main spaces and what one might have foreshadowed as a dense centre, doubled or echoed by perimeter incidents. Views under and through the studios that occupy the middle floors across the ramp's cut suggest this theory.

There is no simple dispersal of focus but more of a constant rebound. Visual waves bound back to confront the initial ripples. In mounting or descending the ramp, the walls of the studios channel and deflect the effect outward. At other moments, a downward vortex effect is created.

When inside, a potential release is denied or multiplied, while energy is bounced back from or ricocheted off all the perimeter incidents: the curving wall, ondulatories, brise-soleils, smooth columns engendering centrifugal forces, and the *aérateurs* (vertical narrow pivoting doors with fly screens) channelling space. There is a peripheral interest in horizontal expansion in the studios containing the concentration of a rather constant nature that slides and swings along vertically when up and over the ramp.

Look at the level-two plan. An apparently regular field of columns is the constant condition in the studio spaces.[17] A sense of discrete room volumes is not the main thing: space does not conclude or ever solidify. Perimeter walls are an end but only in a tentative way.

There is rather a more dominant oblique state creating an effect of space sliding away – one might almost say leaking. There are vectors moving along diagonal lines that spring out through the brise-soleil and that are pushed along by the oblique cut of the end wall in the plan and in the vertical plane. In the Visual Arts Center, the effect of a deferred arrival is similarly achieved, although through different means. Certainly, an artist's apartment perched on the final floor might want to satisfy a desire for a conclusion as a kind of pyramidal cap. If an internal ramp had been built between the second and third floors, then perhaps in Cambridge, the third floor would have gained some hierarchical role, but the ramp was not built.

If the plan is a section in the work of Le Corbusier as claimed by John Hejduk in his 1965 essay, it is equally valid to claim the section is a plan, one recording ambiguous conditions of overlapping forces. Hejduk says, 'A plan is a section.'[18] The square volume is never perceived and is constantly broken up and dissolved. Even in its purest state at level three, the stair and lift forever blur the edges from the sawtooth brise-soleil and create an effect of curious irresolution.

These ambiguities reveal a lingering tendency that might be described as combining facets of Cubist and post-Cubist sensibilities. There is a direction as well as an eccentricity introduced by placement and delineation of walls – one that establishes a dominant direction for organising spatial flow. The orchestration of flows contributes to a constantly shifting centre, or, more simply, it is perhaps the case that the very possibility of a centre is endlessly deferred and literally shifted further away. Differing elevation treatments further complicate the readings with brise-soleil, full-height fixed glass sheets and narrow vertical aérateurs providing different kinds of animation.

This could be interpreted as introducing a Cubistic gesture (directional) in a post-Cubist or neo-plasticist (non-directional, square grid) realm. Plan tensions are introduced between a bias to the vertical against uniform extensive or horizontally explosive forces – not at the points but out to the edges of the level-three diamond plan, which is precariously balanced on the splitting ramp. All this reinforces the ambiguities and fluctuations in the figure and field as well as the matrix and object readings.

II.iv Voided centres

Form relations, concepts of space, and perhaps, as I am proposing, notions of time are all worked on here. At first blush, and as suggested earlier, two composition devices are constantly explored in the Visual Arts Center. The first is an expansion or, to borrow a turn of phrase from Kenneth Frampton, an 'exfoliation toward the periphery and beyond.'[19] A second composition strategy is that of a condensation of space and mass toward an always-voided centre.

This idea of the voided centre confirms a move away from – or beyond – a trabeation logic of post and beam frames, of singular columnar surfaces, and of articulated roof planes toward a groundless architecture of round columns, freestanding partitions, and flat slab floors and ceilings – all forecast in that early sketch of 1 April.

In other words, there is a critical work on the Domino world of column-slab construction, fully engaging the implications and effects of two kinds of architectural freedoms, namely 'liberated space [and] liberated structure,' as Hejduk writes in an undated manuscript sheet from the period, which can be approximately dated to 1965–1966. This is around the time he was writing his homage to *L'Architecture d'aujourd'hui*.[20] Recall that we considered this suggestion of Hejduk in Chapter 2 when examining the Diamond projects.

To begin again, we notice that columns also play a fundamental role in the Visual Arts Center. On closer inspection, however, other conditions are also seen to contribute and cause differences between the Domino flat slab and point column, the brise-soleil window walls, and etched floors. There is a peripheral dispersion of incidence in the case of the Visual Arts Center's middle floors and peripherals. There is a shifting look – an animated vision – that is largely frontal even if following a switchback or Z-shaped pattern in the case of the central volumes and ramp element. In all views, the geometric centre is hollow or hollow and occupied by a ramp, and has outdoor slices of space. It is presented equally as echeloned, oblique, or more front on, with elevator cores, stairs, and slots copenetrating and sometimes attracting attention to the edges. At other times, it resides in a mute middle.

To characterise the Visual Arts Center differently, any assumption of a central focus is relegated to dismembered spaces in a sort of serial installation of interest (organs, events, and ribbon galleries) around the extremities of the plan. A view from Prescott Street reveals the ambiguities in this assemblage which work to contradict the theme of wholeness or unity (see Figure 6.2).

Contradictions and complexity with two different compositional strategies – liberated space and liberated structure – yield similar effects, at least from one point of view. There is no single centre. Instead, it is replaced by a kind of indefinite though not neutral space. This space is never uniform. In fact, it is always potentially fully animated such that hierarchy (of figure over ground, or object over matrix) is shown specifically not to be the intent, as discussed in the previous section. The absence of one dominant centre produces another kind of condition: that of being always already in an ambiguous kind of middle.

So while there is perhaps an idea or promise of a denouement, it is endlessly deferred. I believe this is further evidence of the concept of time at work. You never fully arrive – suggesting time itself has always already passed you by or perhaps the building surpasses time. There is no interior; everything is in a liminal state. This is a shift in emphasis from previous form studies that focus and make manifest the phenomenon of all-over kinetic equilibrium. In the same pendulum arc used

FIGURE 6.2 Visual Arts Center, view from Prescott Street, Le Corbusier

Source: © Le Corbusier, ADAGP/Copyright Agency, 2022

to realize the condition for a neutral container, the two compositional strategies together mimic what Hejduk described as a Michelangelo effect. Hejduk, speaking on this mysterious state of things, says, 'The effect is like in Michelangelo's architecture. At first there's a sense of a perfectly neutral condition. Then when you begin to penetrate, it becomes kinetic and dynamic.'[21]

Look again at the structural system as a further demonstration of this state. The Visual Arts Center is set out in a rectangular bay grid rotated relative to the bounding streets and generally employing round section columns with local incidents. In terms of consequent volumetrics, we have observed narrow horizontal volumes folding back on themselves. The Visual Arts Center is a hybrid of the Domino flat plate point column grid and an assembly of independent organs. A stable interior is of secondary importance, with ascendancy given emphasis – especially in the early schemes, where certain of the key uses were located at the second level ramp's arrival.[22] As already noted, there is a promise of arrival and culmination that is never satisfied.

The voided centre, finally, is revealed in the reading of the horizontal planes of floor and ceiling as dominant in the one reading, the enclosing walls channelling movement and reinforced by a highly articulated and, in parts, transparent ceiling and floor in the experience of the ramp in another observation. Horizontal extensions are reinforced by the shear, taut, unencumbered ceiling plane matched by a vertical pull of the studio organs, themselves staggered diagonally. In the Visual Arts Center, the centre is occupied by a cut of the ramp, marking a spring-point of pinwheeling elements. However, contrary to possible assumptions, there is no tension; rather, there is a state of ambiguous equilibrium. All the architectural energies are moved to the perimeter.

III

The four spatial-formal effects have now been surveyed. We return to the germinal questions and opening propositions around time. Is there a concept of time rendered in VAC – a time concept specific to a work of architecture? What kind of temporal structures are at work, and do they share aspects of being plunged into a kind of direct time? In the preceding analysis, explicit has been the question of pure time – both as an effect created or made manifest in the building and as an interpretive category. In other words, can we claim some evidence of what I have proposed to call diagonal time at work in the Visual Arts Center?

In terms of frontality, which we started with, here is Le Corbusier clearly working to get over or to abandon the limits he sees in a reliance on frontality using at least two moves – that of charging the perimeter and voiding the centre. Linked to all these, and perhaps as a first move, there is the rotation of the building relative to site conditions which allows him to move away from cross-axial planning which characterises so much of the layered site planning in his early career – from the Villa at Garches to the League of Nations. When confronted with receding or encompassing walls as one approaches up the ramp always on the oblique, an observer can be said to be always already in a transverse state, even without moving. Moreover, in the rotation appears a curious, ambiguous notion of time, characterized by Hejduk as a 'moment of the present.' These terms come out during Hejduk's interviews in the 1980s. Hejduk states: 'The place where a perspective or diamond configuration on the horizontal plane flattens out and the focus moves to the lateral peripheral edges. . . . This is the moment of the hypotenuse of the diamond: it is here that you get the extreme condition, what I call the moment of the present.'[23]

It is not just an entry or threshold condition of walls but the entire project that is working on and intensely occupies the present without, however, any hope for or promise of a before or of an after. It is all about what might be called a timeout.

From the earlier analysis, we can perhaps say that the Visual Arts Center renders manifest an idea of time out of joint – time, one that does not rely on movement to gain presence. Thus, Visual Arts Center differs from Le Corbusier's early period which laid emphasis on an acropolian sequence and the motor and visual aspects implied and the parallax effects so immediate and palpable in that whirl of columns and tilting planes proceeding up and through the building. In other words, and despite the combination of oblique movement and peripheral incident dispersed over and across several floors, and the free organs staggered vertically, despite or in addition to all this, time perhaps appears directly: it is on its own, in a state of what we might call diagonal time.

The four aspects, when reviewed together, provide a provisional description of Visual Arts Center's main characteristics: diagonal and transverse relationships and a voided centre that creates intensity independent of any other animating presence. In addition, there is a specific idea of structure: the flat slab and point structure in the Visual Arts Center overlap with dense perimeter conditions and the cantilever, lung-like shapes in an open-ended plan and perhaps supporting or enabling it all – field and ground ambiguities. To varying degrees and with all the qualifications called for, there is a suggestion of an architectural concept of time. It is one that shares qualities with those post-1945 aesthetic phenomena whose consequence were described by Deleuze so aptly: 'We are plunged into time.'[24]

We are confronted with forms of simultaneity and a concept of time as overlapping durations – the consequence of compressions and release, all working to create folds in or give thickness to time. These seem to be valid and real findings and, even if only tentatively, conclusions which nonetheless call for further research with other concrete examples to be sought and terms of reference to be refined and amended. Chapter 7 and 8 contribute to such efforts.

There is a provision for a kind of open unity to the form relations and spatial orders under consideration – a voided centre, peripheral tension, exploded field, and volume becoming a plane, thus creating the conditions for a flat space to appear. The specific notion of time revealed in the Visual Arts Center is, I believe, that dimension which ensures a single whole is never completely given. In this instance, direct or diagonal time would be that function or operation that holds it all together. As suggested in this brief analysis, what we call diagonal time has the strange power to affirm parts that do not make a whole in space or form a succession in time. Time is exactly the diagonal of all possible spaces – those made possible as a result of the freedoms Hejduk found in Le Corbusier, namely that of liberated space and liberated structure. In place of frontality and cross-axial planning, the Visual Arts Center proposes transverse relationships. The ramp's cut displaces a Domino ideal by expressive volumes and partial figures. Table 6.1 is comparative and lists some characteristics of diagonal time as developed earlier.

A number of lines of further research should be followed, with two already alluded to. The study of the diagonal in a plan and in conditions of diagonality as a general condition in late-twentieth-century architecture should be pursued. Efforts might include tracking parallel manifestations of the diagonal in a series of architectural projects and a limited number of theoretical-historical texts. On

TABLE 6.1 Aspects of diagonal time versus linear time in certain works of architecture

Linear time	*Diagonal time*
• Frontality	• Diagonality
• Cross-axial planning	• Transverse planning
• Domino	• Expressive volumes
• Free plan	• Free section
• Contour and simple mass	• Ambiguities in figure-ground relations
• Hierarchy	• Voided centre

Source: table by the author

the side of projects, the research might start with an interrogation of Hejduk's Diamond Projects series, Eisenman's House projects, and Louis Kahn's project for the Philadelphia College of Art that each render different aspects of the diagonal. In parallel to the formal analyses, the research might examine the diagonal and its various manifestations in writings of different periods and teachings of key architectural historians. Colin Rowe, Vincent Scully, and Rudolf Wittkower might provide a start. Each theorises, to different degrees, the modernist project and alludes to the diagonal and related concepts of ambiguity, folding, the oblique, and torquing.

A second line of expanded research should examine more emphatically whether and by what means Deleuze's notion of direct time provides a way to think about and test different architectural concepts of time, which have only been touched on earlier. According to Deleuze, a reversal in the relation of movement and time can be discerned in the realms of philosophy and cinema. For philosophy, the reversal has occurred slowly, whereas in cinema it has occurred since 1945 and thus at a much more accelerated pace with the movement image of classical cinema being supplanted by what Deleuze names a time image. Deleuze describes certain devices which render time manifest in itself, prior to or proceeding movement, and he finds evidence of this condition in certain films of Renoir, Fellini, and Welles among others.

To conclude and as a final token of promise to future research, I return to the concept of pure time in *Cinema 2*. Deleuze succinctly characterises it this way: 'There are certain conditions rendered in works of cinema – and by extension I would claim in certain architectural projects – such that one is taken directly into an experience of time irrespective of any reliance on movement. There are certain kinds of aesthetic works so conceived and constructed,' he writes, that 'we are plunged into time rather than crossing space.'[25]

The aforementioned is a suggestion of the interpretive and creative potential a concept of diagonal time may hold for architecture. An analysis of Le Corbusier's Visual Arts Center has provided an initial case study, and further research on other modernist architects may reveal others.

Notes

1. Hejduk's essay is first published as "Hors du temps dans l'espace" in *L'Architecture d'aujourd'hui* 122 (1965): xi–xxiii. An expanded version referenced in this paper is contained in John Hejduk, *Mask of Medusa: Works 1947–1983*, ed. Kim Shkapich (New York: Rizzoli International, 1985).
2. Gilles Deleuze: *Cinema 2 The Time-Image,* trans. Hugh Tomlinson and Robert Galeta (Minneapolis: University of Minnesota Press, 1989), xi.
3. Deleuze does not specifically propose this effect, but its appropriateness is suggested when he writes in relation to the cinema image: "What is specific to the [time-] image, as soon as it is creative, is to make perceptible, to make visible, relationships of time which cannot be seen in the represented object and do not allow themselves to be reduced to the present." Deleuze, *Cinema 2 The Time-Image,* xii.
4. Standard references include W. E. Boesiger, ed., *Le Corbusier et son atelier rue de Sèvres 35. Oeuvre complete: Volume VII, 1957–1965* (Zurich: Les Editions d'Architecture, 1965),

54–67. Eduard F Sekler, and William, Curtis, *Le Corbusier at Work. The Genesis of the Carpenter Center for the Visual Arts* (Cambridge: Harvard University Press, 1978).
5 Deleuze, *Cinema 2: The Time-Image*, xi.
6 Le Corbusier, *Oeuvre complete 1957–1965 Volume VII*, 54.
7 Colin Rowe, *The Mathematics of the Ideal Villa and Other Essays* (Cambridge: The MIT Press, 1976), 16.
8 Stanislaus von Moos, *Le Corbusier. Elements of a Synthesis* (Cambridge: The MIT Press, 1979), 85, 87.
9 William J. R. Curtis, *Le Corbusier. Ideas and Forms* (London: Phaidon Publishing, Inc., 2015).
10 Alan Colquhoun, "Formal and Functional Interactions: A Study of Two Late Buildings by Le Corbusier," in *Essays in Architectural Criticism: Modern Architecture and Historical Change*. (Cambridge: The MIT Press, 1981), 31–41.
11 Peter Eisenman, *Ten Canonical Buildings 1950–2000* (New York: Rizzoli, 2008).
12 Le Corbusier, *Le Corbusier Sketchbooks Volume 4*, 1957–1964, eds. Architectural History Foundation and Françoise de Franclieu (New York: The Architectural History Foundation, The MIT Press in collaboration with the Fondation Le Corbusier, Paris, 1982). Sketchbook P61, figure 566.
13 Kenneth Frampton, "John Hejduk and the Cult of Humanism," *A+U (Architecture and Urbanism)* 53 (1975): 142.
14 Curtis, *Le Corbusier*, 372–373.
15 W. E. Boesiger, ed., *Le Corbusier et son atelier 35 rue de Sèvres. Oeuvre complete: Volume VI, 1952–1957* (Zurich: Les Editions d'Architecture, 1965), 144–157.
16 Le Corbusier, *Oeuvre complete: Volume VII, 1957–1965,* 152–163.
17 The as built plans published in Sekler and Curtis, *Le Corbusier at Work*, better demonstrate this condition.
18 John Hejduk, "Hors du temps dans l'espace," 73.
19 The term exfoliation is Kenneth Frampton's and is used to characterize tensions in the periphery of Hejduk's contemporary diamond projects and with useful application here. Frampton, "John Hejduk and the Cult of Humanism," 14.
20 Hejduk, annotations on a sheet of unpublished sketches for Diamond House B, Canadian Center for Architecture, John Hejduk Archive/Fonds 145, Series 2: Professional Work, File 15: Diamond Houses, Sub-file 4: Miscellaneous Diamond House Sketches, drawing DR1998_0063_005.
21 John Hejduk, "Interviews with Don Wall," in *Mask of Medusa: Works 1947–1983*, ed. Kim Shkapich (New York: Rizzoli International, 1985), 90. On the idea of kinetic equilibrium, see also Hejduk, "Interviews with Don Wall," 52.
22 As Curtis relates, in the final scheme as built, the administration offices were relocated from level to the ground floor, thus removing the programmatic imperative to take the ramp. Sekler and Curtis, *Le Corbusier at Work*, 139ff.
23 Hejduk, interview with Wall, *Mask of Medusa*, 90.
24 Deleuze, *Cinema 2*, xii.
25 Deleuze, *Cinema 2*, xii.

Bibliography

Besset, Maurice. *Le Corbusier*. (Translated from the French by Robin Kemball). London: Academy Editions, 1976.
Boesiger, W.E., ed. *Le Corbusier et son atelier rue de Sèvres 35. Oeuvre complete: Volume VI, 1952–1957*. Zurich: Les Editions d'Architecture, 1965.
Boesiger, W.E., ed. *Le Corbusier et son atelier rue de Sèvres 35. Oeuvre complete: Volume VII, 1957–1965*. Zurich: Les Editions d'Architecture, 1965.

Colquhoun, Alan. "Die Fassade in ihren modernen Varianten." In *Werk, Bauen + Wohnen* 12 (2005): 12–19.

Colquhoun, Alan. "Formal and Functional Interactions: A Study of Two Late Buildings by Le Corbusier." In *Essays in Architectural Criticism: Modern Architecture and Historical Change*, 31–41. Cambridge: The MIT Press, 1981.

Curtis, William J. R. *Le Corbusier. Ideas and Forms*. London: Phaidon Publishing, Inc., 2015.

Deleuze, Gilles. *Cinema 2 The Time-Image*. (Translated by Hugh Tomlinson and Robert Galeta). Minneapolis: University of Minnesota Press, 1989.

Eisenman, Peter. *Inside Out Selected Writings 1963–1988*. New Haven: Yale University Press, 2004.

Eisenman, Peter. *Ten Canonical Buildings 1950–2000*. New York: Rizzoli, 2008.

Frampton, Kenneth. "John Hejduk and the Cult of Humanism." *A+U (Architecture and Urbanism* 53 (1975): 141–142.

Hejduk, John. "Hors du temps dans l'espace." *L'Architecture d'aujourd'hui* 122 (1965): xxi–sxxiii.

Hejduk, John. "Interviews with Don Wall." In *Mask of Medusa: Works 1947–1983*, edited by Kim Shkapich (interspersed throughout). New York: Rizzoli International, 1985.

Hejduk, John. "Out of Time and Into Space." In *Mask of Medusa: Works 1947–1983*, edited by Kim Shkapich, 71–75. New York: Rizzoli International, 1985.

Le Corbusier. *New World of Space*. New York: Reynal & Hitchcock and The Institute of Contemporary Art, 1948.

Le Corbusier. *Le Corbusier Sketchbooks Volume 4, 1957–1964*, edited by Architectural History Foundation and Françoise de Franclieu. New York: The Architectural History Foundation, The MIT Press, 1982.

Rowe, Colin. *The Mathematics of the Ideal Villa and Other Essays*, Cambridge: The MIT Press, 1976.

Rowe, Colin, and Robert, Slutzky. "Transparency: Literal and Phenomenal." In *Perspecta* 8 (1963): 45–54.

Sekler, Eduard F., and William, Curtis. *Le Corbusier at Work. The Genesis of the Carpenter Centre for the Visual Arts*. Cambridge: Harvard University Press, 1978.

Serenyi, Peter, ed. *Le Corbusier in Perspective*. Englewood Cliffs: Prentice-Hall, Inc., 1975.

von Moos, Stanislaus. *Le Corbusier. Elements of a Synthesis*. Cambridge: The MIT Press, 1979.

7

GROUP FORM

Meeting House and Philadelphia College of Art by Louis I. Kahn

I

In his evocation of memories infused from early-morning impressions of Louis I. Kahn's Yale Center for British Art, Michael Cadwell adopts a turn of phrase that resonates with the trajectory of time we are concerned with in this section. Cadwell suggests that the consequence of Kahn's design, and all those strange details, is to make the very presence of the building uncertain. For Cadwell, the building's existence in time is less than clear.

Here is Cadwell: 'The [Yale] Center [for British Art] remained in emergence – never leaving the darkness, never arriving in crisp light.'[1] As Cadwell then self-reflexively notes, it is curious, and at the very least uncommon, to describe a building as emerging. As Cadwell writes: 'A building is either there as physical fact or not there.'[2] This idea of emergence, of being endlessly out of focus, existing in a state of almost but not quite coming into frame and thus perpetually out of step with time's passage, is another way to start to think about architecture's less-than-conventional relationship with time.

This state of remaining endlessly 'in emergence' can be used to qualify other projects by Kahn. To contribute to understanding aspects of the topic of time and late-twentieth-century architecture, we consider two projects by Kahn. The first of the two projects is that conceived for the Meeting House at the Salk Institute (La Jolla, California, 1960–1962), and the second is the Philadelphia College of Art (Philadelphia, 1964–1966). Let us set the stage by considering how others have approached the question of architecture and time.

We start with Vincent Scully in the early 1950s, in Italy, in the same years that Kahn is based at the American Academy in Rome. Let us pick up the question specifically of the diagonal in an early essay by Scully and consider the idea and its force. In Scully's 'Michelangelo's Fortification Drawings: A Study in the Reflex

Diagonal,' we have a meditation on what he terms the 'reflex diagonal.' The term is used by Scully to identify a new kind of architectural design process, one contained in Michelangelo's Florence fortification drawings. Scully endeavours to capture the force of this sensibility. According to Scully, it is a sensibility that led Michelangelo to resort not to rational but to reflexive drawing, not to static but to dynamic shapes. It is, in short, an inaugural display for what Scully calls a 'reflex diagonal method.' To describe it differently, Scully finds an architecture of movement and gesture, taut and subversive, yet marked by a fluid relation to generative and regulating geometries. Scully discerns, that is, an architecture of contradictions.

Scully returns to these ideas decades later when contemplating digital simulations of Kahn's unbuilt projects for the Meeting House, Salk Institute. Similar contradictions in Kahn's project are claimed to be at work in the specifically modern thinness of the Meeting House. It is a thinness made animate and vital out of a layering of screens such that they are able, within a certain framework, to impregnate time's depth into the architecture.

The first question may be to attend to the effect that Scully had in mind when sending his field report from Italy. Clearly moved by the drawings of Michelangelo for improvements to the Florentine fortifications, Scully's description conveys the energy of ideas and forms that he will try to recreate and channel. Michelangelo's drawings, writes Scully, 'explode': they 'consume the paper.'[3]

Scully's writing mimes the force of the formal and temporal moves under examination. In his Italian text, that is, Scully's prose fully echoes that 'intense effort' and, in turn, relays a message. The message is that beyond their incredible beauty, the real significance of the Michelangelo drawings is as heralds of a new kind of architectural sensibility, one conveyed with a 'sense of power and urgency.'[4] For the new kind of work was characterised by a design sensibility radically different from one distinguished by 'static completeness, spatial definition and rhythmical symmetry.'[5]

Here, by contrast, according to Scully, on display and borne by Michelangelo's drawings, is a design method which favours instinct over intellect, reflex over reason, one privileging that dynamic diagonal over the static right-angled relationship. The prose here is especially dense, Scully darting about, 'literally, a man on fire,' to recall a contemporary characterisation.[6] A close reading reveals what is at issue for him. The lessons are more or less still potential, as there seems to have been little consequence, much less a record, of anyone having taken the essay on board, and it remains missing from subsequent compilations of the journal and from Scully's collected writings.[7]

Certainly, Scully was ready to receive the message. Or perhaps he was ideally placed to transmit it, even if not fully in control of the reach and extent of the impact on the discipline's relationships to the past and the contemporary.

Such as they are, the possible lessons can be arranged in terms of composition (devices, tools), consequences (on character and of effect), and larger evidence of a general condition in architecture (whether of movements – Renaissance, Mannerist, Baroque – or general disciplinary potential).

Two hypotheses can be drawn from Scully, one more on the side of the conceptual, one more on the side of the formal. The first: there is a temporality of infinite becoming contained in Michelangelo's drawings, one whose interpretive and creative potential is yet to be realised for architecture. That infinite becoming shares something of the consequence and moment that Cadwell felt in the Yale Center for British Art that opened this chapter. Cadwell found in the Center for British Art an architecture in a permanent, or at least not infrequent, state of emergence. It also shares something with Heinrich Wölfflin's description of buildings which function to appear as if endlessly 'changing, becoming,'[8] to drop in a figure whose potential capacity to inform knowledge in architecture is still to be unpacked.

The second hypothesis: work on the diagonal as a device, figure, and space type in the thinking, and projects of certain late-twentieth-century architectural acts materialises aspects of that temporality.

Perhaps architecture is the realm which establishes the conditions for us to feel a pure time. The architectural problem then would be that of shaping not only a space of immanence but a temporality which is adequate to it. What figures, what kinds of compositional devices, might contribute to such a practice? The second proposition responds to the first and concerns the diagonal, its relay and modifications through a set of late-twentieth-century architectural acts.

To the extent that Scully describes and puts in play a model of thinking which holds together the determinations which compose it as a set of variables, and ties together the forces of thought which cross it, there is a consistency which constitutes its force. Here, where things comprise lines to be unraveled, surfaces unfolded, the system of knowledge in architecture and the resultant constructions are charged with explaining these lines of force and tension and charting the circumstances and their limits of variation.

Perhaps a different notion of time, of the relation of creating and interpreting a temporality of a work of architecture, can be shown to add to the historiography of modern architecture. It reveals a kind of temporality and a pedagogy that is different from the continuously new, different from the of-its-time modernity and different from the continuously in revolt.

That most stable of things, the work of architecture – how does it come to echo those in front of those drawings whose destiny is still to be met, always already deferred, displaced, put on hold in an architecture of action and gesture?

II. Analysis

We have been endeavouring to isolate across a sampling of architectural acts and writings evidence of general, differential ideas about architecture's temporalities, of architecture's relation to time. These temporalities establish themselves in a position to resist, for example, a logic of form and volume.

As introduced earlier, Wölfflin provides a useful introduction to the critical and interpretive vocabulary we claim to discover in the Meeting House and the Philadelphia College of Art. In 'Clearness and Unclearness (Absolute and Relative

Clearness),' in *Principles of Art History*, Wölfflin distinguishes between two manners for arranging architectural elements, the classical and the baroque. He describes the classical as privileging the clear and the 'absolutely comprehensible.'[9] It finds its expression in the formative elements of wall and joint, pillar and beam, supporting and supported members. The work of classical architecture is an art of 'tangible values.'[10]

On the side of the baroque, Wölfflin discovers an architecture of vital shape, in which the building appears 'like something changing, becoming.'[11] The baroque building avoids frontality; it works instead with material folds and with intersections in order to capture and direct the vectors of changing light, such folds giving effect to what Wölfflin calls a kind of 'veiled distinctness.'[12]

In Kahn's response to the problems of the day, he also employs the fold. Taken as a signal for a specific sensibility, a relevant practice can be demarcated. As we have shown, this includes a tendency away from an optical foundation, whether at the level of the metaphoric or the constructivist. This leads Kahn beyond the visual to a non-optical model. We can use Wölfflin to construct an appropriate vocabulary to express this manner in the realm of thought.

This mode adopts a number of strategies when deployed in the realm of aesthetic constructions. The first is an all-over, flattening manner when confronted by the support. This also reveals itself as an insertion of depth into the flatness of the plane. This includes, in the case of sculpture, coming down off the pedestal, as in the case of the floor piece works of Andre. The second is an additive elementarisation (1 + 1 + 1 + 1 . . .), as in the multiple-element works of Judd. Assemblage by means of montage is a third: as Jean-Luc Nancy has shown, it is a 'showing by doing' according to operations which fold the present and, in so doing, suggest a denial or, at best, an indifference to a logic of foundations and origins.[13] This is a manner which does not rely on a point of origin or a logic of beginnings but tends toward a manner of working from the middle, presuming the capturing of an event already in play, even if invisible or unfelt. There is also a preference for the horizontal over the vertical.

In the visual and plastic arts, this bias can be shown to have been announced but not developed or taken up by others, for example in Michael Fried's article on Frank Stella's shaped canvases. Fried writes, 'Frank Stella's new paintings investigate the viability of shape as such. By *shape as such* I mean not merely the silhouette of the support (which I shall call literal shape), not merely that of the outlines of elements in a given picture (which I shall call depicted shape), but shape as a medium within which choices about both literal and depicted shapes are made, and made mutually responsive. And by the viability of shape, I mean its power to hold, to stamp itself out, and *in* – as verisimilitude and narrative and symbolism used to impress themselves – compelling conviction.'[14]

Shape as a consequent theme and creative goal for an aesthetic system reveals a sensibility not of narration or symbolism but its own self-contained power. Shape, the material limit, can be taken as the medium for conveying conviction and choice. The projects and buildings of Kahn support an extension of the criteria of shape to the creation and interpretation of architecture. In order to explore these ideas, let us turn to specific projects and see if there is evidence or traces of these general qualities or characteristics.

II.i Meeting House, Salk Institute for Biological Studies

Kahn's project for the Meeting House can be read as a systemic expression of the problem of the wall as a surface and as a site of experimentation. It presents a response to the resolution of the conflict between an impulse to transparency and thinness and a demand for presence, thickness, shape, and shadow appropriate to the role of the institution. That is at the level of the building enclosure, if one can talk about enclosure in a project that specifically creates ambiguity in where inside and outside begin and end and, as a consequence, creates something like a time machine. More on that later.

The Meeting House also can be read as revealing a sensibility suddenly sensitive again to what Sigfried Giedion in those same years called the 'space-emanating powers of volumes.'[15] If we substitute time for space, we can perhaps speak about architecture's time-emanating potential.

As in Chapter 1, where we considered De Vore house in its several phases and scales of investigation, in the case of the Meeting House, we examine the expressive and formal manifestations given to the trope of time in relation to differing levels of appearance. This examination will pass from individual elements (the wall section, the duplication of the building enclosure) to the overall group form (from immediate precinct planning to the general master plan).

Doubling the outside

In Ronner and Jhaveri's *Complete Works 1935–1974*, a diagram of Kahn's idea for the wall at the Meeting House is reproduced.[16] The sketch depicts a metamorphosis inflicted on the wall as it passes from a traditional wall to an enclosure characterised by a duplication or doubling of the outside. In this operation, Kahn invents a double outside, or an outside which resists any simple opposition to an inside. In place of a simple opposition inside/outside, he creates the condition for the appearance of a more dynamic and open relation. There are two stages in the transformation. In the first, the wall is hollowed. Where the traditional masonry wall which opens the sequence is diagrammed as solid, Kahn imagines an intermediary stage, one in which the thickness of the barrier retains a uniform profile. The plane of the wall could be either opaque or transparent. In a second stage, the identity of the screen dividing the inside from the outside is interrupted. The barrier function is retained, but a direction is introduced into a previously static entity with the introduction of the arrow of air.

This reference to the movement of fluid elements, whether air, water, or light, suggests that architectural members are assigned the status of trace remains. The built elements are a negative record of forces (whether natural or artificial). In the

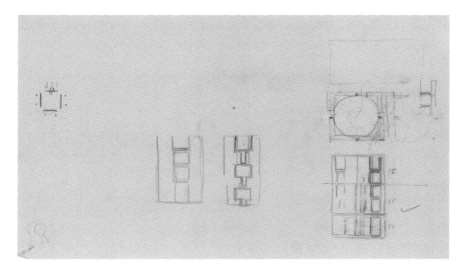

FIGURE 7.1 Meeting House, Salk Institute, La Jolla, exploratory plan sketches of the perimeter duplication, Louis I. Kahn

Source: Louis I. Kahn Collection, University of Pennsylvania and the Pennsylvania Historical and Museum Commission

case of the wall and its transformation into an architectural response to the problem of the surface, a fundamental theme is highlighted in Kahn's investigations. This is the problem of the accommodation of building services (electrical conduits, water lines, air conditioning ducts). In an excerpt of a talk given in 1954 on architectural illumination, Kahn sermonises against the burying of 'tortured unwanted ducts, conduits, and pipelines.'[17] The tussle with the problem and the evolution toward a separation both in terms of geometry and literal gaps can be seen in progress sketches by Kahn. See Figure 7.1 for an early schematic exploration of this idea.

In place of an architecture which encloses these elements according to formal continuity, Kahn searched for an architecture of expression. In relation to De Vore House, discussed in Chapter 1, Kahn sought to achieve an order of construction which expresses the purpose of the various elements in relation to different materials and different devices and the specific circumstances, whether a roof drain, air conditioning, or a simple barrier. In De Vore House, the system of brick piers, roof joists, and alternating brick cavity and glass walls seek to 'express their purpose.'[18]

Returning to the transformation of the wall and the composition more generally in Kahn's studies for the Meeting House, it is appropriate to consider the final stage to be a manifestation of Kahn's response to a system of dynamic elements (wind, glare from light, thermal protection).[19] The wall is no longer a barrier but somehow is in suspension.

The 'o-o' relation which results from the transformative operation effected by Kahn gives the sensation of an outside folded into the plane of the enclosing wall itself. Light, air, and water 'cut' the flesh of the building enclosure, and an attribute is produced, and the design of the wall expresses the effects. He 'dismembers' the inside/outside relation and creates in the process an exteriority within the thickness of the wall.

As a final development, consider the effect of this transformation in relation to the two models of the modern sensibility discussed earlier. Kahn begins with the wall displayed in the Brick Country House. Whether opaque or glazed, the wall is vertical and performs a barrier function between the inside and the outside. In the Project for a Private House by Theo van Doesburg, if the barrier function appears to have been displaced in favour of a multiplied, expansive form, the wall, as physically thin still, is situated within a sensibility which conceives of the wall as a limit.

Peripheral duplication

The doubling of the outside is expanded to become a duplication of the entire peripheral enclosure. It is another example of Kahn's experimentation with the problem of the surface. As Giurgola has suggested, the doubling of the periphery is one of Kahn's 'most important formal contributions to architectural language.'[20] Other examples of peripheral duplication include Kahn's project for the U.S. Consular Office in Luanda, Angola, and the National Assembly in Bangladesh. In the case of the Meeting House, the experiments extend to the relationship between the point columns and the enclosure. To effect a transition from outside to inside, Kahn diagrams three possible configurations of the relation between structural member and enclosing wall. We can see how the drama of the encounter leads Kahn to adopt an abstract practice of diagrams in front of the problem of enclosed space and the outside, which extends further than the experimentation with the thickness of the wall itself discussed earlier. This transformation of the enclosing wall can equally be interpreted as transforming the modern ideal of the relation between the shapes of the container and the contained. In its place, there is an ambiguous relation obtained between the shape of the enclosed room and the external shape.

Group form

A transformation of sensibility is affected in Kahn's successive variations of the precinct planning for the Meeting House. Or if not a transformation, then a trialling of different sensibilities to see if any would stick. It is possible to read a passage from a classic composition characterised by a planar and volumetric order to an arrangement distinguished by surface tension, diagonality, and open shapes. This transformation illustrates Kahn's response to the problematic of the surface extended to the overall group form of the Meeting House.

In the early sketch studies, the project appears as an rectangular platform entered centrally.[21] The building group is arranged in a traditional beaux-arts manner about

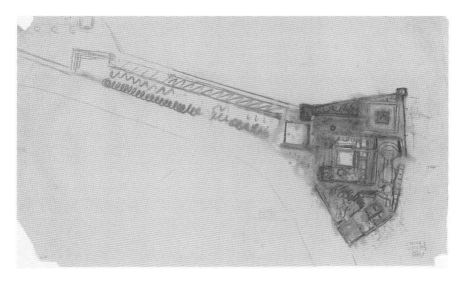

FIGURE 7.2 Meeting House, Salk Institute, La Jolla, site plan schematic group form sketch, Louis I. Kahn

Source: Louis I. Kahn Collection, University of Pennsylvania and the Pennsylvania Historical and Museum Commission

a series of minor cross-axes. It is a continuation of the ordering sensibility present in Kahn's youthful and oft-cited plan for an army post, prepared as his Class A project while at the Beaux-Arts Institute of Design in 1924.[22] This disposition was kept and varied in the early sketches, with the primary transformation occurring in the compaction of the complex from a long rectangle parallel to the sea to a square-like platform organised about a narrow court.

In a latter phase of Kahn's thinking, a tension is introduced into the Meeting House complex. The auditorium is shifted from a location fronting the sea to a position at the entry to the group. A sliding movement is also introduced into the work by shifting the entry off the centre to a side position. See Figure 7.2. This movement is repeated for the entry into the covered hall. The entry road to the group is also shifted to reflect this change of disposition, and a more complicated relation with the exterior of the site is created.

In the final version of the Meeting House, there is an inflection of the relationship of the auditorium and the pool with the general building group. Here, the architectural effects which problematise any simple inside/outside arrangement disappear. Both the auditorium and the pool are rotated away from the primary, centroidal volumetric organisation. This creation of volumetric surface tensions, especially in the case of the auditorium, expresses Kahn's tendency to introduce distortions into strict orthogonal systems. Kahn's notes on a sketch of this stage of design call emphatically for the auditorium to be shifted from a parallel relationship with the other buildings when he describes the relationship as 'not parallel . . . out of parallel.'[23]

At the same time, the character of the groups of rooms around the central hall has been transformed. The lecture halls in particular have responded to the changed organising attitude. They have transformed from unified clusters organised about the radiating force of the hall to locally responsive clusters, creating shifts in the overall site design which create the sensation of independence or autonomy.

II.ii Philadelphia College of Art

In the years just before the commission for the Yale Center for British Art, whose evocation opened this chapter, Kahn was working on a multi-building project in Philadelphia. According to Kathleen James' historical summary, the project for the Philadelphia College of Art came into Kahn's orbit as early as 1960 and initially was proposed to solely include dormitories adjacent to the college's downtown Philadelphia campus.[24] Following delays, by 1964, the program had been expanded to include, in addition to new dormitories, 'a library, a design center and exhibition hall, a theatre, physical education facilities, and space for classrooms, administrative offices, and parking.'[25]

Looking at project materials generated over multiple forays by Kahn and his office to imagine an architectural response to the charge, one soon meets a series of what can properly be characterised as architectural events.

Events in that they are properly architectural, not just in terms of seeing and sensing their state were they to have been realised. Events in that they are properly more than a representation of how the complex group may have been disposed and their inflections onto the other and those elements existing in that charged setting.

So, events understood as outcomes of the plainly visceral battle that Kahn waged on the project. The drawings, heavy though fragile because easily smudged, with no firm contour, tracings of ideas. A sketch held at the Museum of Modern Art gives way to this point of view. As a first preliminary, I shall list half a dozen such episodes.

On folds, or adding depth to a surface

The status of the form in Kahn's project for the Philadelphia College of Art requires confronting the ideas of the fold and of multiplicity. This next part of the chapter examines if and in what manner this concept of the fold accomplishes the traits which were defined as characteristic of the idea of multiplicity. The first step of the consideration will be to indicate in what manner the idea of the fold can be demonstrated to put into motion the idea of secondarity. As a first approach, a linkage at the surface seems to develop between the two terms in Kahn. This introduction of depth into a surface is one of the qualities at the scale of the block that the Philadelphia College of Art can be claimed to exhibit. See Figure 7.3 in which Kahn's effort to instill a depth or presence into the tight site can be sensed in the site elevation.

FIGURE 7.3 Philadelphia College of Art, Philadelphia, early site elevation sketch, Louis I. Kahn

Source: Louis I. Kahn Collection, University of Pennsylvania and the Pennsylvania Historical and Museum Commission

Any fold, by its essence, is a folding of something which precedes it and on which it simultaneously inscribes itself. It will be necessary to return to this double movement of preceding and inscribing and to the extension Kahn provides in relation to the temporality of the fold at multiple scales depending on the project: it appears at the level of the building enclosure, for example, explicitly in the case of the Meeting House as discussed earlier, and at the level of the group plan, we argue now, in the case of the Philadelphia College of Art.

A fold is necessarily something secondary, something derived in relation to the surface which it affects. But this relation of secondarity or externality will not be sufficient, and a second analogy is called for, one which can be found in the microbiological and embryological references of Kahn. For Kahn, the fold appears as the name he assigns to an originating phenomenon which accompanies the construction of any figure. For Kahn, organisms, individuals, and artistic constructions are born within a fold, that is, from an event which is already expressed in material texture. Texture is ontogenetically first. The fold is always, in this case, preformal, at least as compared to the texture. Whatever the hypothesis advanced, a condition of secondarity is perhaps the key characteristic of Kahn's fold, leading the list of other characteristics: preceding, inscribing, externality.

Kahn's manipulations of the fold are marked by a spatiality of ambiguous relations, a simultaneously literal and phenomenal folding, one recognised by its own kind of temporality. This temporality is distinguished, we suggest, by a direct presentation of time. This notion of an open system as a result of a new image of thought leads to an original and necessary consideration of folding. A system which grows in such a manner that the newly embraced is not contained or closed off in the preceding implies some kind of implicating which is not integrated into a superior unity. The Kahnian fold – in the plan, the volume, the section, and the building envelope – produces a conjunctive implication. It is a case of de-multiplication. It is an architecture of difference expressed as a multiplicity away from any simple unity or wholeness. It cannot have as a principle a remembered repetition integral to the history of the form and, accordingly, the liberation of a thought of being hidden as in a metaphysical tradition framed as grounded in ideas of part-to-whole relationships and ideals of continuity and coherence. An architecture of differences can only be considered by way of a description of pure exteriority which is constitutive of the multiple as such.

The fold at work in Kahn's project for the Philadelphia College of Art is not the internal fold of the veil or the enfolding of the difference of being. It is completely other. It is the fold of the multiple, the fold multiplying itself, in an undifferentiating suite of iterations. Not an internal fold but an external fold, or rather a fold engendered from the outside. There is a fold of matter in that which operates a self-differentiation and repetition. There is a diversification of the difference which folds itself, therefore the multiple fold, but this differentiating, far from returning to the intimacy of a secret, is nothing other than the exteriority of an outside which encounters it. It is other than, it is the other element along which this element differentiates itself, but in such a manner that that which is unfolded is the expression of an interior, or of a depth, of a content. This unfolding is a duplication or multiplication which differentiates, one in which the identity of the beginning is not conserved (the illusion of the ideal one) but finds itself projected in a genesis of heterogeneity, until there is nothing remaining in common with that which it appeared to be at the beginning.

There is, in company with the traits isolated in Chapters 1 and 4, an additional formal contribution by Kahn which represents a decisive transformation in the conception of a building plan and section. This is an inflection in response to the problem of exteriority which is realised through the operations of a folding and unfolding in certain projects. The privilege accorded to three-dimensional constructions is signalled by an aesthetic of assembling as distinct from composing, a folding or hollowing as distinct from a carving, a relation of empathy with the surrounding as distinct from a strategy of isolation. This tendency and constructive outcome are already developed in the concept design for the Goldenberg House of 1959.[26] Here, in the Philadelphia Colle of Art, there is at play a transformation of the closed container into a figure which results from the abstraction of a functional program. This abstraction results in a disassembling into major elements and a reassembling which, to adopt Giurgola's words, makes possible 'an immediate, existential unfolding of the building's organisation.'[27] See Figure 7.4.

In the project for the Philadelphia College of Art, Kahn confronts the problem of shape and the operation of folding and unfolding across a number of conditions. Five stand out: the overall campus organisation, the conception of the wall, his handling of light, the ambiguous shapes of the studio buildings, and the character

FIGURE 7.4 Philadelphia College of Art, Philadelphia, site plan and elevation study, Louis I. Kahn

Source: Louis I. Kahn Collection, University of Pennsylvania and the Pennsylvania Historical and Museum Commission

of the public spaces and the overall group form resulting from the form and disposition of the building elements in the site. The combined effect of these operations is to transform the building as a static box into an abstract, ambiguous sign: a time machine working on movement and light.

Leatherbarrow and De Long suggest other affiliations or resonances. Now with suggestions of sharing aesthetic ambitions or tastes to achieve cohesive unity out of isolated elements, an ambition that Leatherbarrow and De Long say is rare in the period, eluding modernist practitioners. The schemes contain complexly angled elements, and the spirit on display is comparable with the spirit of Franz Kline's painting and David Smith's sculpture in its ability to generate complex unity without recourse to balancing mass, for instance.[28] Let us continue to interrogate the resulting conditions.

Folded wall construction

In the College of Art project, Kahn transforms the vertical planes of the enclosing walls into dynamic echeloned figures. The folded wall constructions generate a range of formal interpretations. The walls appear to cascade down the vertical planes of the various buildings, the pressure of the building resulting in the sensation that the walls are sliding off a supporting frame as a consequence of a downward force. Another reading is suggested by the early section sketch which shows the study of light penetrations.[29] A centripetal movement results, with the walls pulling into the base of the building. A third reading is possible, one which sees the folded and canted walls as the shards of a vertically oriented force. It is as if the buildings were bursting from the ground, with the various planes the successive record of an emerging form. The resultant movement would trace a centrifugal line, pushing the four studio wings away from an empty central space. This is already evident in the early site plan and site section study discussed (Figure 7.4) and a subsequent sketch studies of the studio building in particular. See Figure 7.5.

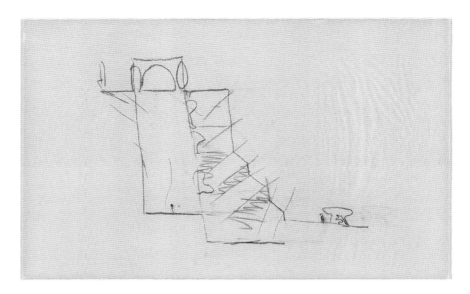

FIGURE 7.5 Philadelphia College of Art, project, Louis I. Kahn, section sketch of studios, Philadelphia, Pennsylvania, 1966. New York, Museum of Modern Art (MoMA), charcoal on paper 29 3/4 × 47 3/4' (75.6 × 121.3 cm) Gift of the architect 429.1967

Source: © 2022, digital image, The Museum of Modern Art, New York/Scala, Florence

A formal reading of the architectural response to the problem of external forces extends into the planimetric disposition of the four studio elements which project into the open space. Approached from Broad Street, there is a stepped movement following the arc shape traced by the various buildings.

Group form: ambiguous shapes

Kahn transforms the regular modern, functional box into a set of ambiguous parallelograms. This transformation is undertaken during the experiments within the design development stages. In the first plan sketches, the studios are placed in rectangular buildings on the rear of the site in three parallel blocks. These pick up and repeat the traditional shape and alignment of the old buildings by Franck Furness on Pine Street. In the second version, a major transformation has occurred. The three separate, parallel blocks have melded into a single figure of multiple parts. Readings from the north and the south would suggest a complexity of the program which is reinforced by the megastructuralist bias of the total proposal. The regular plan forms of the studio buildings have been folded into the central spine and unfolded away from the spine.

A third and final plan version continues this development of ambiguous shapes. The library tower is especially complex, and I will trace the appearance of the notion of a folded exteriority in the College of Art through a reading of the successive variations on the shape and position of the library. The library is, first, located in a free-standing lozenge-shaped building in an inner site location. In another approach, the library changes to a square plan and is rotated 90 degrees. It is also now attached to the college complex and is surrounded by studio wings to the east, south, and west. In a final configuration, the library transforms itself from a simple diamond column into a figure which could be read either as an irregular, truncated octagon, or, especially above the sixth level, as a rotated square. The form further inflects itself away from a generic condition of a square in its variations between the east-west and north-south edges. In the former alignments, the volume pulls itself in and back to finally meet the central regular column. On the north edge, there is a simpler transition repeating the echeloned forms of the studio buildings described.

In this final version of 1966, the library building has also pulled itself forward, right, and up to have direct contact with the Broad Street frontage. The effect is to introduce a fold into the overall site disposition. It achieves this by pulling the centre of the site fully away from the original Pennsylvania Institution for the Deaf and Blind building by Haviland on Broad Street. This is achieved by aligning the spine of the new college complex to the body of the Haviland Building and pulling the ground floor edge of the library tower right up to the sidewalk. As in Kahn's Goldenberg House, and repeating a formal strategy discussed in relation to the problem of the point in Chapter 5, these operations reinforce a diagonality already present in the earlier schemes. Returning to the earlier arrangements will demonstrate the force of this final disposition in folding the open space of the site.

In the first version, the Haviland Building is retained as the primary focus of the entire composition, as is revealed in the sketch elevations onto Broad Street in which the columned portico and flanking volumes are pulled forward and matched by the adjacent Theatre of Performing Arts. The theatre pulls its major massing line down to meet the older building and simultaneously presents a long, neutral wall edge, thus reinforcing the primacy of the Haviland Building. See Figure 7.6. In the second version, Kahn begins to pull the site focus away from the old building toward the corner of Broad and Spruce Streets. This is achieved by relocating the theatre along Spruce Street and rotating the figural elements 90 degrees so that the 'figure' of the theatre now reads as a second primary element in the Broad Street elevation, whereas previously it had been in a perpendicular, reinforcing relation. Supporting this reading is the manner in which the studio building thrusts in between the two figures of the Haviland and theatre buildings. The eastern arm of the studio building is folded away from the Haviland Building toward the theatre, thus beginning to form the strong diagonal force of the final version.

In the last version of the scheme, with the shift in the library building location discussed earlier, the folding of the public open space is complete. The library tower performs a double function. It is a fulcrum around which the old and the new campuses rotate. It focuses the energy of the site toward the corner entry. This reading is reinforced by the chamfered cutting along Broad Street versus the pyramidal cutting along the edge parallel to Spruce Street.

144 Time

FIGURE 7.6 Philadelphia College of Art, Philadelphia, site plan study, Louis I. Kahn

Source: Louis I. Kahn Collection, University of Pennsylvania and the Pennsylvania Historical and Museum Commission

III

In the early 1960s, Sigfried Giedion reflected on the changes in sensibility and temperament over the two decades since *Space, Time and Architecture* first appeared. As one measure of the mood in those years, Giedion was moved to claim a new or restored sense of the force potential in free-standing building mass.

Giedion was driven at that precise moment to add an introduction to the fourth edition of *Space, Time and Architecture* and claim a restored and perhaps reinvigorated sensibility. According to Giedion, a long-absent sensitivity had returned: a sensitivity to the powers of building mass. Here is Giedion: 'Forms are not bounded by their physical limits. Forms emanate and model space. Today we are again becoming aware that shapes, surfaces and planes serve not only to model interior space. They operate just as strongly, far beyond the confines of their actual measured dimensions, as constituent elements of volumes standing freely in the open. . . . Today we have again become sensitive to the space-emanating powers of volumes.'[30]

What caused Giedion at the time to mark a shift in temperament can be used to provide some support to our closing observations on the relationship of the two Kahn projects which were contemporary to Giedion. We conjecture that Kahn's

Meeting House and Philadelphia College of Art projects provide a certain theoretical lens for thinking about architecture and time and that a specific temporality can be detected in each. We framed the analysis around a pair of hypotheses inspired by Scully's parallel claim of changes in temperament. The first hypothesis proposes certain works of architecture fall on the side of an infinite becoming, never fully coming into frame. The second, that devices such as those of the doubling of the enclosing wall in Kahn's Meeting House and the multiple folding strategies in the Philadelphia College of Art work to render such a temporality manifest. To that end, one is left with an unsatisfied desire to explore further what Kahn might have done in the next phase on such issues. The final chapter in this section on time provides one possible pathway around certain of these themes.

Notes

1. Michael Cadwell, *Strange Details* (Cambridge: The MIT Press, 2007), 139.
2. Cadwell, *Strange Details*, 140.
3. Vincent Scully, "Michelangelo's Fortificationi Drawings: A Study in the Reflex Diagonal," *Perspecta* 1 (1952): 39.
4. Scully, "A Study in the Reflex Diagonal," 38, 39.
5. Scully, "A Study in the Reflex Diagonal," 40.
6. Jaquelin Robertson thus characterises the Scully of those years as 'a kind of demonic Irish firefly darting back and forth [during his lectures at Yale] before huge flickering images of White and Sullivan . . . literally a man on fire.' See Robertson cited in Robert Stern, "Yale 1950–1965," *Oppositions* 4 (1974): 45.
7. The "Reflex Diagonal" essay does not appear in the compilation of *Perspecta* issued recently: see Robert A. M. Stern, Alan Plattus, and Peggy Deamer, eds., *(Re)Reading Perspecta: The First Fifty Years of the Yale Architectural Journal* (Cambridge: The MIT Press, 2004). Neil Levine's edited collection of hard-to-find or out-of-print essays by Scully does not refer to it except in the bibliography. Ackerman does list Scully's essay in his 1961 *Michelangelo* in the general bibliography but does not refer to it in the text.
8. Heinrich Wölfflin, *Principles of Art History. The Problem of the Development of Style in Later Art*, trans. M. D. Hottinger (New York: Dover Publications, 1950), 222.
9. Wölfflin, *Principles of Art History*, 221.
10. Wölfflin, *Principles of Art History*, 221.
11. Wölfflin, *Principles of Art History*, 222.
12. Wölfflin, *Principles of Art History*, 223.
13. In his analysis, Jean-Luc Nancy identifies three traits as bracketing in part Deleuze's notion of folding: it concerns a world of virtual concepts, not of things; there is a valorisation of nomination, not of discourse; and it is a world not of beginnings or ends but of continuous creation understood as a crossing over, a traversing of middles. See Jean-Luc Nancy, "The Deleuzian Fold of Thought," in *Deleuze: A Critical Reader*, ed. Paul Patton, trans. Tom Gibson and Anthony Uhlmann (Oxford: Blackwell, 1996), 107–113.
14. Michael Fried, *Art and Objecthood: Essays and Reviews* (Chicago: The University of Chicago Press, 1998), 77.
15. Sigfried Giedion, *Space, Time and Architecture: The Growth of a New Tradition*, 5th ed. (Cambridge, Mass.: Harvard University Press 1967), xlvii.
16. Heinz Ronner and Sharad Jhaveri, eds., *Louis I. Kahn: Complete Work, 1935–1974*, 2nd, revised and enlarged ed. (Basel: Birkhäuser, 1987), 134.
17. Alessandra Latour, ed., *Louis I. Kahn: Writings, Lectures, Interviews* (New York: Rizzoli, 1991), 57.
18. Louis Kahn, "Two Houses," *Perspecta* 3 (1955): 60–61.

19 Kahn relates the function of the duplication of the walls in the Salk project to the modification of glare in "A Statement" of 1962, reproduced in Latour, *Louis I. Kahn: Writings, Lectures, Interviews*, 150.
20 Romaldo Giurgola with Pamille I. Berg, "Kahn, Louis I.," in *Macmillan Encyclopedia of Architects, Volume 2*, ed. Adolf K. Placzek (New York: The Free Press, 1982), 539.
21 See the plan sketch reproduced in Ronner and Jhaveri, *Louis I. Kahn*, 130, SRI.5. See also drawings 540.137, 540.140, and 540.143 reproduced in Louis I. Kahn, *The Louis I. Kahn Archive: Personal Drawings. The Completely Illustrated Catalogue of the Drawings in the Louis I. Kahn Collection, University of Pennsylvania and Pennsylvania Historical and Museum Commission, Vol. 2. Buildings and Projects, 1959–1961* (New York & London: Garland Publishing, Inc., 1987)
22 Kahn's project is reproduced in David Brownlee and David De Long, *Louis I. Kahn: In the Realm of Architecture* (London: Thames and Hudson, 1997), 12. A sustained and well-developed analysis of the composition affinities of the Beaux-Arts approach in Kahn is found in Kenneth Frampton, "Louis Kahn and the French Connection," *Oppositions* 22 (1980): 21–53. See also the plan for a shopping centre from the same early period in Kahn's professional life, reproduced in Vincent Scully, *Louis I. Kahn* (New York: George Braziller, 1962), plate 7.
23 Ronner and Jhaveri: 135, SRI.24.
24 Kathleen James, "Philadelphia College of Art, Philadelphia, Pennsylvania, 1960–66," in *Louis I. Kahn: In the Realm of Architecture*, ed. David Brownlee and David, De Long (New York: Rizzoli International Publications, 1991), 358.
25 James, "Philadelphia College of Art," 358.
26 See Giurgola with Berg, "Kahn," 540; Ronner and Jhaveri, *Louis I. Kahn*, 146–49; Scully, *Louis I. Kahn*, 34–35, plates 92, 93.
27 Giurgola with Berg, "Kahn," 540.
28 Brownlee and De Long, *Louis I. Kahn: In the Realm of Architecture*, 186.
29 Ronner and Jhaveri, *Louis I. Kahn*, 276, PSA.6; 279, PSA.16.
30 Giedion, "Introduction. Architecture of the 1960's," xlvii.

Bibliography

Brownlee, David, and David, De Long. *Louis I. Kahn: In the Realm of Architecture*. London: Thames and Hudson, 1997.

Caldwell, Michael. *Strange Details*. Cambridge: The MIT Press, 2007.

Deleuze, Gilles. *Cinema 2: The Time-Image*. (Translated by Hugh Tomlinson and Robert Galeta). Minneapolis: University of Minnesota Press, 1988.

Deleuze, Gilles, and Félix, Guattari. *What is Philosophy?* (Translated by Hugh Tomlinson and Graham Burchell). London: Verso, 1994.

Fried, Michael. *Art and Objecthood: Essays and Reviews*. Chicago: The University of Chicago Press, 1998.

Giedion, Sigfried. "Introduction: Architecture of the 1960's." In *Space, Time and Architecture: The Growth of a New Tradition*, xlvi–xlviii (5th edition). Cambridge: Harvard University Press, 1967.

Giurgola, Romaldo, with Pamille I. B. "Kahn, Louis I." In *Macmillan Encyclopedia of Architects, Volume 2*, edited by Adolf K. Placzek, 537–546. New York: The Free Press, 1982.

James, Kathleen, "Philadelphia College of Art, Philadelphia, Pennsylvania, 1960–1966." In *Louis I. Kahn: In the Realm of Architecture*, edited by David, Brownlee and David, De Long, 358–360. New York: Rizzoli International Publications, 1991.

Kahn, Louis. "Two Houses," *Perspecta* 3 (1955): 60–61.

Kahn, Louis I. *The Louis I. Kahn Archive: Personal Drawings. The Completely Illustrated Catalogue of the Drawings in the Louis I. Kahn Collection, University of Pennsylvania and Pennsylvania*

Historical and Museum Commission, Vol. 2. Buildings and Projects, 1959–1961. New York: Garland Publishing, Inc., 1987.
Latour, Alessandra, ed. *Louis I. Kahn: Writings, Lectures, Interviews.* New York: Rizzoli, 1991.
Levine, Neil, ed. *Vincent Scully: Modern Architecture and Other Essays.* Princeton: Princeton University Press, 2005.
Nancy, Jean-Luc. "The Deleuzian Fold of Thought." In *Deleuze: A Critical Reader*, edited by Paul Patton (translated by Tom Gibson and Anthony Uhlmann), 107–113. Oxford: Blackwell, 1996.
Rajchman, John. "Out of the Fold." *Architectural Design Profile* 102 (1993): 61–63.
Ronner, Heinz, and Sharad, Jhaveri, eds. *Louis I. Kahn: Complete Work, 1935–1974.* (2nd, revised and enlarged edition). Basel: Birkhäuser, 1987.
Scully, Vincent. *Louis I. Kahn.* New York: George Braziller, 1962.
Scully, Vincent. "Michelangelo's Fortificationi Drawings: A Study in the Reflex Diagonal." *Perspecta* 1 (1952): 38–45.
Stern, Robert A. M. "Yale 1950–1965." *Oppositions* 4 (1974): 35–62.
Stern, Robert A. M., Alan, Plattus, and Peggy, Deamer, eds. *(Re)Reading Perspecta: The First Fifty Years of the Yale Architectural Journal.* Cambridge: The MIT Press, 2004.
Wölfflin, Heinrich. *Principles of Art History: The Problem of the Development of Style in Later Art.* (Translated by M. D. Hottinger). New York: Dover Publications, 1950.

8
FREEDOM
MAXXI by Zaha Hadid

I

Adopting the stance announced in the opening chapter, and as an organising proposition, we conjecture that there is a largely unexamined relationship of architecture to time specific to certain works of late-twentieth-century architecture. This specific kind of architectural temporality is one whose existence is independent of movement. It is proposed, in addition, that a close reading of such projects from the framework of time may reveal the devices and formal moves deployed to achieve effects characteristic of that temporality. In earlier chapters, we considered the Visual Arts Center by Le Corbusier and Louis Kahn's unbuilt projects for the Salk Institute Meeting House and the Philadelphia College of Art. We sought to identify and categorise the attributes and qualities of these projects when read from the lens of time. To expand the investigation, we now turn to Zaha Hadid's MAXXI: Museum of XXI Century Arts.

As suggested in earlier chapters, architecture's relationship to time is not simple or singular in nature. Nor is it a generally foregrounded preoccupation. In the case of Hadid, however, it is appropriate to examine certain of her statements, the observations of colleagues and commentators, and evidence in the projects to get a take on the potential character of the temporality at play in her work. Hadid provides the impetus for such scrutiny. In her contribution to the 1998 *Anytime* conference, for example, Hadid formulates her work as always necessarily read against an engagement with time. As we'll see, an insistence on taking a stance about or on time, however, is there from the beginning.

Architecture experiments with trying to shuttle between times: the past, the now, the moment generated out of a body's motion, the new. This is to claim a value in architecture's potential capacity to introduce ambiguities in shape, to dissolve hard contours. As discussed in Chapter 5, this would be to create a state of

DOI: 10.4324/9781003009641-12

things that mimics those qualities Pei sought when he claimed architecture's ability to manufacture an undulation in space when describing the lobby of Meyerson Symphony Center. Hadid's temporality, taking her at her word and to come to a first quality, is also about the possibility of the new: a new that never fully arrives, for then it would be all over, at the end. By the new, Hadid is imagining something like a new kind of plan.

In this case, the architect's notion of time sets an ambition to develop a new kind of plan, a liberated plan, one that renders ideas of fluid space. The freedom of the plan according to Hadid is a freedom from the ground, from stasis, and from chronology. This freedom from linear time is described by the architect as the capacity to 'move back and forth in time.'[1] In what follows, we track the conceptual significance of the notions of time by considering statements by Hadid, comments and observations by others, and through an examination of traces of time in MAXXI.

As far as time and architecture are concerned, Hadid had a way of classifying their possible configurations. Hadid's way of thinking about, and dealing with relationships to, time is one that maintains degrees of tension. Never fully resolved, never fully dissipated, Hadid's relationships with time rather maintain a creative contradiction, one that takes up different manifestations.

A purely conceptual opposition of space as exteriority and time as interiority, for instance, is contradicted in Hadid's project work by the realities of people's movement, urban fluctuations, and time's literal passage. While others consider the lessons revealed in examining the work from the optic of chronology, consistent with this section's emphasis on the trajectory of time, in what follows, we focus on the conceptual aspects of architecture's relationship with time. We will focus, then, on the temporal logic discerned in MAXXI. There is in MAXXI a confluence, not to say a synthesis of responses to time. For Hadid, time is considered variously to demarcate time past (the 'what came before'[2]), a temporal logic that enables the 'new' to appear, or a process she names 'a kind of oscillational process.'[3] This process is given expression in multiple fashions. It is a process for conceiving and representing form, in this case by x-ray drawings or paintings that show several levels of built and open space form at once. This oscillational process is also one that leads to or facilitates, according to Hadid, an architectural idea of rupture.

Hadid wrote frequently about an ambition to liberate architecture. As if in anticipation of MAXXI, Hadid talked in the early years about a new kind of space, one 'liberated from certain forces.'[4] This is the architect as liberator: the one who liberates architecture from the ground, from the static, from the notion that the plan must be linear.

Elsewhere, in an interview with Alvin Boyarsky, Hadid also suggests the ambition of releasing or instilling freedoms: in the plan, in the section, in injecting change into the programme of use. Here is Hadid: 'What the plan interpreting the programme can do is to manifest the free form and liberate it from the notion that it must be linear.'[5]

Even more direct pronouncements on a desire to liberate, to free life via a new plan, are further laid out in the interview with Boyarsky. The architect's problematic, baldly stated, is to liberate the plan. The question preoccupying Hadid is clear even if the consequences are not when she states: 'How, then, do you liberate the plan?'[6]

Aaron Betsky also recognises in Hadid the ambition to establish the architectural conditions for a new world, a world founded on freedoms. Here is Betsky: 'Hadid has no truck with typologies, applied orders, implied assumptions or gravity: she believes that we could and should build a better world, one marked by freedom, above all else.'[7]

A devotion to freedom finds a further resonance as liberation. This occurs, for example, in a text by Hadid published in 1987. Here we also get a sense of the idea of the plan as indented or marked with a new way of life. Here again, the architect is pushing forward the modernist problematic of dynamic, not static, forms. This foregrounding of the problematic of freedoms again comes out, with Hadid emphasising it's not about formal implications in looking to Suprematist experiments. As she states: 'The dynamic of the architecture stems from early Suprematist exercises, not because of its physical or formal implications but more importantly because of its programmatic implications. The modern project is yet to begin.'[8] Taking Hadid at her word, is there evidence of this sensibility realised in MAXXI?

In order to pursue such questions, the following is organised into four sections. The first sets out the generating propositions and approach. The second section is an analysis of the building according to four tropes: expressive space, structures, figure-figure urbanism, and diagonalities. Section three returns to the question of a specifically architectural concept of time, extending the formal analysis into the realm of contemporary thinking as discussed in the opening chapter of this book. This is done with special reference to Gilles Deleuze's notion of pure or direct time as developed in Deleuze's *Cinema 2: The Time-Image*. The chapter concludes with comparative observations about the different temporal modes present in Le Corbusier's Visual Arts Center, Louis Kahn's Philadelphia College of Art, and MAXXI as a way to bring to an end this part of the book.

Hadid was awarded the commission for MAXXI in 1998, and the 30,000 square metre (323,000 square foot) building opened to the public in 2010. The project has been the object of a series of monographic studies that provide critical and historical information as well as useful documentation.[9]

II

An examination of the building and project materials generated around MAXXI reveals at least four form-shaping tactics in play: expressive space, structures, figure-figure urbanism, and diagonalities. The following section takes each tactic as an opening framework for analysis of the project.

II.i Volume, or: expressive space

MAXXI, at first glance, appears to be mostly about ribbons or lines. See Figure 8.1. If one extends the description and abstracts the reading, then one can generalise the schema. Lines elaborate space in their pull and torsion. Lines can

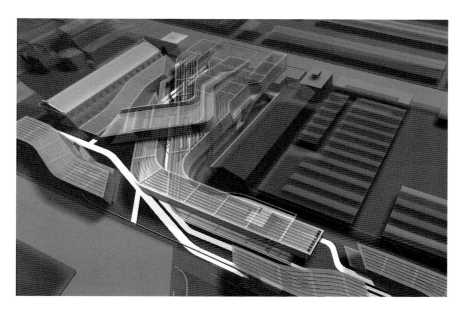

FIGURE 8.1   MAXXI: Museum of XXI Century Arts, Rome, master plan bird's-eye view, Zaha Hadid

Source: courtesy Zaha Hadid Architects

also dissipate, leading the eye away from a static, single-object focus, the effect of which is to remove firm boundaries in order perhaps to establish the conditions of possibility for what Hadid called a 'new reality'[10] to be created.

We can also perhaps then say that the building disposes volume so as to engender a dynamic space. Such a space is distinguished by a facility to produce what can be characterised as expressive space. The demands of expressive space, in other words, refer to Hadid's never-ending 'new life' referenced above. It is there as an ambition of the architect from the beginning, an ambition that might come first, only to be later rationalised in terms of structure or composition or use or destiny. This sensitivity might extend to a divergence equally attracted by continuity, on the one hand, and seduced toward a permanent separation, on the other hand. Alternatively, it might reveal a cast of mind preoccupied with different kinds of continuity, where continuity is understood as a unity of space and structure.

Perhaps this is the separation of parts that Hadid evokes so deliberately in her interview with Boyarsky as an essential part of the architect's programme. By what means and with what forms is the architect to allow certain parts to operate independently?[11]

Look at MAXXI's approach to the site as additional evidence. Occupying a flat urban site, the museum, to a certain extent, creates its own topography. Another consequence of the volume disposition is the use of overlap and the different strategies of central compression, not quite buckling under the weight and peripheral dispersion caused by the momentum of it all.

Perhaps the two attitudes of continuity versus separation are not as different as they may at first appear. Both are in pursuit of an architectural idea. Both are in support of different ideals, neither of which is interested in the modernist fragment. Even if MAXXI's plan is open-ended, in anticipation of future construction phases (the drawings imply at least two), the plan is specifically not about the fragment. MAXXI's section that includes the volumetric modelling provides palpable support to this reading.

Staying with first impressions, the plan is perhaps mostly about open-ended, incomplete forms in a condition of continuous motion at their midpoints such that there are only middles to deal with.

The analysis thus far might suggest that MAXXI is about the movement of volumes, and the plan is, in part, an illustration of the architectural promenade. Thus would be implied a time concept that resists a primarily empirical chronological idea of time, one subordinate to movement: a this then that, a past then present, a before and after. That, however, would be only part of the story.

II.ii Structures

Another title for this section might be the free plan versus the free section. To begin, we notice that columns have almost no role in Hadid's building. Outside, there are six clusters of thin tubes at the cantilevers or overhangs of first- and second-floor volumes.

The multiplication of supporting poles, columns, structural ribs, and functional partitions implies that structure does not define space but channels it. Too thin, surely, to be carrying anything, certainly not the whale-like thrust of the galleries and exhibition corridors above.

Inside there is a single instance of a line of three thin tubes on the edge of the first-floor outer gallery. In the adaptive reuse of the existing Via Guido Reni building, finally, there are four columns in the ground-floor space, now used for exhibitions. Animation and architectural effects are developed from other elements at MAXXI. In other words, at MAXXI, other conditions dominate, set up in part by the difference between the (Domino) flat slab and point column paradigm and in situ concrete wall and stacked cantilever structures of MAXXI felt in the section drawings. See Figure 8.2.

MAXXI's structure, other than the clusters of thin columns supporting the first-floor galleries as noted, is monolithic, exploiting the characteristics of poured-in-place concrete. In terms of consequent volumetrics, MAXXI is a narrow volume folding back on itself. One aspect of MAXXI's solid wall structure is a certain freedom in sectioning which is not allowed in the flat-slab, column-point grid structure. The open plan effects are, in one sense, transferred to a kind of 'free section'[12] at MAXXI. The impacts are not strictly in the nature of the sculptural quality of a building as carving but nearly, Hadid's sectional transmutation and modelling of volume yielding much of the plastic effect. Horizontal extension, reinforced by the sheer, taut, articulated, and unencumbered ceiling plane is matched by vertical pull

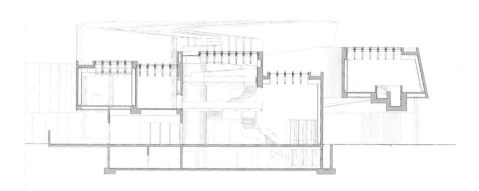

FIGURE 8.2   MAXXI: Museum of XXI Century Arts, Rome, section on main lobby, Zaha Hadid

Source: courtesy Zaha Hadid Architects

at MAXXI. The horizontal planes of floor and ceiling are dominant in the one, the enclosing walls channelling movement and reinforced by a highly articulated and in parts transparent ceiling and floor in the other. MAXXI's reflected ceiling plan is particularly revealing on this point.

II.iii Figure-figure relationships

Thus far, an analysis of MAXXI has explored the tropes of dynamic volumes rendered expressive and the consequences of free-plan and free-section structural ideas. In the general idea, as can be seen in an examination of the plans, the architectural condition is conceived perhaps around diagonal movements with functional spaces disposed as coincident with circulation. The third theme to be developed concerns ambiguities in field/object or figure/ground conditions. The plexiglass study model characterises an aspect of this state of simultaneity. See Figure 8.3.

The building project of MAXXI cannot be absorbed from without. The value of wholeness, the ideal of being able to stand at some point and receive a palpable impression of the whole, is specifically not an aim. Development of focus is something of an arbitrary and, for Hadid, intentionally ambiguous proceeding, as is explicit if her pronouncements are taken at face value. A site's organisation is intended, for example, not to contain, according to Hadid, but to 'make a site much more porous to allow for flows of any kind to move through.'[13]

A potential single, central focus is consistently broken up; concentration in one point is never sought. Rather, a peripheral, shifting look – an animated vision in the case of MAXXI – dominates, one that is also largely frontal even if following a switchback or Z-shaped pattern. The geometric centre is a void, a void occupied

FIGURE 8.3 MAXXI: Museum of XXI Century Arts, Rome, study model in plexiglass, Zaha Hadid

Source: courtesy Zaha Hadid Architects

by the main stairs, atrium, and light slots at MAXXI. Any assumption of a central focus is relegated to dismembered spaces in a sort of serial installation of interest (organs, events, ribbon-galleries) around the extremities of the plan.

So, while this is perhaps too easy a parallel and things are evidently more subtle, can we say that at MAXXI the plan is all field and no object? Are we here confronted with a constant architectural condition of middles or of background intensity, what Peter Eisenman has theorised as a figure-figure urbanism?

This is surely a response, in part, to the fact that at MAXXI, the site and program required intensive development as elaborate external deployment was not possible within the more or less set and limiting boundaries of the site and the constraints obtained by the preservation of existing buildings.

Inversion or intensification is in the place of extension at MAXXI, being bound by those floor and ceiling plates and directed horizontally. This is clear especially if you study the sliding or staggered distribution of main spaces and the dense centre, doubled or echoed by perimeter incidents. There is no simple dispersal of focus but more of a rebound, waves bounding back to confront initial ripples.

There is a contained concentration of a rather constant nature, sliding and swung along vertically at MAXXI. A variety of space strategies yielding in one regard, however, similar effects: no one centre, a kind of indefinite though not neutral space. Never uniform; in fact, it is always potentially fully animated such that hierarchy (of figure over ground or object over field) is shown specifically not to be the intent. The absence of one dominant centre produces this other kind of condition, of being always already in an ambiguous kind of middle condition.

At MAXXI, in other words, you never fully arrive. This suggests that time has always already passed: or perhaps time is always deferred. Look at the plans. At MAXXI, the interest is the figure as a constant condition. Patrick Schumacher highlights in the same vein the persistence of the field.[14]

Suite V, that gallery reproduced so frequently in external photographs, does not pretend to be the main thing, and it certainly does not conclude. It is the provisional end but only in a tentative way, an effect of the sloping floor, the view slot, the oblique cut of the end wall in plan and plane, the promise of something more to come.

So, while there is perhaps the idea or promise of a denouement, it is endlessly deferred. I believe this is a further attribute of an idea of time at work, not narrative or chronological in kind.

II.iv Transversalities

As discussed earlier, a fourth attribute or ambition that Hadid announced all those years ago is a freedom from stasis. MAXXI provided a kind of manifesto to explore that desire.

MAXXI is centrifugally ordered, channelled, and vertically stacked. An overall effect of flight from the ground, and thus of gravity as a stabilising force, is rendered in plastic terms by a variety of means. As we saw with Kahn's Philadelphia College

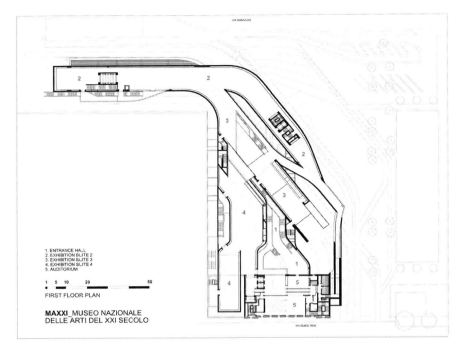

FIGURE 8.4   MAXXI: Museum of XXI Century Arts, Rome, first-floor plan, Zaha Hadid

Source: courtesy Zaha Hadid Architects

of Art in Chapter 7, a frontal approach and frontal views are difficult to achieve and are deemed static; three-quarter views are also favoured in MAXXI.

Peripheral intensities are sought over centralised. Interpenetration is favoured over isolation and separation, with MAXXI emphasising the vertical over the horizontal. Out of these relations, a general, fairly constant diagonal condition can be claimed to exist. From there, a further review of the plans reveals a disposition different from the enfilade (room to room) plan and the poché (served and servant) plan. It is a case of an open plan if different from the Domino free plan. See Figure 8.4.

MAXXI favours transverse over cross-axial or longitudinal arrangements. Springing off the zigzag work on the building through the site, one enters on the oblique and continually slides in either an echelon or a counter-clockwise or clockwise motion up the building and then back down again, sliding always on the edge. MAXXI's plan is layered by open Ls (boomerangs) or flattened S-shaped volumes – no rooms – with circulation slipping along the edges in a sidling manner. Galleries thrust forward, as in Exhibition Suite V, in part in a burst of energy or, as in Gallery Exhibition Suite II, in the promise of future extension. Design drawings and renderings suggest future phased elements to the south, extending Suite II to the northwest. The oddly truncated corridor or narrow gallery which swings away from the building to the north is intersected by another corridor from the east which, in study sketches, is fully developed into another flattened 'S.' The building folds over itself in an almost Boolean movement.

What does this tell us about Hadid's sense of time, if anything? Do traces of a reflex diagonal imprint on the work a relationship to time that is more than or different from the dialectical? In general, MAXXI operates by means of the device of diagonality to create temporal ambiguity: walls become floors, ceilings bend, the entry is not clearly marked. These qualities resist a discourse and practice of what Eisenman and Iturbe identify as 'temporal integrity.'[15]

III

In order to further enhance our understanding of architecture's different relationships with time, we now turn to a comparative look at the differences among the case studies illustrating the trajectory of time. We focus initially on differences between Le Corbusier's Visual Arts Center, considered in Chapter 6, and MAXXI.

If VAC is mostly about horizontal volumes formed by floor and ceiling planes, MAXXI is about ribbons or volumetric vectors. Look at their respective sites as additional evidence. Both MAXXI and the Visual Arts Center occupy flat urban sites and, to a certain extent, create their own topography. Another consequence of the volume disposition is the use in both cases of overlapping and the different strategies of central compression and peripheral dispersion. Perhaps the two attitudes are not as different as they may at first appear. Both are in pursuit of an architectural idea. It is an idea that includes at least something about being in time and in support of a continuity ideal.

It is clear that neither project is interested in the fragment. Even if MAXXI's plan is open-ended, in anticipation of future construction phases (the drawings imply at least two), the plan is specifically not about the fragment. And the Visual Arts Center is adamantly complete, not to say static. MAXXI's section where the volumetric modelling is palpable supports this reading. Still, it is generalised. The plan is perhaps, staying with first impressions, about open-ended, incomplete forms in a condition of continuous motion at their midpoints.

The analysis thus far might suggest that MAXXI is about the movement of volumes, and the plan is in part an illustration of the architectural promenade. Thus would be implied a time concept aligned with a primarily empirical (chronological) idea of time, one subordinate to movement: a this then that, a past then present, a before and after. And equally, in the Visual Arts Center, we are only ever satisfied (satiated) with an experience of space triggered by and supported in movement (the Acropolis effect).

On the other hand, we can observe that in the Visual Arts Center, an intensification of local conditions might be a first obvious finding. Those mandolin-shaped organs capture in a spiralling disposition the edges of their Georgian neighbours, organising the elements such that a vector, or multiple forces, are shaped and temporarily brought into focus only to be quickly dispersed so that even in the absence of a peripatetic eye, there is still a vibration, a momentum produced in that building and between the buildings and its neighbours.

In this manner, perhaps a record is created of a pure time independent of any reliance on motion or movement to bring it forth. If it is perhaps too early to state a preliminary finding, one might thus far be justified in claiming that MAXXI works on the concept of space, and the Visual Arts Center on problems of time (though which form of time is unclear).

In both, other conditions dominate, set up in part by the difference between the (Domino) flat slab and point column in the Visual Arts Center on the one hand and the cast-in-place concrete wall and stacked cantilevered structures of MAXXI on the other. The structural systems are entirely different, and both look to some extent to structure as a justification for their plan dispositions. The Visual Arts Center is set out in a rectangular bay grid rotated relative to the bounding streets, generally employing round section columns with local incidents. MAXXI's structure, other than the clusters of thin columns supporting sections of the first-floor galleries as noted, is monolithic, exploiting the characteristics of the poured-in-place concrete.

In terms of consequent volumetrics, MAXXI is a narrow tube-like volume folding back on itself. Or alternately attempting to break free and drift upward. The Visual Arts Center is a hybrid of the Domino flat-plate point-column grid and an assembly of independent organs. The ground is of secondary importance, with ascendancy given emphasis.

The impacts are not strictly in the nature of the sculptural quality of a building as a carving but nearly, Hadid's sectional transmutation and modelling of volume yielding much of the plastic effect. Horizontal extension, reinforced by the sheer, taut, unencumbered ceiling plane of the Visual Arts Center is matched by vertical pulls at MAXXI. The horizontal planes of floor and ceiling are dominant in the one, the enclosing walls channelling movement and reinforced by a highly articulated and, in parts, transparent ceiling and floor in the other.

Both MAXXI and the Visual Arts Center are centrifugally ordered, one channelled and vertically stacked, the other self-bifurcating and horizontally distributed. An overall effect of continuity is rendered in plastic terms by a variety of means. As discussed earlier, frontal views are difficult to achieve and are deemed static; three-quarter views are favoured in both buildings. Peripheral composition is sought over centralised, and interpenetration preferred over separation, though in MAXXI, the emphasis is on the vertical, and in the Visual Arts Center, on the horizontal.

Out of these relations, a general, fairly constant diagonal condition is shown to exist. From there, a review of the plans reveals a disposition different from the enfilade (room to room) plan and the poché (served and servant) plan: it is a case of an open plan in the one and a free plan in the other.

Thus far, a diagrammatic comparison of MAXXI and the Visual Arts Center has explored the themes of diagonal or transverse relationships, of internal volumes rendered expressive, and the consequences of free-plan and free-section structural ideas.

In their general idea, as can be seen in my cursory examination of the plans, the overall architectural systems of the two works bear some similarities. They are both conceived perhaps around diagonal movements, with functional spaces disposed either as coincident with circulation (MAXXI) or as appendages to lines of circulation (Visual Arts Center). The fourth theme to be developed concerns ambiguities in object/field or figure/ground conditions, which disrupt a critical approach to part-to-whole logics.

Neither building can be absorbed from without. The value of wholeness, the ideal of being able to stand at some point and receive a palpable impression of the whole, is specifically not an aim, as already discussed. Development of focus is something of an arbitrary and, for Hadid, intentionally ambiguous proceeding. In this regard, the inability to bring things sharply into focus leads to a blurring or a fluidity if her pronouncements are taken at face value. Listen to Hadid discussing this aspect of her work in an interview with Mohsen Mostafavi: 'I begin to see a similarity between liquid space and rock. . . . We have found ways to articulate these concepts [of spatial overlap, interpenetrations, and juxtapositions] in a much more fluid way.'[16]

It is a case therefore of inversion and intensification in the place of extension: more fluid at MAXXI, no less concentrated at the Visual Arts Center for being bound by those floor and ceiling plates and directed horizontally. Especially if you study the sliding or staggered distribution of main spaces and the dense centre, doubled or echoed by perimeter incidents at the Visual Arts Center. No simple dispersal of focus due to bounding elements. It is a case, rather, or more specifically, of space rebounding: waves bounding back to confront initial ripples. In MAXXI, the concrete walls of the galleries channel the effect. At the Visual Arts Center, potential release is denied, energy bounced back from or ricocheted off all those perimeter vertical incidents: curving walls, undulatories, brise soleils, columns.

The eye never settles, is never at rest. This quality may be taken as another instance of the nature of time rendered by MAXXI. Peripheral interests are driven to horizontal expansion in the Visual Arts Center. Differently, interests are moved in a contained concentration of a rather constant nature, sliding and swung along, ramping up and down at MAXXI. The two different strategies yield in one regard, however, similar effects: no one centre, a kind of indefinite though certainly not neutral space. Never uniform: no grid. In fact, it is always potentially fully animated such that hierarchy (of figure over ground or object over field) is shown specifically not to be the intent. The absence of one dominant centre produces this other kind of condition, of being always already in an ambiguous kind of middle condition. So, another quality of MAXXI's temporality is this resistance to a clear middle.

What motivates this drive away from a centre? It is perhaps Hadid's abandonment to a certain force that she characterised as exhilarating. That 'certain exhilaration' contained in a certain lineage of modernity that persuaded Hadid that the architect's task was to reinvestigate modernity, to further develop and 'unleash' its potential.[17]

So, while there is perhaps the idea or promise of a denouement in both, it is endlessly deferred. I believe this is further evidence of a specific nature of time at work. In neither do you ever fully arrive, suggesting alternatively that time has always already passed. Or is it always in motion but never researched? A definite time has yet to arrive. Look again at the plans. In MAXXI, the interest is the field as a constant condition.[18]

A key aim of this chapter in this part of the book devoted to the idea of time and architecture is to begin to identify elements for a theory of those temporal structures that certain modern works of architecture may be able to channel and reveal. Though tentative, and calling for further development, I believe there is evidence of a concept of time at work in each of the buildings considered. The multiple aspects explored in relation to the Visual Arts Center in Chapter 6 and further, when reviewed together, thus perhaps provide a provisional description of its main characteristics: diagonal and transverse relationships; a voided centre that creates intensity independent of any other animating presence. In addition, there is a specific idea of structure: the flat slab-and-point structure in the Visual Arts Center overlapping with dense perimeter conditions and the cantilever, ribbon-like shapes in the open-ended plan of MAXXI. And perhaps supporting or enabling all are the field and ground ambiguities. This includes the vibration introduced by Kahn in the plans for the Philadelphia College of Art. To varying degrees, and with all the qualifications called for, there is a suggestion of terms for describing another architectural concept of time. It is one that shares aspects with those post-1945 phenomena that Deleuze describes.

From the earlier analysis, we can now perhaps say that, though employing different means, MAXXI, the Visual Arts Center, and the Philadelphia College of Art are equally about movement and about a temporal structure. All three projects render manifest an idea of time out of joint, one that does not rely on movement to gain presence. Contrary to Le Corbusier's emphasis on the Acropolitan sequence, and the motor and visual aspects that implies and the parallax effects so immediate and palpable in that whirl of columns and tilting planes proceeding up and through the building; and despite the combination of oblique movement and peripheral incident dispersed over and across several floors, and the 'free organs' staggered vertically; despite or in addition to all this, time perhaps appears directly, independent of an animating movement.

Equally true, it can be claimed, MAXXI freezes a moment in time and thus illustrates a Deleuzian pure time by means of the strategies examined here: oblique movements already underway, folding volumes, an animated middle (no beginning or end), describing part-to-whole logics.

Thus, we are confronted with conditions of simultaneity, with concepts of time as overlapping durations, the consequence of compressions and release, all working to create folds in, or give thickness to, time. Perhaps we now see the Philadelphia College of Art as a machine that manufactures time in frozen shadows. These seem to be valid and real findings, if only tentative conclusions which nonetheless support further research with other concrete examples to be sought and terms of reference refined and amended.

Notes

1. Zaha Hadid, "The Ambition of the New," in *Anytime*, ed. Cynthia C. Davidson (Cambridge: The MIT Press, 1998), 91.
2. Hadid, "The Ambition of the New," 91.
3. Hadid, "The Ambition of the New," 91.
4. Zaha Hadid, "The Calligraphy of the Plan," *Oz: Journal of the College of Architecture, Planning & Design Kansas State University* 9 (1987): 38. https://doi.org/10.4148/2378-5853.1140.
5. Zaha Hadid from a 1987 interview with Alvin Boyarsky, "The Calligraphy of the Plan," in *The Idea of the City*, ed. Robin Middleton (London: Architectural Association and Cambridge: The MIT Press, 1996), 68.
6. Hadid interview with Boyarsky, "The Calligraphy of the Plan," 65.
7. Aaron Betsky, "Beyond 89 Degrees," in *Zaha Hadid: The Complete Buildings and Projects* (London: Thames and Hudson, 1988), 6.
8. Zaha Hadid, "The Calligraphy of the Plan," *Oz Journal of the College of Architecture, Planning & Design Kansas State University* 9 (1987): 38. Accessed 11 May 2022. https://doi.org/10.4148/2378-5853.1140.
9. Key published sources on the project include the following: Fernando Marquez Cecilia and Richard Levene, eds., "Zaha Hadid, Contemporary Arts Centre in Rome," in *Zaha Hadid 1983–2004* (Madrid, El Croquis, 2004), 414–25. Gianluca Racana and Manon Janssens, eds., *MAXXI: Museum of XXI Century Arts* (New York, Rizzoli International Publications, 2010). Mario Avagnina, Margherita Guccione, and Silvia La Pergola, eds., *MAXXI materia grigia. Il racconto della costruzione* (Milano, Mondadori Electa, 2010). A good selection of preliminary drawings, images, and as-built photographs can be found on the office website, accessed 14 June 2022, www.zaha-hadid.com/wp-content/uploads/2019/12/maxxi.pdf.
10. Project description on the office website, accessed 14 June 2022, www.zaha-hadid.com/wp-content/uploads/2019/12/maxxi.pdf.
11. Zaha Hadid, from a 1987 interview with Alvin Boyarsky published as "The Calligraphy of the Plan," in *The Idea of the City*, ed. Robin Middleton (London: Architectural Association and Cambridge, Mass.: MIT Press, 1996), 65.
12. Rowe employs this term to describe the difference of Palladio's Malcontenta as compared to Le Corbusier's Villa at Garches. Rowe, *The Mathematics of the Ideal Villa and Other Essays*, 11.
13. Zaha Hadid with Mohsen Mostafavi, "Landscape as Plan [A Conversation with Zaha Hadid]," in *Zaha Hadid, 1983–2004* (Madrid: El Croquis Editorial, 2004), 49.
14. For a discussion of the concept of field, see Patrick Schumacher, "The Meaning of MAXXI – Concepts, Ambitions, Achievements", in *MAXXI: Museum of XXI Century Arts*, ed. Gianluca Racana and Manon Janssens (New York: Rizzoli International Publications, 2010), 39.
15. Peter Eisenman with Elisa Iturbe, *Lateness* (Princeton: Princeton University Press, 2020), 3. A future study should consider the formal and conceptual openings contained in *Lateness* for rereading architecture's recent past and contemporaneity.
16. Zaha Hadid with Mohsen Mostafavi, "Landscape as Plan," 52, 54.
17. Zaha Hadid, "The Eighty-Nine Degrees," in *Planetary Architecture Two* (London: Architectural Association, 1983), unnumbered plate.
18. Schumacher, "The Meaning of MAXXI – Concepts, Ambitions, Achievements," 39.

Bibliography

Avagnina, Mario, Margherita, Guccione, and Silvia, La Pergola, eds. *MAXXI materia grigia. Il racconto della costruzione*. Milano: Mondadori Electa, 2010.

Betsky, Aaron. "Beyond 89 Degrees." In *Zaha Hadid: The Complete Buildings and Projects*, 6–14. London: Thames and Hudson, 1988.

Boesiger, W., ed. *Le Corbusier. The Complete Architectural Works, Volume VII 1957–1965*. London: Thames and Hudson, 1965.

Cecilia, Fernando Marquez, and Richard, Levene, eds. *Zaha Hadid 1983–2004*. Madrid: El Croquis, 2004.

Deleuze, Gilles. *Cinema 2: The Time-Image*. (Translated by H. Tomlinson and R. Galeta). Minneapolis: University of Minnesota Press, 1989.

Hadid, Zaha. "The Ambition of the New." In *Anytime*, edited by Cynthia C. Davidson, 90–97. Cambridge: The MIT Press, 1998.

Hadid, Zaha. "The Calligraphy of the Plan." *Oz Journal of the College of Architecture, Planning & Design Kansas State University* 9 (1987): 38–41. Accessed 11 May 2022. https://doi.org/10.4148/2378-5853.1140

Hadid, Zaha. "The Eighty-Nine Degrees." In *Planetary Architecture Two*. London: Architectural Association, 1983.

Hadid, Zaha. *Zaha Hadid: The Complete Buildings and Projects*. London: Thames and Hudson, 1988.

Hadid, Zaha, and Alvin, Boyarsky. "The Calligraphy of the Plan." In *The Idea of the City*, edited by Robin Middleton, 64–83. London/Cambridge: Architectural Association and MIT Press, 1996.

Hadid, Zaha, with Mohsen, Mostafavi. "Landscape as Plan [A Conversation with Zaha Hadid]." In *Zaha Hadid 1983–2004*, 40–69. Madrid: El Croquis Editorial, 2004.

Le Corbusier. *Toward an Architecture*. (Translated by J. Goodman). Los Angeles: Getty Research Institute, 2007.

Racana, Gianluca. "Competition to Construction." In *MAXXI: Museum of XXI Century Arts*, edited by Gianluca Racana and Manon Janssens, 45–55. New York, Rizzoli, 2010.

Racana, Gianluca, and Manon, Janssens, eds. *MAXXI: Museum of XXI Century Arts*. New York: Rizzoli International Publications, 2010.

Rowe, Colin. *The Mathematics of the Ideal Villa and Other Essays*. Cambridge: The MIT Press, 1976.

Schumacher, Patrick. "The Meaning of MAXXI – Concepts, Ambitions, Achievements." In *MAXXI: Museum of XXI Century Arts*, edited by Gianluca Racana and Manon Janssens, 18–39. New York: Rizzoli International Publications, 2010. www.patrikschumacher.com/Texts/The%20Meaning%20of%20MAXXI.html.

Sekler, Eduard F., and William, Curtis. *Le Corbusier at Work. The Genesis of the Carpenter Center for the Visual Arts*. Cambridge: Harvard University Press, 1978.

DISCONTINUITY

Trajectories redux

In the opening chapter, continuities were imagined across diverse characters and objects, brought into proximity on the premise that certain ideas, certain terms, and certain architectural acts over the second half of the twentieth century have garnered too little scrutiny. We suggested, in other words, that a range of yet to be fully explored and exploited thematic frameworks directly or indirectly are in evidence in architecture culture over the latter half of the twentieth century.

Stated differently, we started with observations on approximate configurations of architectural forms and ideas. We then moved to identify contiguities among a set of case studies in order to test how certain motives and tendencies might be generalized into an attitude or mode with enough common momentum to justify their categorisations as more than isolated concerns. We labelled such shared attitudes as trajectories.

The continuity alluded to in the title of the opening chapter, thus, might refer to a continuum calling us to look retrospectively again at such acts and their accompanying sensibilities. This was done with a view to glean, identify, and perhaps take lessons from such qualities. Others have also commented on such an endeavour and can provide an additional framework for thinking about the effort and its continued resonance or quiet demise.

In contemplating the thinking and pronouncements of one of the key protagonists in architecture's scene over the period under review, and to adopt another take on those years, Sanford Kwinter characterises as non-static the elemental qualities of a select set of architects. For Kwinter, the underlying qualities and, by implication, temperament are always already in perpetual movement, such qualities operating 'through invasion, disruption, and the release of temporarily trapped forces into free motion and recombination.'[1] If Kwinter is accurate in his appraisal, such

DOI: 10.4324/9781003009641-13

trajectories can only, at best, coalesce for a brief moment, destined to then break apart from their temporary entrapment.

Springing from such a position, the opening chapter can be said to have thus ventured to put forward a set of thematic continuities or trajectories accompanying the work of a number of architects between the 1960s and 1990s. The following chapters, however, took on faith the potential or provisional existence of such trajectories across a range of architectural acts. Such trajectories in the subsequent four decades, however, will have bifurcated, become in many instances densely articulated or encrusted by diversions and disruptions. They will have been distracted by exigencies, stresses, and unforeseen or unimagined priorities such as to be almost unrecognisable today. Were we to wish to reveal their traces, it would be a case of following Kwinter's various disruptions, diversions, swerves: in short, various forms of discontinuity. This is to invert and then adopt for our own use Kwinter's characterisation of the impossible attempt to maintain stable boundaries and 'new forms of consistency.'[2]

Another period commentator, Stan Allen, can be called up to provide a similar though differently useful synthetic model of the pursuit. Mimicking the structure of detective novels, the chase that this book might be claimed to have followed is one trailing circular patterns moving forward in time. This happens while simultaneously providing interlaced and interlayered readings of past events whose meaning is amplified by that self-same effort. As Allen describes it: 'This is part of the immense attraction that detective fiction enjoys: a story that is entirely conventional and straightforward in its narrative structure, and at the same time looping, circular, and topologically complex, all the while promising a satisfactory resolution. The rest is atmosphere.'[3] Allen's 'looping' and 'topologically complex' seems also to come close the events we have considered and an implied underlying narrative.

A third protagonist, Hubert Damisch, can be equally mined to contribute to forming and refining the instruments for proselytizing about futures to turn specifically to what's next. In thinking about the strictures of that manifest when thinking the situation as always already 'late' or 'post,' Damisch warns of the limitations such a stance imposes on our capacity to imagine possible futures. 'I think our incapacity to imagine a future is related to this sense of living in a situation defined by its belatedness. Are we going to dwell unceasingly in the "late," the "post"?'[4] The burden in the late 1980s, the time of Damisch's statement and at the end of the period considered here, was certainly palpable for Damisch who felt compelled, though not provoked by those interviewing him, to say something about the 'post.'

Which instruments and procedures might be turned to in order to start to address such ends and to build a capacity to imagine that Damisch found lacking? In lieu of, or alongside, a reappraisal of the impacts and effects of certain architectural acts from the lens of those theoretico-historical objects,[5] situations at the distance of some four decades now feel more concrete. It is no longer fashionable, or possible, to claim the comfort of a post anything, so divergent are the calls on the architect's focus.

Imperatives

If the theoretical object, sensation, and temporality, no matter how well disguised, were present in the late-twentieth-century cases considered, which today are their problems that should or could preoccupy architecture as discipline and practice? Which responses might suggest themselves to such preoccupations? Without launching into a new research endeavour, the problematics that may surface as most appropriate for consideration now seems of another nature and from a place foreign to those claiming attention to the sensibilities of the 1960s, 1970s, and 1980s examined earlier.

If receiving various formulations, let us take Henry Cobb's 2018 depiction of matters most pressing as a starting point. The occasion was an event sponsored by Mohsen Mostafavi who invited Cobb, Peter Eisenman, and Raphael Moneo to respond to the question: how will architecture be conceived? Cobb, in his response, suggests one configuration. None of the terms or imperatives in that configuration identified by Cobb will be surprising. At that place and on that occasion, Cobb described the imperatives as follows:

'I expect that architecture as discipline and practice will be directed during the next quarter century to three primary ends all of which I take to be moral imperatives that have been widely acknowledged if only imperfectly treated in recent decades. These are, first, to sustain diversity both in the natural world and in human culture; second, to alleviate human suffering caused by economic asymmetry and political dysfunction; third, to minimize the harmful effects of human activity on the ecosystems of our planet.'[6]

To sustain diversity, to alleviate suffering, to minimise the effects of climate change: such are the thematic frameworks for Cobb most evident today. More could be said, other vectors sought, and others called on to witness, to testify, to refute. As alluded to by Cobb, however, and to take just one line, the next effort would surely include work on the nature and range of academic agendas put forward as parallel laboratories to the practice-based work considered in the main sections of this book.

If the ends are more or less agreed, as many who concur with Cobb imply, the means to achieve these ends are equally and appropriately in debate in practice, in professional societies, and within universities. Such ends will necessarily call on all our energies and imaginations – disciplinary, private, professional – to address. If such ends are agreed, then the gift we have is the clarity of the imperative, and the momentum demanded is to focus on the means to achieve them. If a gift, it is also a burden and a responsibility.

Notes

1 Sanford Kwinter, "Introduction: The Eisenman Wave," in *Eisenman Architects: Selected and Current Works*, ed. Stephen Dobney (Mulgrave: The Images Publishing Group Pty Ltd, 1995), 7.
2 Sanford Kwinter, "Can One Go Beyond Piranesi? (Liner Notes for a Building Revisited)," in *Eleven Authors in Search of a Building: The Aronoff Center for Design and Art at*

the University of Cincinnati, ed. Cynthia C. Davidson (New York: The Monacelli Press, 1996), 162.
3 Stan Allen, "Trace Elements," in *Tracing Eisenman: Peter Eisenman Complete Works*, ed. Cynthia Davidson (New York: Rizzoli, 2006), 49.
4 Hubert Damisch with Yve-Alain Bois, Denis Hollier and Rosalind Krauss, "A Conversation with Hubert Damisch," *October* 85 (Summer 1988): 5.
5 Damisch, "A Conversation with Hubert Damisch," 8.
6 Henry Cobb, "Response to the Question: How will Architecture be Conceived?," in *How Will Achitecture Be Conceived* (An Event Held at Harvard University Graduate School of Design on 13 April 2018). Accessed 27 July 2018. www.youtube.com/watch?v=xkejyPt6n-g

Bibliography

Allen, Stan. "Trace Elements." In *Tracing Eisenman: Peter Eisenman Complete Works*, edited by Cynthia Davidson, 48–65. New York: Rizzoli, 2006.
Cobb, Henry. "Response to the Question: How Will Architecture be Conceived?" *How Will Architecture be Conceived* (An Event Held at Harvard University Graduate School of Design on 13 April 2018). Accessed 27 July 2018. www.youtube.com/watch?v=xkejyPt6n-g
Damisch, Hubert, with Yve-Alain, Bois, Denis, Hollier, and Rosalind, Krauss. "A Conversation with Hubert Damisch." *October* 85 (Summer 1988): 3–17.
Kwinter, Sanford. "Can One Go Beyond Piranesi? (Liner Notes for a Building Revisited)." In *Eleven Authors in Search of a Building: The Aronoff Center for Design and Art at the University of Cincinnati*, edited by Cynthia C. Davidson, 152–163. New York: The Monacelli Press, 1996,
Kwinter, Sanford. "Introduction: The Eisenman Wave." In *Eisenman Architects: Selected and Current Works*, edited by Stephen Dobney, 7–15. Mulgrave: The Images Publishing Group Pty Ltd, 1995.

INDEX

1/2 Series (Hejduk) 64
1/4 Series (Hejduk) 64
3/4 Series (Hejduk) 64

accumulation 24–25
Adath Jeshurun Synagogue (Kahn) 22
additive strategy 79
Adler House (Kahn) 22, 27
Alberti, Leon Battista 48
Allen, Stan 55, 164
ambiguity 3, 5, 7, 11, 36, 38, 42, 46, 48–49, 64, 81, 113, 115, 117, 118, 121, 122, 123, 126, 127, 134, 142–143, 148, 153, 157, 159, 160
American Academy in Rome 23, 79, 130
American organicism 75
Architectural League 55, 63
Architecture's Desire (Hays) 9
Argan, Giulio Carlo 9, 10, 93–99, 106, 108
Artec 105
atemporality 25
a+u [*Architecture and Urbanism*] (magazine) 2

Bank of China Tower (Pei) 97
Barcelona Pavilion 42
Baroque 108, 131, 133
Baxandall, Michael 48
Beaux-Arts Institute of Design 137
Beaux-Arts plan 1, 2, 21, 27, 82, 86, 91n45
Berg, Pamela 74
Betsky, Aaron 150
Bibliothèque Sainte Geneviève 85
binuclear plan 27
Blenheim 27

Boehm, Gero von 98, 100, 102, 103
Bois, Yve-Alain 30, 51
Bonnefoi, Christian 24–25, 30
Bottero, Maria 29, 75, 79, 80, 82, 86
Boullée, Étienne-Louis 75
boundless field extensions 3
Boyarsky, Alvin 149, 151
Brown, Frank 79
Brownlee, David 19, 21, 26, 75, 78, 86
Bryn Mawr College Dormitory (Kahn) 9, 73–89, 95, 113
building fabric 82–87
butterfly mind 48
B/W XVI (Held) 107

Cadwell, Michael 86, 130, 132
California Institute of Technology 23
calligraphy 12
Canadian Centre for Architecture 34, 56, 64
Casabella (magazine) 40, *41*
centralisation 27, 45
Cézanne, Paul 100–101
Choate Rosemary Hall Science Center (Pei) 105
Choisy, August 79
Cinema 2 (Deleuze) 10, 64–65, 115, 150
classical architecture 133
'Clearness and Unclearness' (Wölfflin) 132–133
Cobb, Henry 40, 165
Colosseum 81
Colquhoun, Alan 88–89, 116
column/wall ambiguities 36–40, 46–47, 50

168 Index

Compass Rose (Held) 107
compression 34, 126
Congress Hall (Le Corbusier) 120
Constructivism 89
Creative Artists Agency (Pei) 105
cross-axial planning 2, 21, 27, 42, 47, 50, 117–118, 125, 126, 156
Cubism 2–3, 21, 99, 103, 108, 122
Curtis, William 116

Damisch, Hubert 6–7, 21, 29, 33, 36, 38, 40, 42–43, 50–52, 56, 113, 164
Deleuze, Gilles 10, 64–65, 114, 115, 126, 127, 150, 160
De Long, David 19, 21, 26, 75, 78, 86, 139
De Stijl 89
De Vore House (Kahn) 7, 19–30, 34, 75, 87, 113, 135
diachronicity 20
diagonalities 3–4, 34, 117–119, 126, 143
diagonal time 66
Diamond House A (Hejduk) 28, 55, 56, 63–64
Diamond House B (Hejduk) 28, 55, 56, 63–64
Diamond Museum C (Hejduk) 28, 55, 56, 63–64
Diamond Projects (Hejduk) 7, 28, 40, 55–66, 113
'Diamond Thesis' (Hejduk) 55, 57, 59, 63, 66, 67n7
direct time 65–66
dispersal 34
'Dominican Monastery of La Tourette, Eveux-Sur Arbresle, Lyon' (Rowe) 8
Domino 40, 46, 61, 62, 63, 119, 123, 124, 126, 152, 158
doubling 134–136, 145
Dubuffet, Jean 103, 104
Durand, J. N. L. 1

École des Beaux-Arts, Paris 2
Eisenman, Peter 1, 2, 5, 21, 33, 82, 88, 165; "The Futility of Objects" 88; House II 7, 26, 27, 34–40, 47, 48–52, 113; House III 48; House IV 7, 27, 34–35, 38, 40–48, 113; House Projects 127; "In My Father's House Are Many Mansions" 88; *Ten Canonical Buildings 1950–2000* 20, 116
elastic space 93–98, 102–103, 108–110
emergence 130, 145
entry hall 79–82
European rationalism 75

Everson Museum of Art (Pei) 97, 99–101, 103, 105
Expressionism 89
expressive volumes 113, 115, 117, 126, 150–152

Farnsworth House (Mies van der Rohe) 20
Fellini, Federico 65, 127
figure-figure relations 116, 153–155
figure-ground relations 117
First Unitarian Church (Kahn) 74, 79, 81, 82, 83, 86
Five Architects (George Wittenborn and Company, N.Y.) 34
Florence fortification drawings (Michelangelo) 3–4
folds 133, 138–142, 160
formal-spatial characteristics 2–3, 35
four-square plan 21, 25–28, 42, 46
Frampton, Kenneth 1, 49, 75, 119, 122–123
free plan 21, 28, 42, 62, 79, 82, 87, 115, 118, 119, 121, 152, 153, 156, 158–159
free section 119, 121, 152, 153, 159
Fried, Michael 133
frontality 40, 48, 49, 50, 56, 61, 62–64, 66, 117–119, 121, 125, 126, 133
"Futility of Objects, The" (Eisenman) 88
Futurism 89

Genel House (Kahn) 27
German History Museum (Pei) 105
Giedion, Sigfried 134, 144
Giotto 80, 88
Giurgola, Romaldo 21, 23, 73–74, 75, 76, 78, 136, 139
Goldenberg House (Kahn) 139, 143
Gowan, James 20, 33
Greek revival 49
Greenberg, Alan 1
Gropius, Walter 30
group form 136–138, 139, 142–143

Hadid, Zaha 5; MAXXI 12, 148–160; plan-focused nature of work 11–12
Hays, K. Michael 9, 55
Hejduk, John 2, 5, 11, 113–114, 122, 126; 1/2 Series 64; 1/4 Series 64; 3/4 Series 64; Diamond House A 28, 55, 56, 63–64; Diamond House B 28, 55, 56, 63–64; Diamond Museum C 28, 55, 56, 63–64; Diamond Projects 7, 28, 40, 55–66, 113; 'Diamond Thesis' 55, 57, 59, 63, 66, 67n7; *Mask of Medusa* 63;

Index

'Out of Time and into Space' 2, 64, 66, 67n7, 67n8; Texas Houses 2, 55–56, 57, 62, 64; *Three Projects* 57, 63; Wall Houses 55–56
Held, Al 107
Hernandez, Antonio 1
hierarchy 27, 45, 106, 126, 155, 159
Hollier, Denis 51
House II (Eisenman) 7, 26, 27, 34–40, 47, 48–52, 113
House III (Eisenman) 48
House IV (Eisenman) 7, 27, 34–35, 38, 40–52, 113
House Projects (Eisenman) 127
Houses of Cards (Eisenman) 34

I. M. Pei & Associates 98
I. M. Pei & Partners 93
I. M. Pei (Wiseman) 107
'Importance of Sammicheli in the Formation of Palladio, The' (Argan) 93
Indian Institute of Management Ahmedaba (Kahn) 80
informal 30
"In My Father's House Are Many Mansions" (Eisenman) 88
International Style 47
isolation 79

Jacob K. Javits Convention Center (Pei) 97
James, Kathleen 138
Jewish Community Center (Kahn) 20, 28
Jhaveri, Sharad 74, 76, 134
Jodidio, Philip 98
John Hejduk Archive 56, 64
Johnson, Russell 105

Kahn, Louis 4, 5; Adath Jeshurun Synagogue 22; Adler House 22, 27; Bryn Mawr College Dormitory 9, 73–89, 95, 113; De Vore House 7, 19–30, 34, 75, 87, 113, 135; First Unitarian Church 74, 79, 81, 82, 83, 86; Genel House 27; Goldenberg House 139, 143; Indian Institute of Management Ahmedaba 80; Jewish Community Center 20, 28; Korman House 28; *The Louis I. Kahn Archive. Personal Drawings* 75; Meeting House 29; Meeting House at the Salk Institute for Biological Studies 29, 75, 80, 81, 130–138, 139, 145, 148; National Assembly Building in Dhaka 80; Philadelphia College of Art 29, 127, 130, 138–143, 145, 148, 155–156, 160; Phillips Exeter Academy Library 74, 84, 86; Richards Medical Research Laboratories 74, 83, 86; Salk Institute for Biological Studies 74; Tribune Review Publishing Company Building 74, 86; 'Two Houses' 30; United States Consulate [Luanda, Angola] 74, 136; Weiss House 27; Yale Center for British Art 83, 85, 86, 130, 132, 138
Kline, Franz 139
Korman House (Kahn) 28
Krauss, Rosalind 30, 51
Kwinter, Sanford 163–164

Labrouste, Henri 79, 85
L'Architecture d'aujourd'hui (magazine) 2, 123
Larson, Kent 80, 81
League of Nations (Le Corbusier) 125
Leatherbarrow, David 139
Le Corbusier 5, 81; Congress Hall 120; League of Nations 125; Millowners' Association Building 120; Monastery of Sainte-Marie de la Tourette 3, 8; *Oeuvre complète* 115, 116, 117; plan-focused nature of work 11; *Toward an Architecture* 8; Villa Stein 2–3, 4, 56, 61, 63, 66, 125; Visual Arts Center 2–3, 12, 56, 57, 63, 66, 113–127, 148, 157–160
Ledoux, Claude Nicolas 75
Lewis, Michael 74, 77
liberation 149–150
Library of Congress 98
Linder, Mark 55
line 22–23
longitudinal planning 118
Louis I. Kahn Archive. Personal Drawings, The (Kahn) 75
Louis I. Kahn (Brownlee and De Long) 75
Louis I. Kahn Collection 25
Louis I. Kahn (Giurgola and Mehta) 75
Louis I. Kahn (McCarter) 75
Louis I. Kahn (Ronner and Jhaveri) 74, 76, 134
Louis I. Kahn (Scully) 75
Louvre Pyramid (Pei) 98
Lucan, Jacques 88
Lutyens, Edwin 1

Maison de Verre 1
Maki, Fumihiko 104, 108
Maniaque, Caroline 29
Mannerism 131

'Mannerism and Modern Architecture'
    (Rowe) 8
Mask of Medusa (Shkapich) 57, 63
materiality 9–10
Maxwell, Robert 9
MAXXI (Hadid) 12, 148–160
McCarter, Robert 75
Meeting House at the Salk Institute for
    Biological Studies (Kahn) 29, 75, 80, 81,
    130–138, 139, 145, 148
Mehta, Jaimini 23, 75, 76
Michelangelo 3–4, 63, 123, 130–132
'Michelangelo's Fortification Drawings'
    (Scully) 130–131
Mies van der Rohe, Ludwig 9, 20, 42,
    102–103
Miho Museum (Pei) 97
Mile High Center (Pei) 97
Millowners' Association Building
    (Le Corbusier) 120
minimalist artists 24–25, 30
Miró, Joan 103
modernism 1, 50, 82
Monastery of Sainte-Marie de la Tourette
    [La Tourette] (Le Corbusier) 3, 8
Mondrian, Piet 2, 63
Moneo, Raphael 1, 5, 13, 165
Moore, Henry 103, 104
Moos, Stanislaus von 116
Morris, Robert 24, 25
Morton H. Meyerson Symphony Center
    (Pei) 97, 105–107, 108, 149
Mostafavi, Moshen 159, 165
movement 6, 10–12, 21, 27, 28, 34, 36,
    38–40, 46–48, 50, 56, 62, 64–66, 81,
    82, 87, 88, 94, 95, 103, 108, 114–115,
    119, 120, 121, 124, 125, 127, 131, 134,
    137, 139, 141–142, 148, 149, 152, 153,
    157–160, 163

Nancy, Jean-Luc 133
National Assembly Building in Dhaka
    (Kahn) 80
National Center for Atmospheric Research
    (Pei) 100–101
National Gallery of Art East Building (Pei)
    97, 101–104, 105, 108
National Mall 101
'Neo-Classicism and Modern Architecture II'
    (Rowe) 49
neo-plasticistism 2–3, 108
nine-square plan 2, 27, 42, 45–46, 55–56
non-perspectival space 93–98

Oeuvre complète (Le Corbusier) 115, 116, 117
Oles, Steve 103, 108
Olinski, Jules 24
opacities 120–122
"Organic and Rational Morphology in
    Louis Kahn" (Bottero) 75
'Out of Time and into Space' (Hejduk) 2,
    64, 66, 67n7, 67n9

Palladian plan 27
Palladio, Andrea 93–95, 99, 108
part-to-part logic 27
part-to-whole logic 160
part-to-whole relation 27, 45
Pei Cobb Freed & Partners 98
Pei, I.M. 5, 9, 10; Bank of China Tower
    97; Choate Rosemary Hall Science
    Center 105; Creative Artists Agency 105;
    Everson Museum of Art 97, 99–101, 103,
    105; German History Museum 105; Jacob
    K. Javits Convention Center 97; Louvre
    Pyramid 98; Miho Museum 97; Mile
    High Center 97; Morton H. Meyerson
    Symphony Center 97, 105–107, 108,
    149; National Center for Atmospheric
    Research 100–101; National Gallery of
    Art East Building 97, 101–104, 105, 108;
    Webb & Knapp, Inc. 93
peripheral duplication 136
peripheral tensions 3
Perspecta (journal) 1, 22, 23, 30
perspectival space 93–98
Philadelphia College of Art (Kahn) 29, 127,
    130, 138–143, 145, 148, 155–156, 160
Phillips Exeter Academy Library (Kahn) 74,
    84, 86
pinwheel plan 27, 34, 48, 61, 62, 64, 99, 125
Piranesi, Giovanni Battista 80
plan 1–2, 4, 5–8, 11–12, 21–22, 24,
    25–28, 30, 34, 35, 36, 38, 40–52,
    57–58, 59, 61, 62, 63, 74–75, 76–79,
    81–82, 84, 87–88, 94–95, 99, 113,
    115, 117–119, 122, 123, 126, 139, 140,
    142–143, 149–150, 152–159
poché 29, 82, 88, 118, 156, 158
post-Cubism 2, 122
practice-based research 35
Principles of Art History (Wölfflin) 133
Progressive Architecture (magazine) 73
Project for a Private House
    (van Doesburg) 136
promenade architecturale 115, 120
Pusey, Nathan 119

Index

rational drawing 3, 131
rationalism 8, 49, 75, 85
reflex diagonal 3–4, 131
reflexive drawing 3–4, 131
Renaissance 63, 79, 131
Renoir, Jean 65, 127
Richards Medical Research Laboratories (Kahn) 74, 83, 86
right-angle relationships 3, 4, 50
Ronner, Heinz 74, 76, 134
rotation 34, 47, 49, 55, 57, 63, 76, 78, 117, 120–121, 125
Rowe, Colin 3, 4, 35, 76, 97, 116, 127; 'Dominican Monastery of La Tourette, Eveux-Sur Arbresle, Lyon' 8; 'Mannerism and Modern Architecture' 8; 'Neo-Classicism and Modern Architecture II' 49
Royal Academy of Arts 1, 5
Rudolph, Paul 33
Rykwert, Joseph 74, 75, 83
Ryman, Robert 24

Salk Institute for Biological Studies (Kahn) 29, 74; *see also* Meeting House at the Salk Institute for Biological Studies (Kahn)
Sanmicheli, Michele 93
Schumacher, Patrick 155
Scope of Total Architecture (Gropius) 30
Scully, Vincent 3–4, 21, 23, 73, 75, 78, 79, 80, 81, 82, 85, 86, 127, 130–132, 145
Sekler, Eduard 116
sensation 2, 3, 4, 5, 6, 8–10, 12, 13, 34, 49, 76–89, 93–109, 113, 135, 138, 141, 165
Serenyi, Peter 116
shape 133–134
simultaneity 7, 21, 50, 65–66, 79, 97, 114, 126, 153, 160
Slutzky, Robert 55, 97
Smith, David 139
Smithson, Alison 19, 21, 27, 28
Smithson, Peter 19, 21, 27, 28
Soane Medal lecture 5, 13
Solà-Morales, Ignasi de 9–10
Solar Wind I (Held) 107–108
Solomon, Susan 20
Space, Time and Architecture (Giedion) 144
spacing 23–25, 30
spatial warps 3
square-bay plan 57
Stella, Frank 133
Stirling, James 20, 33

Strong, Janet Adams 98, 101
structures 152–153
studio-based research 35
Sullivan, Louis 75

Tafuri, Manfredo 33, 40, 48
Ten Canonical Buildings 1950–2000 (Eisenman) 20, 116
Texas Houses (Hejduk) 2, 55–56, 57, 62, 64
text-based research 35
theoretical object 6–7, 21, 29, 33, 38, 50–52, 56, 113, 164–165
Three Projects (Hejduk) 57, 63
time 2–3, 4, 5, 6, 9, 10–12, 13, 20, 25, 29, 35, 56, 61–66, 108, 113, 114–116, 120–121, 123, 125–127, 130, 131, 132, 134, 141, 145, 148–150, 152, 155, 157–158, 159, 160
Toward an Architecture (Le Corbusier) 8
transverse planning 115, 117, 118, 120, 125, 155–157, 158, 160
Tribune Review Publishing Company Building (Kahn) 74, 82, 86
Tschumi, Bernard 9
'Two Houses' (Kahn) 30
Tyng, Anne 77

United States Consulate [Luanda, Angola] (Kahn) 74, 136
University of Leicester Engineering Building (Stirling and Gowan) 20, 33
University of Pennsylvania 25
University of Texas at Austin 2

van Doesburg, Theo 136
Vignola, Giacomo Barozzi da 97
Villa Farnese (Vignola) 97
Villa Stein (Le Corbusier) 2–3, 4, 56, 61, 63, 66, 125
Viollet-le-Duc, Eugène 7
Visual Arts Center [Carpenter Center for the Visual Arts] (Le Corbusier) 2–3, 12, 56, 57, 63, 65, 66, 113–127, 148, 157–160
voided centres 3, 28, 38, 62, 66, 76, 113, 115, 117, 122–125, 126, 153–155, 160

Wall, Don 57, 63
Wall Houses (Hejduk) 55–56
Webb & Knapp, Inc. 93
Weiss House (Kahn) 27
Welles, Orson 65, 127

Wiseman, Carter 98, 107
Wittkower, Rudolf 127
Wölfflin, Heinrich 132–133
Wright, Frank Llyod 75

Yale Center for British Art (Kahn) 83, 85, 86, 130, 132, 138
Yale School of Architecture 1, 33, 34

Zeckendorf, William 93, 101